D1566626

Wildflowers of the Coastal Plain

WILDFLOWERS

OF THE COASTAL PLAIN

A Field Guide

INCLUDES THE *Lower Mississippi River Valley,*
Gulf, AND *Atlantic Coastal States*

RAY NEYLAND

Louisiana State University Press
Baton Rouge

Published by Louisiana State University Press
Copyright © 2009 by Louisiana State University Press
All rights reserved
Manufactured in China
First printing

DESIGNER: Michelle A. Neustrom
TYPEFACE: Adobe Caslon Pro
PRINTER AND BINDER: Everbest Printing Co. through Four Colour Imports, Ltd., Louisville, Kentucky

All photographs and the map are by the author. Drawings in the appendix are by Sisley Badolato.

LIBRARY OF CONGRESS CATALOGING-IN-PUBLICATION DATA

Neyland, Ray.
    Wildflowers of the coastal plain : a field guide / Ray Neyland.
        p. cm.
    Includes bibliographical references and index.
    ISBN 978-0-8071-3407-8 (cloth : alk. paper) 1. Wild flowers—Gulf States—Handbooks,
manuals, etc. 2. Wild flowers—Atlantic Coast (U.S.)—Handbooks, manuals, etc. I. Title.
    QK115.N49 2009
    582.130976—dc22

                                                        2008031571

To my favorite person

CONTENTS

Wildflowers of the Coastal Plain

INTRODUCTION

The Coastal Plain

Most wildflower guides cover a particular geographical or political region such as Missouri, Florida, or the Southeast. Plant associations, however, typically do not coincide with state or regional boundaries. This guide encompasses the wildflowers that grow in one of the great floristic provinces of the United States—the coastal plain (see map later in this introduction). The coastal plain province extends from southeast Texas eastward to Florida and includes the Mississippi River flood plain, which stretches from southern Illinois to the Gulf of Mexico. It embraces all but the southern tip of the Florida peninsula and reaches northward along the eastern seaboard into southern New Jersey and even parts of Long Island and Cape Cod.

Plants that grow in the coastal plain are part of a recognizable association. For example, a plant species found in eastern Texas is also likely to be found from that point northward to Illinois and eastward to Florida and northward to Long Island. But it is not likely to be found in any other place in the country. There are exceptions—usually transplants introduced by man. Because those exceptions are now permanent elements of the flora, they are also included in this guide.

Scope and Purpose of This Guide

As a field guide, this book's main purpose is to assist the amateur botanist in identifying the conspicuous wildflowers of the coastal plain. It accomplishes that aim at several levels. First, the guide features color photographs of 535 wildflower species in their natural state. Second, it describes each of those species in precise terms. Although a minimum of technical language is used, some standard botanical terms are unavoidable in a field guide. Most of the terms are used repeatedly; therefore, the short amount of time necessary to learn their meaning will increase the reader's ability to identify plants. A glossary and an appendix with illustrations of plant structures provide the reader with an understanding of these botanical terms. Third, the guide offers dichotomous keys to aid the more serious student in making identifications. With a little practice, anyone can soon make good use of the keys.

This guide comprises herbaceous plants, vines, and shrubs. Although the term *wildflower* is not specific, flowering trees are generally not considered wildflowers and are not included here. Nonflowering plants such as ferns, lycopods, and mosses are also excluded.

PLANT DESCRIPTIONS

The text accompanying each plant includes its scientific name, a common name, a brief description, and its range and blooming time. Plants are listed by family and scientific name in alphabetical order. Therefore, no phylogenetic or systematic treatment is implied. When relevant, other closely related species are mentioned in each description to help avoid confusion in identification. In some cases, modern, traditional, and ethnobotanical uses of a plant are mentioned. Botanical terms used in the descriptions are defined in the glossary and depicted in the appendix.

PLANT NAMES

The common names of plants may be useful and convenient in a local setting but may become confusing in a broader spectrum. For example, in the United States, *Monotropa uniflora* is called Indian pipe, corpse plant, or ice plant; in Japan, it is called akino-ginryoso or ginryoso-modoki. The advantage of using scientific names is that worldwide the same name is recognized for a particular plant, thus eliminating confusion concerning a plant's identity. The rules governing the naming of plants are promulgated in the International Code of Botanical Nomenclature.

The scientific name consists of two Latin or Latinized words followed by the author citation. The first word is called the generic name and the second word is called the specific epithet. The author citation is attributed to the first person who described the species. When this person's name is placed within parentheses and followed by a second name, this indicates that the second person has changed the original scientific name to the one shown. Author citations are often abbreviated. The full names of these authors can be determined by referencing the book *Authors of Plant Names*, by R. K. Brummitt and C. E. Powell, or the Web site "International Plants Name Index" (www.ipni.org).

Geologic History of the Coastal Plain

A dominant feature of the coastal plain is the Mississippi Embayment. It is a large floodplain that extends from the confluence of the Mississippi and Ohio rivers in southern Illinois to the Mississippi River Delta in southern Louisiana. The embayment is a rift in the North American continent that was formed in the Precambrian period (>543 million years ago [MYA]) as a result of tectonic forces and was subsequently filled with Precambrian and Cambrian period (495–543 MYA) sediments.

Rifting ceased with the collision of Africa in eastern North America and with South America in southern North America during the Carboniferous period (290–354 MYA). As part of the process that contributed to the formation of the supercontinent Pangaea, these collisions created the Ouachita and Appalachian Mountains. During the Triassic period (206–251 MYA), the movement of Africa and South America away from North America began the formation of the Atlantic Ocean and Gulf of Mexico, respectively. It was also during this time that peninsular Florida was formed.

During the Cretaceous period (65–144 MYA), the area now occupied by the coastal plain was a shallow sea. It was also during this time that the Rocky Mountains were forming. In the early Tertiary period (starting about 65 MYA), the coastal plain began to form as a result of river and stream deposition into an ever-widening Gulf of Mexico and Atlantic Ocean. The Gulf of Mexico portion of the coastal plain primarily was formed by interior continental sediments from the Mississippi and Ohio rivers and by Rocky Mountain deposits from the Rio Grande, Missouri, Platte, and Pecos rivers. Sediment from rivers and streams of the Appalachian Mountains built the Atlantic coastal plain. A line of sandhills in the upper coastal plain along the fall line from Virginia to Alabama presently marks these ancient Cretaceous shorelines.

Throughout the Pleistocene epoch (1.8–0.1 MYA), the coastal plain was repeatedly inundated during the warm interglacial periods. Cool, dry conditions prevailed during the periods of glaciation.

The geologic coastal plain presently extends from southern Texas to peninsular Florida and northward into southern New Jersey and also includes the Mississippi River floodplain that extends from southern Illinois to the Gulf of Mexico. The region is characterized as low and flat with high rainfall and warm temperatures. Major habitats include pinelands, savannas, river floodplains, swamps, marshes, and upland forests. Because the soil is of marine origin, it is often sandy and acidic.

The Coastal Plain Floristic Province

The coastal plain floristic province is an area with a relatively uniform composition of plant species and generally coincides with the geologic coastal plain with some exceptions. In Texas, the floristic province occupies a narrow strip in the southeastern part of the state, whereas the geologic coastal plain continues farther westward and southward. All of Florida is considered part of the geologic coastal plain; however, the flora of the southern tip of the peninsula is more closely associated with the West Indian Province of the Caribbean. Although the northern limit of the geologic coastal plain is southern New Jersey, an element of the flora continues into Long Island, New York; Cape Cod, Massachusetts; and beyond. (The opposite map illustrates the extent of the coastal plain floristic province.)

Compared with the flora of the Appalachian Province, the coastal plain flora is younger. This is due to the younger geological substrate of the coastal plain and to the Pleistocene inundations that repeatedly have decimated the flora. Plants surviving in refugia during these long periods of inundation have resulted in high numbers of endemic species on the coastal plain. Areas where a large number of endemics persist include the line of sandhills in the upper coastal plain, the banks of the Apalachicola River in northern Florida, flatwoods in the Florida Panhandle, and Orange Island in central Florida.

Several pine species represent the dominant plants of the coastal plain floristic province. These include pitch pine in the north and longleaf, shortleaf, slash, and loblolly in the south. Pinelands are fire adapted and must burn regularly, or they become replaced by hardwoods such as oak, hickory, beech, and magnolia. Conspicuous herbaceous elements in the pinelands include pitcher plants, sundews, orchids, star grass, yellow-eyed grass, meadow beauties, and butterworts.

The incidence of swamps is extensive on the coastal plain. Notably large swamps include the Atchafalaya in southern Louisiana, the Dismal in southeastern Virginia, and the Okefenokee in southern Georgia. Swamps that are flooded for extensive periods are dominated by cypress. Swamps that flood only part of the year are dominated by water tupelo, ash, American elm, and red maple. Common herbaceous species here include arrowheads, spider lilies, water lilies, floating hearts, tuckahoe, iris, hibiscus, lizard's tail, and bladderwort.

Coastal marshes represent a substantial feature on the coastal plain and are dominated by grasses and sedges. Marshes may be either fresh or brackish. In general, marshes become more saline the closer they lie to the coast. The degree of salinity is a critical factor in determining where marsh species are distributed. In addition to grasses and sedges, other conspicuous plants include cattail, water hyacinth, pickerelweed, arrowheads, swamp lilies, water lilies, bladderwort, hibiscus, and fanwort.

The coastal plain is drained by numerous rivers including the Mississippi and its tributaries. Bottomland forests are a prevalent feature in the alluvial floodplains associated with these rivers. These forests are dominated by cypress, magnolia, ash, water oak, sweet gum, red maple, gordonia, American elm, titi, buckeye, fringe tree, button bush, and buckwheat tree. Notable herbaceous species here include green dragon, Jack in the pulpit, lady's tresses, greenbrier, lousewort, spider lily, lizard's tail, and St. Johnswort.

Although not part of the native flora, numerous species introduced to the coastal plain have become naturalized. Most of these species have been introduced (accidentally or deliberately) through human activity. Notable introductions on the coastal plain include tallow tree, water thyme, water hyacinth, dandelion, henbit, wild carrot, water lettuce, rattlebox, chicken spike, kudzu, and mullein.

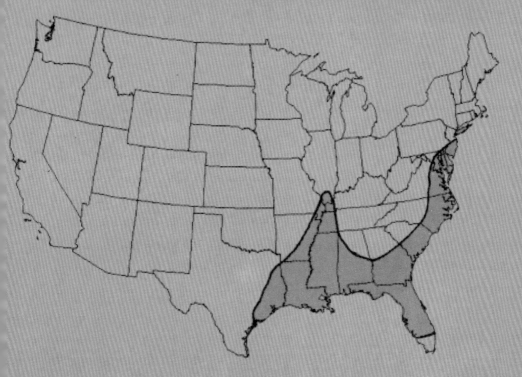

The coastal plain floristic province. Although not part of the geologic coastal plain, elements of the flora are found in Long Island, New York; and Cape Cod, Massachusetts.

SPECIES DESCRIPTIONS
AND PHOTOGRAPHS

Justicia ovata (Walt.) Lindau var. *lanceolata* (Chapman) R.W. Long

WATER WILLOW

From slender rhizomes, this glabrous perennial herb produces angled stems each up to 5 dm tall. The oppositely arranged sessile leaves are narrowly elliptic or lanceolate and somewhat membranous. Arranged in loose terminal and axillary spikes, the pale lavender or purplish flowers are bilabiate; the lower lip is marked with dark purple. Fruits are club-shaped capsules with disk-shaped seeds. Blooming from spring to fall, water willow inhabits wet woods, swamp margins, and stream banks throughout much of the Southeast. Densely arranged in spikes, the flowers of *J. americana* (L.) Vahl, American water willow, are white and marked with brown-purple on their lower lips. This species inhabits sandy or rocky streambeds, and its range extends throughout much of the eastern U.S.

Ruellia caroliniensis (J. F. Gmel.) Steud. ssp. *carolinensis* var. *caroliniensis*

WILD PETUNIA

Up to 3 dm tall, the stems of this rhizomatous perennial herb are hairy and often branched. The oppositely arranged petiolate leaves are lanceolate, narrowly elliptic, or obovate. Leaves of the upper nodes are often densely clustered. Arranged in terminal and axillary cymes, the funnelform flowers are blue, purple, or violet. Blooming from spring to summer, wild petunia inhabits open woods, fields, and thickets throughout much of the eastern U.S. *R. humilis* Nutt., fringeleaf wild petunia, has sessile leaves. This species inhabits open woods and prairies, and its range extends throughout much of the eastern U.S.

Ruellia nudiflora (Engelm. & Gray) Urban var. *nudiflora*

VIOLET WILD PETUNIA

This perennial produces erect stems each up to 7 dm tall. The oppositely arranged leaves are oblong or ovate with undulate and toothed margins. Blue or purple funnelform flowers are arranged in terminal panicles. The sepals are densely glandular-pubescent. Fruits are puberulent capsules with dark brown seeds. Blooming in summer, violet wild petunia inhabits open woods and roadsides from eastern TX to MS. With stems up to 4 dm long, *R. ciliatiflora* Hook., hairyflower wild petunia, has lower leaves that are spathulate and upper leaves that are ovate or elliptic. Inhabiting roadsides and disturbed sites in southern LA and peninsular FL, this escape from cultivation is native to South America and has become naturalized in the warmer parts of the coastal plain.

Manfreda virginica (L.) Salisb. ex Rose

FALSE ALOE

This rhizomatous perennial herb produces a basal rosette of succulent linear-lanceolate leaves that are often spotted with purple. Several-to-many tubular flowers are arranged along a scape up to 1.4 m tall. Each flower is composed of linear green tepals, stamens with prominent anthers, and a three-lobed stigma. Fruits are globose capsules. Blooming in summer, false aloe inhabits open woods throughout much of the Southeast as far north as KY and WV but is absent in peninsular FL. Native Americans used an infusion of the roots for snakebite and worms.

Yucca filamentosa L.

ADAM'S NEEDLE

This is a woody evergreen shrub with a short erect stem. Arranged in a basal rosette, the lanceolate leaves are somewhat soft and either held erect or reflexed near the middle. The margins are entire with prominent filamentous curly threads. Terminating a scapelike peduncle up to 3 m tall, the pendulous campanulate white flowers are arranged in a terminal panicle. Fruits are erect capsules with many dull black seeds. Blooming in spring, Adam's needle inhabits open woods throughout much of the eastern U.S. *Y. aloifolia* L., aloe yucca, has thickened erect leaves that bear sharp teeth on their margins. This species inhabits dunes near the coast, and its range extends from southeastern TX to FL and north to southeastern VA.

Sesuvium portulacastrum (L.) L.

SEA PURSLANE

This is a glabrous succulent perennial herb. Rooting at their nodes, the trailing stems are often mat-forming. Oppositely arranged leaves are clasping with blades that may be oblanceolate or spathulate. Flowers are solitary in the leaf axils. Each calyx is bright pink and corollas are absent. Fruits are conic circumscissile capsules with glossy black seeds. Blooming from spring to fall, sea purslane inhabits dunes and brackish marsh margins along the coast from southeastern TX to FL and north to southeastern VA. *S. maritimum* (Walt.) B.S.P., slender sea purslane, has flowers that bear only five stamens each. This species inhabits coastal beaches, and its range extends from southeastern TX to FL and north to Long Island, NY.

Alismataceae

Echinodorus cordifolius (L.) Griseb.

BURRHEAD

This aquatic perennial herb produces arching or decumbent scapes each up to 1 m long. The emergent basal leaves are ovate or elliptic with cordate or truncate bases and prominent veins. White flowers are arranged in few to several whorls. Fruits are plump oblanceolate achenes with many seeds. Blooming from spring to summer, burrhead inhabits lake margins, sluggish streams, marshes, and ditches from TX and OK to northern FL and north to eastern VA. *E. berteroi* (Spreng.) Fassett, upright burrhead, has scapes that stand erect. This species inhabits ponds and sluggish streams, and its range extends from TX to southern LA.

Sagittaria graminea Michx. ssp. *graminea*

GRASSY ARROWHEAD

From a short, stout rhizome this perennial herb produces both submergent strap-shaped phyllodia and emergent petiolate leaves with blades that are linear, lanceolate, or elliptic. Positioned in whorls, the white flowers are arranged along a scape that is usually shorter than the leaves. Flowers of the lower whorls are carpellate; those above are staminate. On ascending stalks, the fruiting heads contain achenes that are winged, ridged, and beaked. Blooming from summer to fall, grassy arrowhead inhabits swamps, marshes, ditches, and lake margins throughout much of the U.S. east of the Rocky Mountains. *S. platyphylla* (Engelm.) J.G. Sm., delta arrowhead, has its fruiting heads on recurved stalks. This species inhabits marshes, sluggish streams, and ditches, and its range extends from eastern TX, southeastern OK, southern MO, and western KY to northwestern FL.

Sagittaria lancifolia L. ssp. *media* (Micheli) Bogin

BULL TONGUE

From a stout rhizome, this perennial herb produces leaves with long, spongy petioles and elliptic or lanceolate blades. Arranged in whorls, the flowers are borne in an elongated raceme that terminates a scape up to 1.5 m tall. The lower flowers are carpellate; the upper flowers are staminate. Fruits are aggregates of falcate beaked achenes. Blooming from summer to fall, bull tongue inhabits marshes, swamps, ditches, and canals from southeastern TX and OK to FL and north to southern DE. *S. papillosa* Buch., nipplebract arrowhead, produces phyllodial leaves with spongy bases that become linear distally. This species inhabits bogs, swamps, ponds, and marshes, and its range extends from eastern TX and OK to southern MS.

Sagittaria latifolia Willd.

WAPATO

From a corm, this perennial herb produces broadly sagittate leaves with long, spongy petioles. Flowers with three uniformly white petals are arranged in a raceme atop a scape up to 8 dm tall. Whorls of staminate flowers are positioned above the lower whorls of carpellate flowers. Fruits are globose heads of aggregated, beaked lanceolate achenes. Blooming from summer to fall, wapato inhabits marshes, swamps, ditches, and canals throughout much of the eastern U.S. *S. montevidensis* Cham. & Schlecht., giant arrowhead, has petals that bear a purple or green spot at the base. This species inhabits swamps, ponds, and ditches, and its range extends from eastern TX to southern NE and east to the Atlantic coastal states as far north as southern ME.

Alliaceae

Allium canadense L. var. *canadense*
MEADOW GARLIC

This is a perennial glabrous herb with an ovoid bulb clothed in grayish or brownish fibers. The several basal leaves are linear and flattened. Subtended by three or four membraneous bracts, the pinkish or whitish campanulate flowers are arranged in a terminal umbel. Flowers often are partially or entirely replaced by bulbils. Fruits are capsules with glossy black, reticulate seeds. Blooming from spring to summer, meadow garlic inhabits open woods, fields, and roadsides throughout much of the eastern half of the U.S. The entire plant emits a strong odor of garlic.

Allium canadense L. var. *mobilense*
(Regel) Ownbey
MEADOW GARLIC

In many respects, this variety is similar to *A. canadense* var. *canadense* described above, but it can be distinguished by its tendency to produce an inflorescence of flowers only. It blooms in spring, and its range extends from southeastern TX to IL and east to the Atlantic coastal states as far north as NC. *A. canadense* L. var. *ecristatum* (M.E. Jones) Ownbey is a stouter plant that inhabits prairies near the coast in southeastern TX. Native Americans and early settlers used all parts of the plant for food.

Nothoscordum bivalve (L.) Britt.

FALSE GARLIC

This perennial herb produces a globose bulb sheathed with brownish outer bracts. Up to 3 dm tall, the basal leaves are terete or narrowly linear. Subtended by two membranous bracts, each umbel terminates a solitary scape up to 4 dm tall. The cream-colored tepals are free and marked with red or green along their midveins. Fruits are brown capsules with glossy black seeds. Blooming throughout the year, false garlic inhabits open woods, prairies, pinelands, lawns, and roadsides from southeastern NM to southern IL and east to the Atlantic coastal states as far north as VA. *N. gracilie* (Dryander) Stearn, slender false garlic, has fragrant flowers with tepals that are basally connate for at least a third of their length. This species inhabits open woods, roadsides, and disturbed sites, and its range extends from LA to northwestern FL and along the Atlantic coast from central FL to SC.

Alternanthera phiolxeroides (Mart.) Griseb.

ALLIGATORWEED

Either from a taproot or freely floating, this perennial herb produces prostrate, decumbent, or erect branching hollow stems. The oppositely arranged leaves are elliptic or oblanceolate and somewhat succulent. With clasping bases, each forms a small sheath around the stem. Pedunculate, headlike spikes of silvery white flowers are terminal or axillary. Fruits are bladderlike capsules; the seeds typically are nonviable. Blooming from spring to summer, alligatorweed inhabits lake margins, marshes, ditches, and disturbed sites from southeastern TX and OK to FL and north to southeastern VA. This introduction from South America can become invasive under favorable conditions.

Amaranthus viridis L.

GREEN AMARANTH

From a taproot, this annual monoecious herb produces succulent simple
or branching greenish or reddish stems
each up to 1 m long. The alternately arranged leaves are ovate or rhombic with
a small notch at each apex. Short spikes
of small greenish flowers are aggregated in elongated terminal and axillary
panicles. The inconspicuous staminate
flowers are situated above the larger
carpellate flowers. Fruits are ovoid utricles with brown or black seeds. Blooming from summer to fall, green amaranth inhabits fields, roadsides, gardens,
dunes, and disturbed sites from AZ to
the Atlantic coastal states as far north
as MA. *A. spinosus* L., spiny amaranth,
has sharp-spined stipules. This species
inhabits fields, roadsides, and disturbed
sites, and its range extends throughout
much of the eastern half of the U.S.

Froelichia floridana (Nutt.) Moq.

PLAINS SNAKECOTTON

From a taproot, this annual herb produces a solitary, sparingly branched, gray
or white, pubescent stem up to 1.8 m tall.
The oppositely arranged petiolate leaves
are linear, lanceolate, oblanceolate, or
oblong. Flowers are spirally arranged in
dense pedunculate spikes. Each bilabiate perianth is greenish or whitish and
clothed with dense woolly hair. Fruits
are flask-shaped utricles, each enclosed
by its persistent perianth. Blooming in
summer, plains snakecotton inhabits
open woods, prairies, and roadsides from
TX and western LA to SD and MI and
also from southeastern LA to FL and
north to southern NJ. *F. gracilis* (Hook.)
Moq.-Tandon, slender snakecotton, typically produces several branches from its
base. This species inhabits open woods,
prairies, and disturbed sites, and its
range extends from southeastern AZ
to WI and east to the Atlantic coastal
states as far north as ME.

Crinum americanum L. var. *americanum*

SWAMP LILY

Habranthus tubispathus (L'Hér.) Traub

COPPER LILY

From a large bulb, this aquatic perennial herb produces a rosette of ligulate leaves with scabrous margins. Subtended by two lanceolate bracts, an umbel of white sessile flowers terminates a scape up to 1.2 m tall. Each fragrant flower is composed of six linear tepals that are basally fused to form a short tube. Fruits are capsules with fleshy seeds. Blooming throughout the year, swamp lily inhabits swamps, marshes, and pine flatwoods along the outer coastal plain from eastern TX to FL and north to SC. An escape from cultivation, *C. zeylanicum* (L.) L., Ceylon swamp lily, has purplish red flowers. This species inhabits wet fields and disturbed sites, and it occurs in LA and peninsular FL.

From a bulb, this perennial herb produces linear leaves. Each bright yellow, funnelform flower terminates a hollow scape. Arranged in bundles, filaments are of four different lengths. Fruits are subglobose capsules with D-shaped seeds. Blooming from summer to fall, copper lily inhabits grasslands, prairies, and disturbed sites from southeastern TX to northwestern FL and central AL. It is uncertain whether this species is native or introduced. Also with yellow flowers, *Zephyranthes citrina* Baker, citron zephyrlily, has filaments that are of two different lengths but are not bundled. This species inhabits lawns, roadsides, and disturbed sites, and its range extends from southeastern LA to FL.

Hymenocallis lirisome (Raf.) Shinners

SPIDER LILY

From a large bulb, this perennial herb produces several leathery basal leaves that are linear or narrowly lanceolate. White fragrant flowers, arranged in an umbel, terminate a flattened scape. A conspicuous corona exhibits a yellow-green center; margins between the filaments are undulate or toothed. Fruits are leathery capsules with large fleshy seeds. Blooming in spring, spider lily inhabits ditches, swamps, marshes, and wet woods from eastern TX and southeastern OK to northwestern FL. *H. occidentalis* (J. Le Conte) Kunth, hammock spider lily, has oblanceolate leaves. This species inhabits hammocks and alluvial woods, and its range extends from eastern TX, OK, and southern IL to northern FL and GA.

Zephyranthes atamasca (L.) Herbert

ATAMASCO LILY

From a bulb, this perennial herb produces linear leaves with sheathing bases. Subtended by a bractlike spathe, each solitary white or pinkish, funnelform flower terminates a hollow scape. The six tepals are basally fused and form a greenish tube. Each of the six filaments is about twice the length of the tube. Fruits are globose capsules with numerous black seeds. Blooming from winter to spring, Atamasco lily inhabits mesic to wet forests, pastures, and roadsides from eastern MS to northern FL and north to VA. *Z. treatiae* S. Watson has a perianth tube that is about the same length as the filaments. This species inhabits wet pinelands and roadsides, and its range extends from peninsular FL to southeastern GA.

Zephyranthes chlorosolen (Herb.)
D. Dietrich

RAIN LILY

From a blackened bulb, this perennial herb produces several sheathing
linear leaves. Subtended by a greenish
spathe, each solitary white or pinkish
salverform flower terminates a hollow
scape. Stigmas are three-lobed. Leaves
emerge in fall when plants begin to
bloom. Fruits are globose capsules with
numerous black seeds. Rain lily inhabits wet woods, meadows, and roadsides
from TX, OK, and northwestern AR
to southern MS. *Z. drummondii* D.
Don, prairie lily, has a head-shaped
stigma. This species inhabits sandy
or rocky sites, and its range extends
from eastern TX to southwestern LA;
it also occurs in northwestern FL.

Asimina incana (Bartr.) Exell

FLAG PAWPAW

This is a much-branching deciduous
woody shrub up to 1.5 m tall. The alternately arranged leaves are obovate or
oblong, coriaceous, and densely pubescent with blonde hairs. One to several
fragrant, nodding flowers are borne in
the leaf axils of the previous year. Corolla lobes are in two unequal series.
The lobes of the outer series are creamy
white, and those of the inner series are
yellowish and shorter. Fruits are yellow-
green berries with brown seeds. Blooming in spring, flag pawpaw inhabits
sandy pinelands and scrub oak forests
from peninsular and northeastern FL
to southeastern GA. *A. longifolia* Kral,
polecat bush, has narrow ascending
leaves, solitary flowers, and inner corolla
lobes that are maroon, red, or white.
This species inhabits sandy pinelands
and occurs in southern AL, southern
GA, and northern and peninsular FL.

Apiaceae

Chaerophyllum tainturieri Hook. var. *tainturieri*

WILD CHERVIL

From a taproot, this annual herb produces an erect, branching pubescent stem up to 9 dm tall. The alternately arranged ovate leaves are pinnately compound; the ultimate leaflets are dissected. Small white flowers are arranged in compound axillary umbels. Each umbel is subtended by ovate green bracts that are reflexed at maturity. Fruits are oblong ribbed mericarps. Blooming from winter to spring, wild chervil inhabits prairies, alluvial woods, roadsides, and disturbed sites from eastern TX to southeastern NE and east to the Atlantic coastal states as far north as DE. *C. procumbens* (L.) Crantz, spreading chervil, has a glabrous stem. It inhabits alluvial woods from OK to northern FL and north to MI and NY.

Cicuta maculata L. var. *maculata*

WATER HEMLOCK

From fleshy tuberous roots, this biennial or perennial herb produces a simple or branching purplish green stem up to 2 m tall. The alternately arranged ovate leaves are pinnately compound. The leaflets are lanceolate with sharply toothed margins. Small white flowers are arranged in terminal and axillary compound umbels with an involucre that is composed of a few linear bracts or is lacking. Fruits are orbicular, glabrous ribbed mericarps. Blooming from spring to fall, water hemlock inhabits marshes, swamps, and ditches throughout much of the eastern half of the U.S. All parts of the plant are considered toxic. Native Americans used the root as a contraceptive.

Cyclospermum leptophyllum (Pers.) Sprague ex Britt. & P. Wilson

MARSH PARSLEY

From a slender taproot, this introduced annual herb produces glabrous, branching stems each up to 6 dm long. The alternately arranged ovate leaves are pinnately compound; the segments are linear or filiform. Sessile or borne on peduncles, umbels of small white flowers are simple or compound. Fruits are ovoid, glabrous ribbed mericarps. Blooming from spring to summer, marsh parsley inhabits ditches, prairies, roadsides, and disturbed sites from CA to FL and north to NY. Similar in appearance, *Apium graveolens* L., wild celery, is a Eurasian perennial herb up to 1.5 m tall. An escape from cultivation, this species occurs throughout the southern half of the U.S. and along the Atlantic coastal states as far north as MA.

Daucus carota L

QUEEN ANNE'S LACE

From a taproot, this herbaceous biennial introduction from Europe produces a solitary, freely branching stem up to 2 m tall. The alternately arranged leaves are oblong and pinnately dissected. Compound umbels of small white flowers are subtended by a series of pinnately divided bracts. The central flower may be white or purplish. Fruits are ovoid, flattened, ribbed, bristly mericarps. Blooming from spring to fall, Queen Anne's lace inhabits fields, roadsides, gardens, and disturbed sites throughout much of the U.S. The cultivated carrot is the domesticated form of this species. A native annual, *D. pusillus* Michx., American wild carrot, is a shorter species with a simple or sparingly branched stem. This species inhabits roadsides and disturbed sites, and its range extends throughout much of the southern half of the U.S.

Eryngium aquaticum L. var. *aquaticum*

RATTLESNAKEMASTER

This biennial or perennial herb produces a solitary branching stem up to 2 m tall. The alternately arranged linear or lanceolate toothed leaves are sheathing. Heads of bluish flowers are arranged in open cymes. Bluish-reflexed bracts subtend each head. Fruits are angled mericarps with prominent scales on the edges. Blooming from spring to summer, rattlesnakemaster inhabits fresh or brackish marshes, wet pinelands, savannas, bogs, and ditches from southern MS to FL and north to NY. *E. prostratum* Nutt. ex DC., creeping eryngo, is a smaller plant with prostrate stems. This species inhabits swamps, alluvial woods, and ditches, and its range extends from TX, OK, and MO east to the Atlantic coastal states as far north as VA.

Eryngium yuccifolium Michx. var. *yuccifolium*

SNAKEROOT

From bunched tuberous roots, this perennial herb produces a single branched stem up to 1 m long. The thickened leaves are mostly linear with a few bristles. The basal leaves may exceed 1 dm long. Dense floral heads, subtended by spiny leaflike bracts, are arranged in terminal cymes. The rigid, erect sepals are persistent, and the corollas are white. Fruits are pyramid-shaped mericarps with prominent scales on the angles. Blooming from spring to summer, snakeroot inhabits savannas, pinelands, prairies, open woods, and bogs throughout much of the eastern U.S. *E. integrifolium* Walt., blueflower eryngo, has basal leaves that are generally less than 1 dm long. This species inhabits wet pinelands, savannas, and bogs, and its range extends from TX and OK to FL and north to VA.

Hydrocotyl umbellata L.

Hydrocotyl bonariensis Comm. ex Lam.

LARGELEAF MARSH PENNYWORT

This is a glabrous perennial herb with
creeping stems that root at the nodes.
On long petioles, the peltate and somewhat thickened alternate leaves are orbicular to broadly ovate with rounded
teeth on the margins. The inflorescence
is a much-branched series of compound
umbels. Each umbel is subtended by
an involucre of lanceolate bracts. The
greenish white or yellow flowers are arranged in interrupted verticils. Fruits
are ellipsoid mericarps that divide into
sharp-ribbed mericarps. Blooming from
spring to fall, largeleaf marsh pennywort inhabits coastal sand dunes, wet
savannas, prairies, and ditches from
southeastern TX to FL and north to
southeastern VA. *H. verticillata* Thunb.,
whorled marsh pennywort, has an inflorescence that is composed of one to
several interrupted spikes. This species
inhabits swamps, stream banks, and
ditches, and its range extends from
CA to FL and north to MA.

This is a perennial herb with creeping or
floating stems rooting at the nodes. The
alternately arranged leaves are peltate
and orbicular with shallowly lobed margins. Simple umbels of small white flowers terminate axillary peduncles. Fruits
are reniform schizocarps. Blooming
from spring to fall, marsh pennywort
inhabits swamps, marshes, lake margins,
and ditches from eastern TX and OK to
FL and north to eastern MA. Often mat
forming, *H. ranunculoides* L. f., floating
marsh pennywort, has leaves that are
not peltate as the petiole attaches to
the sinus at the base of the leaf blade.
This species inhabits lake margins and
ditches, and its range extends from eastern TX to KS and east to the Atlantic
coastal states as far north as NY.

Limnosciadium pinnatum (DC.) Mathias & Constance

TANSY DOGSHADE

From a fascicle of fibrous roots, this annual herb produces branching stems, each up to 8 dm long. Both basal and stem leaves are entire or pinnately divided into linear or lanceolate lobes. Compound umbels of small white flowers are subtended by linear or lanceolate reflexed bracts. Individual umbels are subtended by linear bractlets. Fruits are oblong, glabrous ribbed mericarps. Blooming from spring to summer, tansy dogshade inhabits open wet woods and ditches from eastern TX to western MS and north to southern IL and MO. *L. pumilum* (Engelm. & Gray) Mathias & Constance, prairie dogshade, is a low, diffuse annual herb from eastern TX, southwestern LA, and southeastern AR.

Oxypolis filiformis (Walt.) Britt.

HOG FENNEL

From a cluster of fibrous roots, this perennial herb produces a solitary stem up to 1.8 m tall. Sheathing on the stem, the alternately arranged hollow leaves are reduced to bladeless expanded petioles. Small white flowers are arranged in compound umbels along the upper stem. Each umbel is subtended by an involucre of narrowly lanceolate bracts. Fruits are flattened, ovoid winged mericarps. Blooming from summer to fall, hog fennel inhabits wet pinelands, savannas, prairies, bogs, and ditches from TX to FL and north to NC. *O. rigidior* (L.) Raf., stiff cowbane, has pinnately compound leaves. It inhabits stream banks, bogs, wet woods, swamps, and marshes throughout much of the eastern U.S.

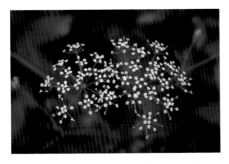

Ptilimnium capillaceum (Michx.) Raf.

BISHOP'S WEED

From fibrous roots, this annual herb produces erect, branching, glabrous stems each up to 8 dm tall. The alternately arranged oblong leaves are pinnately dissected and verticillate with three leaves per node. Terminal and axillary compound umbels of small white flowers are subtended by an involucre of simple and pinnately three-cleft filiform bracts. Fruits are corky-banded, ovoid ribbed mericarps. Blooming from spring to summer, bishop's weed inhabits wet woods, marshes, lake margins, and ditches from eastern TX to KS and east to the Atlantic coastal states as far north as MA. *P. nuttallii* (DC.) Britt., laceflower, bears two leaves per node, and its involucral bracts are entire. This species inhabits wet prairies, low fields, and ditches, and its range extends from eastern TX to southern IL and east to southwestern AL.

Sanicula canadensis L. var. *canadensis*

BLACK SNAKEROOT

From a fascicle of fibrous roots, this biennial or perennial herb produces a solitary stem that is simple or dichotomously branched above. The alternately arranged leaves are palmately divided into ovate or obovate sharply toothed leaflets. The upper stems are terminated by compound umbels of greenish white flowers. Each umbel is subtended by small leaflike bracts. Globose mericarps bear numerous hooked bristles. Blooming from spring to summer, black snakeroot inhabits mesic woods throughout much of the eastern half of the U.S. *S. smallii* Bickn., Small's snakeroot, has tuberous roots. This species inhabits rich woods, and its range extends from eastern TX to IL and east to the Atlantic coastal states as far north as VA.

Zizia aurea (L.) W.D.J. Koch

GOLDEN ALEXANDER

From a cluster of thickened roots, this perennial herb produces glabrous, branching stems each up to 8 dm tall. The alternately arranged leaves are mostly ternately compound. The leaflets are lanceolate with toothed margins and are often irregularly lobed. Bright yellow flowers are arranged in terminal compound umbels. Fruits are ellipsoid ribbed mericarps. Blooming from spring to summer, golden Alexander inhabits alluvial woods, prairies, and fields throughout much of the eastern half of the U.S. Native Americans used the plant for the treatment of fever and headache.

Apocynaceae

Amsonia tabernaemontana Walt. var. tabernaemontana

BLUESTAR

This showy perennial herb produces several stems, each up to 1 m tall. Alternately arranged glabrous leaves are lanceolate or narrowly elliptic. The blue pubescent flowers are salverform and arranged in loose terminal cymes. Stamens are adnate to the corolla tube; the anthers are orange. Fruits are terete follicles with many corky seeds. Blooming in spring, bluestar inhabits wet woods and savannas from TX, OK, and KS east to the Atlantic coastal states as far north as NY and MA. *A. rigida* Shuttlw. ex Small, stiff bluestar, has glabrous corollas. This species inhabits wet pinelands, swamps, and pond margins, and its range extends from LA to FL and GA.

Araceae

Arisaema dracontium (L.) Schott

GREEN DRAGON

From a large corm, this monoecious or dioecious perennial herb produces one or two leaves, each with a stem-like petiole. The blade is pedately divided into several elliptic or oblanceolate leaflets. Terminating a solitary peduncle, the inflorescence consists of a pale green, sheathlike spathe that surrounds the unisexual flowers at the base of an elongated yellow spadix. The fruit is an aggregate of orange-red berries. Blooming from spring to summer, green dragon inhabits mesic and wet woods throughout much of the eastern U.S. Native Americans used this plant in the treatment of female disorders and to inspire supernatural dreams.

Arisaema triphyllum (L.) Schott ssp. *triphyllum*

JACK IN THE PULPIT

From a globose corm this monoecious or dioecious perennial herb produces one or two palmately divided leaves. Each leaflet is broadly elliptic. The unisexual flowers are embedded in the base of a white or purple spadix. A green spathe, striped with either purple or white, surrounds and arches over the spadix. The fruit is an aggregate of bright red berries. Blooming in spring, Jack in the pulpit inhabits mesic and wet woods throughout much of the eastern U.S. Larger plants are typically female and smaller plants are male. Native Americans roasted the corm for food and placed the dried fruits in gourds to make rattles.

Orontium aquaticum L.
GOLDENCLUB

From a stout rhizome, this aquatic perennial herb produces emergent blue-
green basal leaves with long petioles and
broadly elliptic blades. Terminating an
erect scape, small flowers are borne in a
bright yellow spadix that is subtended
by an inconspicuous sheathlike spathe.
Flowers along the base of the spadix are
bisexual; those toward the distal end are
staminate. The fruit is a cluster of blue-
green berries. Blooming in spring, goldenclub inhabits marshes, swamps, and
streams from southern LA to FL and
north to MA. Native Americans ate
the dried or roasted fruit.

Peltandra sagittifolia (Michx.)
Morong
SPOON FLOWER

From a robust corm, this species produces a scape up to 6 dm tall. The long-
petioled hastate leaves are somewhat
glaucous. Unisexual flowers, devoid of
perianth parts, are embedded in an
orange-yellow spadix. The lower portion
of the spathe is green and constricted
into a closed tube that surrounds the
flowers; the upper portion is white, open,
and concave. The fruit is an aggregate of
bright red berries that is subtended by a
persistent spathe. Blooming from spring
to summer, spoon flower inhabits acidic
swamps, bogs, and hammocks along the
outer coastal plain from southeastern
LA to FL and north to NC.

Pistia stratiotes L.

This free-floating aquatic perennial herb produces a dense growth of feather-shaped roots. Arranged in a basal rosette, the prominently ridged, spongy leaves are obovate to spathulate. The inconspicuous unisexual flowers are embedded in a short spadix that is adnate to a whitish green spathe. Fruits are brown berries with cylindrical seeds. Blooming from summer to winter, water lettuce inhabits canals, ditches, ponds, and marshes along the outer coastal plain from southeastern TX to LA; it also occurs in peninsular FL. Because plants rapidly reproduce asexually from stolons, they can become weedy and choke waterways. It is unclear whether this is a native or introduced species in the U.S.

Peltandra virginica (L.) Schott

TUCKAHOE

This is a perennial herb with thickened fibrous roots. Hastate leaves are glossy green and glaucous. One to several scapes extend up to 6 dm long. Embedded with small unisexual flowers, the lower portion of each cream-colored spadix is enclosed by a thickened green spathe. At flowering, the upper spathe opens slightly, allowing the entry of pollinators. Each fruit is an aggregate of dark green berries surrounded by the persistent spathe. Blooming from spring to summer, tuckahoe inhabits swamps, marshes, and ditches throughout much of the eastern U.S. Its berries are an important food source for waterfowl. Native Americans used the roots for food and medicine.

Arecaceae

Sabal minor (Jacq.) Pers.

DWARF PALMETTO

The stem of this evergreen species typically remains subterranean. The fan-
shaped leaves are plicate with short
midribs and unarmed petioles. A sparingly branched axillary inflorescence
bears panicles of small, creamy white,
fragrant flowers. Fruits are brownish black spheroid drupes with glossy
seeds. Blooming from spring to summer, dwarf palmetto inhabits hammocks, alluvial woods, and swamps
from eastern TX and southern AR to
FL and north to southeastern NC. *S.
palmetto* (Walt.) Lodd. ex J.A. & J.H.
Schultes, cabbage palm, has an aerial
stem. This species inhabits open woods,
dunes, and coastal marshes, and occurs
in FL and southern GA and also in
northeastern SC and southeastern NC.

Serenoa repens (Bart.) Small

SAW PALMETTO

This perennial produces a robust underground branching stem that may become aerial and trunklike. On stout
petioles with recurved spines, the green
or bluish leaves are palmately divided.
One to several persistent bracts subtends stout axillary panicles of creamy
white flowers. Fruits are black, ellipsoid
drupes. Blooming in spring, saw palmetto inhabits pinelands, scrub forests,
and dunes from southeastern LA to FL
and north to southeastern SC. Fruits
provide food for numerous animals including raccoons, bears, deer, and birds.

Asclepiadaceae

Asclepias connivens Baldw.

LARGE-FLOWER MILKWEED

From a well-developed obconic rhizome, this perennial herb produces a solitary branched stem up to 8 dm tall. The oppositely arranged leaves are sessile and vary from ovate to oblanceolate. The yellowish green flowers are arranged in axillary umbels. Corolla lobes are reflexed and the hoods are incurved so that the tips meet over the gynostegium. Fruits are fusiform capsules with comose seeds. Blooming in spring, large-flower milkweed inhabits wet pinelands and savannas from southern AL to FL and southern GA. This species is listed as rare by the Georgia Department of Natural Resources in that state.

Asclepias humistrata Walt.

PINEWOODS MILKWEED

This perennial herb produces one to several spreading stout stems each up to 7 dm long. The succulent, alternately arranged leaves are sessile with auriculate bases. The conspicuous veins are lavender or pale pink. Umbels of pale rose or lavender-colored flowers are borne in the upper leaf axils. Horns of the corona are slightly shorter than the hoods. Fruits are erect follicles with comose seeds. Blooming from spring to summer, pinewoods milkweed inhabits open sandy woods and sandhills from southeastern LA to FL and north to NC. *A. amplexicaulis* Sm., creeping milkweed, has erect stems and rose-purple flowers. This species inhabits open woods, roadsides, and fields, and its range extends throughout much of the eastern U.S.

Asclepias lanceolata Walt.

LANCE-LEAVED MILKWEED

From a rhizome with tuberous roots, this perennial herb produces a solitary simple stem up to 1.2 m tall. The oppositely arranged leaves are linear or lanceolate and perpendicular to the stem. One or several umbels are arranged in a terminal inflorescence. The corolla lobes are reflexed and orange-red; the hoods and horns are orange. Fruits are narrowly fusiform, glabrous follicles. Blooming from spring to summer, lance-leaved milkweed inhabits wet pinelands, savannas, bogs, ditches, seeps, and ditches from eastern TX to FL and north to southern NJ. *A. curassavica* L., bloodflower, is an introduced annual herb with ascending leaves and umbels borne in the leaf axils. This species inhabits wet woods, pastures, and disturbed sites, and it occurs in eastern TX, southern LA, and peninsular FL.

Asclepias longifolia Michx.

LONGLEAF MILKWEED

From a stout tuberous rhizome, this perennial herb produces a solitary stem up to 7 dm tall. The numerous leaves are linear and sessile. Flowers are arranged in terminal and axillary umbels. The hornless corollas are greenish white and marked with maroon. Fruits are fusiform follicles with comose seeds. Blooming from spring to summer, longleaf milkweed inhabits wet pinelands and savannas from eastern TX to FL and north to DE. This and other milkweed species produce steroidal glycosides that are toxic to many vertebrates including humans. Feeding on milkweed plants, monarch butterfly caterpillars deposit these compounds in their tissues. After metamorphosis, the butterflies are toxic to most birds.

Asclepias obovata Ell.

PINELAND MILKWEED

From a slender rhizome, this perennial herb produces a simple or sparingly branched, softly pubescent stem up to 7 dm tall. The oppositely arranged leaves are ovate, oblong, or elliptic and densely tomentose on the abaxial surfaces. Pale, greenish yellow flowers are densely arranged in terminal and axillary umbels. The sharply curved falcate horns are shorter than the hoods. Fruits are fusiform pubescent follicles. Blooming from spring to summer, pineland milkweed inhabits pinelands, savannas, open woods, and fields from eastern TX and OK to northwestern FL and north to southeastern SC. Also with pale greenish yellow flowers, *A. tomentosa* Ell., tuba milkweed, has horns that are longer than the hoods. This species inhabits open woods and sandhills, and its range extends from eastern TX to FL and north to southeastern NC.

Asclepias pedicellata Walt.

SAVANNA MILKWEED

From a knotty, elongated rhizome, this perennial herb produces a solitary pubescent stem up to 3 dm long. Oppositely arranged sessile leaves are lanceolate or linear-oblong. The greenish-yellow flowers are arranged in axillary and terminal umbels. The corolla lobes are held erect, and the gynostegium is elevated above the hoods. Fruits are follicles with comose seeds. Blooming from spring to summer, savanna milkweed inhabits wet pinelands and savannas from FL to southeastern NC. Also with green flowers, *A. viridiflora* Raf., green comet milkweed, is a robust species with a gynostegium that is not elevated above the hoods. It inhabits fields, roadsides, and disturbed sites, and its range extends throughout much of the U.S. excluding the West Coast.

Asclepias perennis Walt.

AQUATIC MILKWEED

From a thickened rootstock, this perennial herb produces several stems each up to 4 dm tall. The opposite, narrowly elliptic leaves are nearly glabrous. White flowers are arranged in terminal and axillary umbels. The gynostegium is light purple. Coronas bear small horns. Blooming from spring to fall, aquatic milkweed grows in wet woods, swamps, and lake margins throughout much of the southeastern U.S. and lower Midwest. Unlike most members of the genus that produce comose wind-dispersed seeds, this species bears seeds that are specialized for water dispersal.

Asclepias rubra L.

RED MILKWEED

From a filiform rhizome, this perennial herb produces a solitary simple stem up to 1 m tall. The oppositely arranged sessile leaves are lanceolate or ovate with rounded or cordate bases. Flowers are arranged in axillary and terminal umbels. The reflexed corolla lobes are dull red, purplish, or lavender; the hoods are pinkish. Fruits are glabrous, filiform follicles with comose seeds. Blooming in summer, red milkweed inhabits wet pinelands, savannas, swamps, bogs, and seeps from eastern TX to northwestern FL and north to Long Island, NY. This uncommon species is listed as endangered in MD and extirpated in PA.

Asclepias tuberosa L. ssp. *tuberosa*

BUTTERFLY WEED

This showy perennial herb produces one to several stems from a large branching rhizome. The alternately arranged lanceolate leaves are roughly hairy. Orange, red, or yellow flowers are arranged in umbels. Sepals and petals are reflexed. The connate filaments bear appendages that form a prominent petaloid corona with small horns. Fruits are fusiform follicles with wind-dispersed comose seeds. Blooming from spring to summer, butterfly weed inhabits open sandy woods, fields, and pinelands throughout much of the U.S. excluding the Northeast. Not only for butterflies, this species provides nectar for bees and beetles as well.

Asclepias viridis Walt.

ANTELOPE HORN

From a fusiform caudex, this perennial produces one to several erect or decumbent stems. The alternately arranged leaves are lanceolate with entire margins. Hoods are purple and marked with white; horns are absent. Fruits are green fusiform follicles with numerous comose seeds. Blooming from spring to summer, antelope horn inhabits open locations in fields, roadsides, and wood margins from TX to NE and east to the Atlantic coastal states as far north as SC. Although numerous follicles are set initially, very few develop and mature. This phenomenon has been attributed to a late-acting self-incompatibility pollination strategy in the genus.

Matelea gonocarpos (Walt.) Shinners

ANGLE POD

This is a high-climbing or trailing, herbaceous perennial vine. The oppositely arranged leaves are broadly ovate or elliptic with cordate bases. Arranged in axillary umbels, flowers are green or yellow and often suffused with purple. Fruits are sharply angled follicles with comose seeds. Blooming from spring to summer, angle pod inhabits wet woods and stream banks from eastern TX to FL and north to MO, IL, IN, and MD. *M. carolinense* (Jacq.) Woods, Carolina milkweed, has maroon petals. This species inhabits rich woods along stream banks, and its range extends throughout much of the Southeast excluding FL.

Acmella repens (Walt.) L.C. Rich.

CREEPING SPOTFLOWER

From a rhizome, this perennial herb produces creeping or erect stems that bear adventitious roots at their nodes. The oppositely arranged leaves are rhombic, ovate, or lanceolate with petioles up to 4 cm long and margins that are toothed or entire. Hemispheric heads of orange or yellow ray and disk florets are solitary or arranged in corymbs. Bearing whitish glandular hairs, the phyllaries are ovate or linear. Fruits are angled, ellipsoid, blackish achenes. Blooming throughout the year, creeping spotflower inhabits stream banks, lake margins, and ditches from southeastern TX to southeastern MO and east to the Atlantic coastal states as far north as southern NC. *A. pusilla* (Hook. & Arn.) R.K. Jansen, dwarf spotflower, has petioles that are less than 4 mm long. This species inhabits disturbed sites, and its range extends from northwestern FL to NC.

Aphanostephus skirrhobasis (DC.)
Trel. var. *thalassius* Shinners

LAZY DAISY

From a taproot, this freely branching annual herb produces gray-pubescent stems, each up to 4 dm long. The alternately arranged leaves are woolly gray pubescent with pinnately lobed or entire margins. Hemispheric heads are solitary. The disk florets are yellow, and the ligules of the ray florets are white with rose-colored striations on their abaxial surfaces. The phyllaries are lanceolate or oblong and pubescent with ciliated margins. Fruits are ribbed achenes that are tipped with pointed scales. Blooming throughout the year, lazy daisy inhabits coastal sand dunes and beaches from southeastern TX to northern FL. Plants are grazed by deer and cattle.

Arnoglossum ovatum (Walt.)
H.E. Robins.

CACALIA

From a caudex, this perennial herb produces a simple glabrous stem up to 3 m tall. The alternately arranged leaves are mostly lanceolate or narrowly ovate. Petiolate on the lower stem, the leaves become sessile and reduced distally. Arranged in corymbs, the cylindrical-shaped heads bear greenish white or yellow florets that are sometimes tinged with lavender. Phyllaries are linear with hyaline margins. Fruits are brown, fusiform ribbed achenes. Blooming from spring to summer, cacalia inhabits wet pinelands, savannas, and ditches from southeastern TX to FL and north to southeastern NC. *A. sulcatum* (Fern.) H.E. Robins., Georgia Indian plantain, has phyllaries with conspicuously winged midveins. This species inhabits swamps and hillside seeps, and its range extends from southern AL to northwestern FL and southwestern GA.

Balduina uniflora Nutt.

HONEYCOMB HEAD

Baccharis halimifolia L.

SEA MYRTLE

This is a freely branching, dioecious, suffruticose deciduous shrub up to 6 m tall. The alternately arranged leaves are elliptic, obovate, oblanceolate, or rhombic with cuneate bases and toothed margins. Campanulate heads bearing white disk florets are arranged in terminal leafy panicles. Phyllaries are ovate or lanceolate and greenish white with hyaline margins. Fruits are ribbed achenes with white, fluffy, conspicuous pappus. Blooming in fall, sea myrtle inhabits open woods, roadsides, marshes, beaches, and disturbed sites from eastern TX to FL and north to MA. *B. angustifolia* Michx., saltwater false willow, has fleshy entire leaves. This species inhabits coastal marshes, and its range extends from LA to FL and north to NC.

From fibrous roots, this perennial herb produces one to several erect stems, each bearing a solitary floral head. Typically absent at flowering, the mostly oblanceolate leaves form a basal rosette. Leaves along the stem are alternately arranged and linear. An involucre of imbricate, ovate bracts subtends each head. Both ray and disk florets are yellow. Fruits are obconic achenes. Blooming from summer to fall, honeycomb head inhabits wet pinelands and savannas along the coastal plain from southeastern LA to northern FL and north to southeastern NC. *B. atropurpurea* Harper, purpledisk honeycomb head, has purple disk florets. This species inhabits wet pinelands and savannas, and its range extends along the coastal plain from southern MS to northern FL and north to southeastern NC.

Berlandiera pumila (Michx.) Nutt.

GREENEYES

From a fleshy-rooted crown, this suffruticose perennial produces one to several
erect stems, each up to 1.1 m tall. The
ovate, petiolate leaves are velvety pubescent with toothed margins. Arranged
in panicles, the hemispheric heads bear
red-maroon disk florets and ray florets
with yellow ligules veined with green
on their abaxial surfaces. Phyllaries are
ovate or elliptic and imbricate. Fruits
are densely pubescent, flattened achenes
that remain attached to the persistent
phyllaries. Blooming from spring to
summer, greeneyes inhabits open woods
and fields from eastern TX to northern
FL and north to northern NC. *B.*
X *betonicifolia* (Hook.) Small, Texas
greeneyes, has scabrous leaves that are
deltoid, lanceolate, or ovate. This species inhabits open sandy woods, and
its range extends from eastern NM to
western LA and north to southern KS
and southern MO.

Bidens aristosa (Michx.) Britt.

BEARDED BEGGARTICKS

This is an annual herb with stems up
to 1.5 m tall. The oppositely arranged
leaves are petiolate and pinnately compound. The leaflets are coarsely toothed
or lobed. The showy, campanulate floral
heads are arranged in corymbs. Ligules
of the ray florets are yellow with purplish striations; the disk florets are
yellow. Arranged in several series, the
phyllaries are linear or lanceolate. Fruits
are flattened achenes with barbed awns.
Blooming from summer to fall, bearded
beggarticks inhabits wet woods, fields,
and roadsides throughout much of the
eastern U.S. *B. bipinnata* L., Spanish
needles, has smaller floral heads and
fusiform achenes. This species inhabits
fields, forests, and disturbed sites, and its
range also extends throughout much of
the eastern U.S.

Bidens laevis (L.) B.S.P.

SMOOTH BEGGARTICKS

This is an annual or perennial herb with stems up to 1.5 m tall. Plants growing in standing water produce freely branching, decumbent, mat-forming stems. Otherwise, the stems are simple and erect. The oppositely arranged leaves are lanceolate or elliptic and sessile with finely toothed margins. Hemispheric-shaped heads bear yellow-orange ray and disk florets. The outer series of phyllaries are green with toothed margins and somewhat leaflike; the inner series are yellow-orange and raylike. Fruits are flattened achenes with barbed awns. Blooming from summer to fall, smooth beggarticks inhabits marshes, swamps, ditches, and canals from CA to the Atlantic coastal states as far north as southern NJ. *B. mitis* (Michx.) Sherff, smallfruit beggarticks, has petiolate leaves. This species inhabits marshes, and its range extends from southeastern TX to FL and north to southern NJ.

Bidens pilosa L.

HAIRY BEGGARTICKS

This is an introduced, annual, erect branching herb up to 1.8 m tall. The leaves are oppositely arranged and petiolate. Leaflets are ovate or lanceolate with entire or toothed margins. Campanulate heads of white ray and yellow disk florets are solitary or in open corymbs. The phyllaries are lanceolate or oblong with ciliated margins. Fruits are linear fusiform achenes with erect awns. Blooming throughout the year, hairy beggarticks inhabits roadsides, ditches, and disturbed sites from CA to FL and north to MA. Found throughout the warm regions of the world, this species is used as a traditional herbal medicine to treat a variety of ailments.

Borrichia frutescens (L.) DC.

SEA OXEYE DAISY

Bigelowia nuttallii L.C. Anders.

RAYLESS GOLDENROD

From a small caudex this perennial herb produces stems up to 6 dm tall. A basal rosette of linear leaves is present at flowering. Leaves along the stem are alternately arranged and linear. The discoid heads of bright yellow florets are arranged in a flat-topped corymb. The involucre is cylindrical shaped with closely appressed yellow bracts. Phyllaries are lanceolate and yellowish. Fruits are sparsely pubescent, turbinate achenes. Blooming from summer to fall, rayless goldenrod inhabits pinelands, savannas, and stream banks from eastern TX to central FL and GA. *B. nudata* (Michx.) DC., pineland rayless goldenrod, has leaves that are elliptic or oblanceolate. This species inhabits wet prairies and pinelands, and its range extends from eastern TX to northern FL and north to NC.

Up to 1 m tall, this rhizomatous, freely branched, colonial perennial herb produces erect, decumbent, or arching stems. The oppositely arranged fleshy leaves are obovate or oblanceolate and densely pubescent with margins that are sometimes finely toothed. Some petioles bear spine-tipped teeth. A hemispheric head of yellow ray and disk florets terminates each stem. Phyllaries are leaf-like with mucronate or spine-tipped apices. Fruits are gray, obconic, angled achenes. Blooming from spring to summer, sea oxeye daisy inhabits brackish marshes, mud flats, and roadsides along the outer coastal plain from southeastern TX to FL and north to southeastern VA. Butterflies, especially the Gulf fritillary, are its primary pollinators.

Calyptocarpus vialis Less.

STRAGGLER DAISY

This is a perennial herb with freely
branching prostrate or decumbent
stems. The oppositely arranged petiolate leaves are mostly deltoid with finely
toothed margins. Obconic heads of yellow ray and disk florets are borne singly
on axillary peduncles. Phyllaries are
linear or lanceolate and leaflike with
stiff, white, appressed hairs. Fruits are
flattened, tuberculate achenes with erect
awns. Blooming throughout the year,
straggler daisy inhabits disturbed sites
from TX to FL. This species can become
an invasive weed in lawns and gardens.

Carphephorus corymbosus (Nutt.)
Torr. & Gray

CHAFF HEAD

From a stout basal crown, this perennial
herb produces a solitary simple green
stem up to 1.5 m tall. Typically absent
a flowering, the basal leaves are mostly
spathulate. Leaves along the stem are
sessile, oblong-spathulate, punctate, and
reduced distally. Subtended by thin, oblong phyllaries, the discoid floral heads
are arranged in panicles. Corollas are
lavender or pink. Fruits are brown, pubescent achenes. Blooming from summer to fall, chaff head inhabits wet to
dry pinelands from FL to southeastern GA. Up to 8 dm tall, *C. tomentosus*
(Michx.) Torr. & Gray, woolly chaff
head, is a shorter plant with purple
stems. This species inhabits pinelands
and savannas, and its range extends
from southeastern GA to eastern VA.

Carphephorus odoratissimus (J.F. Gmel.) Herbert var. *odoratissimus*

VANILLA LEAF

From a crown this fragrant perennial herb produces a solitary glabrous stem up to 1.5 m tall. Leaf blades are oblanceolate or obovate. Petiolate leaves of the basal rosette typically are withered at flowering. Leaves along the stem are sessile and reduced distally. Campanulate heads of pinkish or purple disk florets are arranged in flat-topped corymbs. Closely imbricated, the oblong phyllaries are thin, membranous, and punctate. Fruits are brown, pubescent achenes. Blooming from summer to fall, vanilla leaf inhabits wood margins, pinelands, savannas, and bogs from southeastern LA to FL and north to NC. *C. paniculatus* (J.F. Gmel.) Herbert, hairy chaff head, has a pubescent stem. This species inhabits wet pinelands, savannas, and prairies, and its range extends from southeastern AL to FL and north to NC.

Chaptalia tomentosa Vent.

WOOLLY SUNBONNETS

This is an acaulescent perennial herb with fibrous roots. Arranged in a basal rosette, the leaves are oblong, elliptic, or oblanceolate with short remote teeth on their margins. The adaxial surfaces are thickly clothed in woolly pubescence. Solitary on elongated peduncles, campanulate-shaped heads bear ray florets with ligules that are white above and purplish below. The disk florets are cream colored. Phyllaries are closely imbricated and bear felty pubescence. Fruits are fusiform ribbed achenes with persistent glandular-pubescent pappus. Blooming in spring, woolly sunbonnets inhabits wet pinelands, savannas, and bogs from eastern TX to FL and north to eastern NC. The Seminoles used this herb to treat a condition called deer sickness, wherein the arms or legs become weak and painful.

Cirsium carolinianum (Walt.)
Fern. & Schub.

CAROLINA THISTLE

From a stubby taproot, this biennial
typically produces a solitary stem that
is branching above. Arranged in a
basal rosette and alternately along the
stem, leaves are weakly lobed and bear
spines only on the margins. A head of
densely arranged disk florets is purple
or pink. The closely imbricate phyllaries are spine tipped with a sticky white
gland on the midrib. Fruits are comose
achenes. Blooming from spring to summer, Carolina thistle occurs in open
woods and thickets from TX, AR, and
OK to FL and north to VA. *C. nuttallii*
DC., Nuttall's thistle, has a conspicuously winged lower stem. This species
inhabits woodlands, roadsides, and
ditches, and its range extends from
LA to FL and north to VA.

Cirsium horridulum Michx.
var. *horridulum*

BULL THISTLE

This biennial herb produces a solitary
hollow stem up to 1.5 m tall. Arranged
in basal rosettes and along the stem,
the spiny-margined leaves are pinnately lobed. Purple, pink, yellow, or
white disc florets are densely arranged
in a head that is subtended by an inner series of pubescent, spiny-margined,
involucral bracts and an outer series
of erect, spine-toothed, leaflike bracts.
Fruits are tan-colored comose achenes.
Blooming from winter to spring, bull
thistle inhabits fields, open woods, pastures, savannas, and pinelands from
TX, OK, and AR to FL and north to
ME. Flowers are pollinated by bees
and butterflies, and the stem plays host
to insect larvae. Young stems can be
chewed, juiced, or served in salads.

Conoclinium coelestinum (L.) DC.

MISTFLOWER

From a long, slender rhizome, this much-branching colonial perennial produces stems up to 1 m tall. The oppositely arranged leaves are ovate, toothed, and marked with resin dots. Arranged in leafy corymbs, each campanulate head bears blue or lavender florets. Arranged in three series, the phyllaries are linear and pubescent. Fruits are five-angled achenes bearing resin glands. Blooming from summer to fall, mistflower inhabits low woods, stream banks, ditches, and fields throughout much of the eastern U.S. *C. betonicifolium* (P. Mill.) King & H.E. Robins., betony-leaf mistflower, has oblong leaf blades. This species inhabits open woods, marshes, and beaches, and it occurs on the coastal plain of TX.

Coreopsis basalis (A. Dietr.) Blake

GOLDENMANE TICKSEED

From a taproot, this annual herb produces numerous stems, each up to 4 dm long. The oppositely arranged leaves are pinnately compound; the leaflets are linear, elliptic, or ovate. Arranged in diffuse corymbs, the heads bear purple disk florets and ray florets that are purple, yellow, or yellow with purple bases. Phyllaries of the inner series are lanceolate or ovate; those of the outer series are conspicuously shorter and linear. Fruits are ellipsoid, brown, papillate achenes. Blooming from spring to summer, goldenmane tickseed inhabits sandy fields and roadsides from southeastern TX to FL and north to southeastern NC. *C. tripteris* L., tall tickseed, is a tall, rhizomatous perennial herb with stems up to 2 m tall. This species inhabits prairies, alluvial areas, and upland woods, and its range extends from eastern TX to southern MI and east to the Atlantic coastal states as far north as southeastern MA.

Coreopsis lanceolata L.

LANCELEAF TICKSEED

From a short rhizome with wiry roots, this sparingly branched perennial herb produces stems each up to 6 dm long. Leaves are glabrous and lanceolate or oblanceolate. The basal leaves are petiolate; those on the stem are opposite and sessile. Solitary floral heads bearing yellow ray and disk florets are subtended by lanceolate or broadly ovate involucral bracts with hyaline margins. Achenes are black and winged. Blooming from spring to summer, lanceleaf tickseed inhabits open woods, roadsides, and disturbed sites throughout much of the eastern U.S. Seeds are sown along roadsides for beautification and erosion control.

Coreopsis nudata Nutt.

GEORGIA TICKSEED

From a short rhizome, this perennial herb produces a flowering stem up to 1 m tall. Leaves are alternately arranged and consist of rounded petioles with no discernable blades. Ligules of the ray florets are pink or purplish, and the disk florets are yellow. The heads are subtended by an outer series of triangular-shaped and an inner series of oblong, reflexed phyllaries. Fruits are oblong, purplish brown winged achenes. Blooming in spring, Georgia tickseed inhabits wet pinelands, swamps, lake margins, ditches, and prairies from southeastern LA to northern FL and southern GA. This showy species is commercially available as a garden ornamental.

Coreopsis pubescens Ell.

STAR TICKSEED

From short rhizomes, this perennial
herb produces erect, leafy stems up to
9 dm tall. The oppositely arranged leaves
are petiolate on the lower stem and sessile on the upper portion. The blades are
lanceolate or elliptic and typically not
lobed. Both ray and disk florets are yellow; the phyllaries are lanceolate to narrowly ovate. Fruits are winged achenes.
Blooming from spring to summer, star
tickseed inhabits open woods, ditches,
and roadsides throughout much of the
southeastern U.S. *C. grandiflora* Hogg ex
Sweet, largeflower tickseed, has irregularly lobed leaves. This species inhabits
fields, roadsides, and disturbed sites, and
its range extends throughout much of
the eastern U.S.

Coreopsis tinctoria Nutt.

GOLDEN TICKSEED

From a taproot, this annual herb produces erect stems, each up to 1.2 m
long. The oppositely arranged leaves are
pinnately divided into linear or narrowly lanceolate segments. Subtended
by loosely imbricate ovate or lanceolate phyllaries, the floral heads are arranged in a loose corymb. Ray ligules
are yellow and marked with red-brown
on their bases; the disk florets are reddish purple. Fruits are oblong black
achenes that are winged or wingless.
Blooming throughout the year, golden
tickseed inhabits wood margins, roadsides, and fields throughout much of
the U.S. *C. gladiata* Walt., Texas tickseed, has narrowly oblanceolate leaves
that are not lobed. This species inhabits wet pinelands, savannas, and bogs,
and its range extends along the outer
coastal plain from southeastern TX
to northern FL and north to VA.

Echinacea sanguinea Nutt.

SANGUINE PURPLE CONEFLOWER

Eclipta prostrata (L.) L.

FALSE DAISY

From a branching taproot, this perennial herb produces a solitary or branching stem up to 1.2 m tall. The alternately arranged leaves are lanceolate or elliptic with attenuated bases and entire margins. On elongated peduncles, the hemispheric heads bear purple disk florets and pink or purplish ray ligules. The phyllaries are lanceolate with ciliated margins. Fruits are tan achenes, often with a dark distal band. Blooming from spring to summer, sanguine purple coneflower inhabits prairies, pinelands, and roadsides from eastern TX to western LA and north to southwestern AR and southeastern OK. *E. purpurea* (L.) Moench, eastern purple coneflower, has fibrous roots and ovate toothed leaves that are rounded or cordate basally. This species inhabits open woods and prairies, and its range extends throughout much of the eastern half of the U.S. excluding New England.

From a taproot, this annual or perennial herb produces decumbent stems, each up to 1 m long. The oppositely arranged leaves are lanceolate or elliptic, sessile or short petiolate with obscurely toothed margins. Borne in leaf axils, campanulate-shaped heads of white ray and disk florets are solitary or arranged in corymbs. Phyllaries are greenish with stiff, appressed hairs and acute or acuminate apices. Fruits are obovoid, brown achenes with rounded tubercles. Blooming throughout the year, false daisy inhabits wet woods, lake margins, marshes, and bogs throughout much of the eastern U.S. This species is used in traditional Chinese herbal medicine as a liver tonic and for the treatment of hair and scalp disorders.

Erigeron philadelphicus L. var. *philadelphicus*

DAISY FLEABANE

Elephantopus elatus Bertol.

TALL ELEPHANT'S FOOT

From a rhizome, this perennial herb produces one to several branching stems, each up to 7 dm tall. At flowering, the oblanceolate leaves are mostly basal; the cauline leaves are few or absent. White, pink, or purple disk florets are arranged in cylindric heads. Each cluster of heads is subtended by deltoid bracts. The phyllaries are arranged in two series; the inner series are clothed in long, dense hairs. Fruits are ribbed achenes with persistent pappi. Blooming from summer to fall, tall elephant's foot inhabits mixed woods, pinelands, and savannas from southeastern LA to FL and north to southeastern SC. *E. nudatus* Gray, smooth elephant's foot, has inner phyllaries that are only sparsely hairy. This species inhabits pinelands and savannas, and its range extends from eastern TX to northern FL and north to NJ.

From a mass of fibrous roots, this biennial or short-lived perennial herb produces one to several hairy stems, each up to 7 dm tall. Leaves of the basal rosette are oblanceolate or obovate and coarsely toothed or lobed. The alternately arranged leaves along the stem are clasping or sessile. Hemispheric heads of white or pinkish ray florets and yellow disk florets are arranged in loose, bracteate cymes. The glandular-pubescent phyllaries are green with membraneous margins. Fruits are pubescent achenes with barbed pappus. Blooming from spring to summer, daisy fleabane inhabits open woods, fields, roadsides, and disturbed sites throughout much of the U.S. *E. pulchellus* Michx., hairy fleabane, is a stoloniferous species. It inhabits swamps, woodlands, and roadsides, and its range extends throughout much of the eastern half of the U.S.

Eupatorium capillifolium (Lam.) Small

DOGFENNEL

From a rhizome this perennial herb produces shaggy, pubescent stems each up to 3 m tall. The lower leaves are oppositely arranged, petiolate, and pinnately divided into linear segments. The upper leaves are alternately arranged, sessile, and divided into filiform segments each about .5 mm broad. Cylindrical-shaped floral heads bearing several white disk florets are arranged in branching, leafy, wandlike panicles. Phyllaries are oblong or lanceolate with hyaline margins. Fruits are obconic, glabrous achenes with persistent pappus. Blooming from summer to fall, dogfennel inhabits lowland fields, lake margins, and roadsides from eastern TX, OK, and MO east to the Atlantic coastal states as far north as MA. *E. compositifolium* Walt., yankeeweed, has upper leaf segments that are up to 2 mm broad. This species inhabits pinelands, dunes, roadsides, and disturbed sites, and its range extends from eastern TX and OK east to the Atlantic coastal states as far north as southeastern VA.

Eupatorium leucolepis (DC.) Torr. & Gray var. *leucolepis*

JUSTICEWEED

From a knotty crown, this perennial herb produces a solitary gray-pubescent stem up to 1.2 m tall. The oppositely arranged sessile leaves are broadly linear or narrowly oblong with toothed margins. Arranged in corymbs, the obconic-shaped flower heads bear dull white disk florets and are subtended by white-margined pubescent phyllaries. Fruits are dark gray, obconic, glandular-dotted achenes. Blooming from summer to fall, justiceweed inhabits pinelands and savannas from southeastern TX to northern FL and north to Long Island, NY. *E. rotundifolium* L., roundleaf thoroughwort, has broadly ovate or deltoid leaves. This species inhabits pond margins and low roadsides, and its range extends throughout much of the eastern U.S.

Eupatorium perfoliatum L.
BONESET

From a rhizome, this colonial perennial herb produces several branching stems, each up to 2 m tall. Oppositely arranged lanceolate leaves with round-toothed margins and amber punctae on their abaxial surfaces have clasping bases. Arranged in corymbs, ellipsoid heads of white disk florets are subtended by pubescent, lanceolate bracts. Fusiform achenes are black with amber punctae. Blooming from summer to fall, boneset inhabits wet woods, bogs, and stream banks throughout much of the U.S. east of the Rocky Mountains. *E. serotinum* Michx., lateflowering thoroughwort, has petiolate leaves. This species inhabits open woodlands and roadsides, and its range also extends throughout much of the U.S. east of the Rocky Mountains.

Eurybia hemispherica (Alexander) Nesom
PRAIRIE ASTER

From a knotty rhizome, this perennial herb produces one to several simple stems, each up to 1 m tall. The alternately arranged linear leaves are firm, ascending, and sessile. Showy flower heads are hemispheric with violet-purple ray florets and yellow disk florets. The spreading phyllaries are linear with obtuse tips. Fruits are brown fusiform achenes. Blooming from summer to fall, prairie aster inhabits pinelands, savannas, and prairies from eastern TX to northwestern FL. *E. eryngiifolia* (Torr. & Gray) Nesom, thistleleaf aster, has coriaceous, spiny-margined leaves and white or pinkish florets. This species inhabits wet pinelands, savannas, and bogs, and its range extends from southeastern AL to northwestern FL and southwestern GA.

Euthamia leptocephala (Torr. & Gray) Greene ex Porter & Britt.

FLAT-TOPPED GOLDENROD

From a rhizome this perennial herb produces a stem that is freely branching above. The alternately arranged leaves are sessile, linear, or narrowly lanceolate. Flowers are arranged in a leafy, flat-topped corymb. The involucre is turban-shaped with oblong phyllaries that are yellowish with green apices. Both ray and disk florets are yellow. Fruits are hairy achenes. Blooming in fall, flat-topped goldenrod inhabits wet woods, pinelands, savannas, and prairies from eastern TX to southern IL and east to western GA. *E. caroliniana* (L.) Greene ex Porter & Britt., coastal plain goldentop, has punctate leaves. This species inhabits lake margins and dunes, and its range extends from LA to FL and north to ME.

Eutrochium fistulosum (Barratt) E.E. Lamont

JOE PYE WEED

From a rhizome this perennial herb produces a solitary purplish, hollow stem up to 3.5 m tall. The whorled leaves are lanceolate with finely toothed margins. Cylindrical heads of purplish or pinkish disk florets are arranged in a dome- or flat-shaped panicle of corymbs. The purplish phyllaries are tightly imbricate in about four series; the outer ones are notably shorter than the inner ones. Fruits are slender ribbed achenes with purplish or tan pappi. Blooming from summer to fall, Joe Pye weed inhabits wet woods, stream banks, bogs, marshes, and ditches from eastern TX to southeastern MI and east to the Atlantic coastal states as far north as ME. *E. purpureum* (L.) E.E. Lamont, sweet Joe Pye weed, has solid stems that are mostly greenish. This species inhabits woodlands, and its range extends throughout much of the eastern half of the U.S.

Flaveria linearis Lag.

NARROWLEAF YELLOWTOPS

Up to 8 dm tall, this is a bushy-branched perennial herb. The oppositely arranged sessile leaves are linear or narrowly lanceolate with a single prominent vein and revolute margins. Cylindrical heads bearing yellow florets are densely arranged in corymbs. The phyllaries are elliptic or lanceolate and keeled. Fruits are obconic ribbed achenes, each with a truncated apex. Blooming throughout the year, narrowleaf yellowtops inhabits roadsides, pinelands, marshes, swamps, and hammocks in FL. *F. bidentis* (L.) Kuntze, coastal plain yellowtops, is an annual with toothed, narrowly elliptic, three-veined leaves. This species inhabits pinelands and occurs in southern AL, northwestern FL, and southern GA.

Flaveria trinervia (Spreng.) C. Mohr

CLUSTERED YELLOWTOPS

This is a freely branching, taprooted annual herb. The oppositely arranged leaves are sessile and mostly lanceolate with finely toothed margins. Individual heads composed of a single ray or disk floret are tightly arranged in sessile axillary clusters. One or two concave phyllaries subtend each head. Fruits are black, club-shaped achenes. Blooming throughout the year, clustered yellowtops inhabits wet saline areas on beaches and roadsides in southeastern TX, southern AL, the southern Gulf coast of FL, and southeastern VA. *F. floridana* J.R. Johnston, Florida yellowtops, has heads that bear as many as fifteen florets. It inhabits beaches and dunes along the western Gulf coast of FL.

Gaillardia aestivalis (Walt.)
H. Rock

LANCELEAF BLANKETFLOWER

From a slender taproot, this sparingly
branching annual or short-lived perennial produces stems up to 7 dm long.
Lower leaves, often absent at flowering,
are oblanceolate and petiolate; the upper leaves are alternate, sessile, and lanceolate. Hemispheric heads are solitary.
Sometimes absent, ray floret ligules are
yellow and three-toothed apically; the
disk florets are red-purple. The lanceolate phyllaries bear beadlike hairs. Fruits
are pubescent achenes. Blooming from
summer to fall, lanceleaf blanketflower
inhabits open woods, pinelands, and
savannas from TX to IL and east to
the Atlantic coastal states as far north
as NC. Easily grown from seed, this
species is occasionally used as a garden
ornamental.

Gaillardia pulchella Foug.

BLANKETFLOWER

From a taproot, this branching annual or
short-lived perennial produces stems up
to 6 dm long. The coarsely toothed sessile leaves are mostly oblanceolate. Ray
floret ligules are typically red and tipped
with yellow. Disk floret corollas are purplish red. The leaflike phyllaries are lanceolate and reflexed. Fruits are comose
achenes. Blooming throughout the year,
blanketflower occurs in sandy or gravelly soils of prairies, wood margins, and
beaches throughout much of the U.S.
excluding the Northwest. This species is
often seeded along highways for beautification. Several cultivars are commercially available for ornamental plantings.

Gamochaeta purpurea (L.) Cabrera
PURPLE CUDWEED

From a taproot, this annual herb produces several ascending or decumbent stems, each up to 3 dm tall. The alternately arranged leaves are oblanceolate or spathulate with feltlike hairs on the abaxial surfaces. The adaxial surfaces are green and sparsely pubescent. Arranged in spikes, the turbinate heads of white or pinkish disk florets are borne in the upper leaf axils. The papery phyllaries are woolly on their bases. Fruits are oblong, glabrous achenes with bristly pappus. Blooming in spring, purple cudweed inhabits fields, roadsides, pastures, and lawns throughout much of the eastern half of the U.S. *G. pensylvanica* (Willd.) Cabrea, Pennsylvania cudweed, has gray-green adaxial leaf surfaces and phyllaries that are densely woolly throughout. This species inhabits disturbed sites, and its range extends from eastern TX and OK to FL and north to VA.

Helenium amarum (Raf.) H. Rock var. *amarum*
BITTERWEED

From a taproot this bushy-branched, herbaceous annual grows up to 8 dm tall. Often withered at flowering, the basal leaves are pinnately lobed; the upper leaves are mostly linear and alternate. Arranged in panicles, the hemispheric-shaped heads bear yellow ray florets and yellow or purple disk florets. The narrowly lanceolate phyllaries are greenish yellow and hairy. Fruits are dark brown, hairy achenes. Blooming from spring to fall, bitterweed inhabits fields, roadsides, and disturbed sites from TX, OK, KS, and NE east to the Atlantic coastal states as far north as MA. Cattle grazing on this toxic species produce bitter milk.

Helenium drummondii H. Rock

FRINGED SNEEZEWEED

From a taproot, this perennial herb produces a solitary simple stem up to 6 dm tall. Leaves in the basal rosette are often absent at flowering; those along the stem are linear, strongly reduced distally, and alternately arranged. Florets are arranged in a solitary hemispheric head that is subtended by two series of linear bracts. Ray and disk florets are yellow; the rays are apically three-lobed. Cylindrical-shaped achenes are hairy on their ribs. Blooming in spring, fringed sneezeweed inhabits wet woods, savannas, and pinelands from southeastern TX to LA. *H. brevifolium* (Nutt.) Wood, shortleaf sneezeweed, has basal leaves that are present at flowering and reddish disk florets. This species inhabits stream banks and bogs, and its range extends from southeastern LA to northwestern FL and north to southern VA.

Helenium flexuosum Raf.

PURPLEHEAD SNEEZEWEED

From a fibrous-rooted crown, this perennial herb produces one to several branching stems, each up to 1 m tall. Absent at flowering, the basal leaves are elliptic or oblanceolate with entire or toothed margins. The stem leaves are linear or lanceolate and decurrent so that the stem appears winged. Arranged in globose heads, the fertile disk florets are reddish brown or purplish, and the sterile ray florets are wholly yellow or suffused with red or purple. Phyllaries are greenish, linear, and curly. Fruits are brown, pubescent achenes with a pappus of awn-tipped scales. Blooming from spring to fall, purplehead sneezeweed inhabits wet open woods, prairies, pastures, ditches, and roadsides throughout much of the eastern half of the U.S. *H. autumnale* L., common sneezeweed, has yellow disk florets and its ray flowers are fertile. This species inhabits bogs, ditches, and low pastures, and its range extends throughout much of the eastern half of the U.S.

Helenium pinnatifidum (Schweinitz ex Nutt.) Rydb.

SOUTHERN SNEEZEWEED

From a short crown, this perennial herb produces one to several stems, each up to 8 dm tall. Arranged in a basal rosette, the leaves are linear, elliptic, or oblanceolate with a few teeth. Leaves on the stem are reduced, sessile, decurrent, and alternately arranged. Solitary hemispheric heads terminate each stem. Ray floret ligules are yellow and toothed; the disk florets are also yellow. Fruits are brown, pubescent achenes. Blooming in spring, southern sneezeweed inhabits wet pinelands, savannas, prairies, and swamp margins from southern AL to FL and north to southeastern NC. *H. vernale* Walt., savanna sneezeweed, has glabrous achenes. This species inhabits wet woods, bogs, and swamp margins, and its range extends from southeastern LA to northern FL and north to southeastern NC.

Helianthus angustifolius L.

SWAMP SUNFLOWER

From a short rhizome with fibrous roots, this perennial herb produces stems up to 2 m tall. Opposite below, the linear or lanceolate sessile leaves become alternately arranged above. Leaf blades bear short, stiff hairs and amber-colored resin dots; the margins are strongly revolute. Hemispheric heads are subtended by narrowly lanceolate bracts. Ray ligules are yellow and three-toothed apically; the disk florets are dark purple. Fruits are slender, brown achenes. Blooming from summer to fall, swamp sunflower inhabits wet pinelands, savannas, bogs, and upland woods from eastern TX to FL and north to southeastern NY. *H. floridanus* Gray ex Chapman, Florida sunflower, has broadly lanceolate leaves. This species inhabits open woods and fields, and its range extends from LA to FL and north to NC.

Helianthus annuus L.

SUNFLOWER

From a taproot, this annual herb produces a simple or branching stem up to 3 m tall. The alternately arranged leaves are ovate and petiolate with toothed margins. Large, showy heads are subtended by oblong phyllaries with ciliated margins and acuminate tips. Corollas of the disk florets are reddish or purplish; the ray floret ligules are yellow. Fruits are obovate, striped achenes. Blooming from summer to fall, sunflower inhabits roadsides, fields, and wood margins throughout much of the U.S. Up to 1.2 m tall, *H. heterophyllus* Nutt., wetland sunflower, has oppositely arranged leaves and lanceolate phyllaries. This species inhabits wet pinelands and savannas, and its range extends from southeastern LA to northwestern FL and north to NC.

Helianthus hirsutus Raf.

HAIRY SUNFLOWER

From a stout, branching rhizome, this scabrous perennial herb produces a solitary stem up to 2 m tall. The oppositely arranged stem leaves are lanceolate to narrowly elliptic with serrated or entire margins. Arranged in a hemispheric head, both ray and disk florets are yellow. Phyllaries are lanceolate and recurved. Fruits are dark brown achenes, each bearing two awns. Blooming from summer to fall, hairy sunflower inhabits woodlands, pastures, and roadsides throughout much of the eastern U.S. *H. tuberosus* L., Jerusalem artichoke, has leaves that are opposite below and alternate above. This species inhabits fields, roadsides, and disturbed sites, and its range extends throughout much of the U.S.

Heterotheca subaxillaris (Lam.) Brit. & Rusby ssp. *subaxillaris*

CAMPHORWEED

From a taproot, this hirsute annual herb produces erect or procumbent stems, each up to 1.5 m tall. The alternately arranged leaves are elliptic, ovate, or lanceolate with entire or toothed margins. Leaves positioned on the lower stem are petiolate; those on the upper stem are sessile. Campanulate heads of yellow ray and disk florets are arranged in diffuse corymbs. Phyllaries are linear, densely hirsute, and glandular. Fruits are ovoid achenes; those of the ray florets are glabrous and those of the disk florets are densely pubescent. Blooming throughout the year, camphorweed inhabits open woods, roadsides, fields, and sand dunes from eastern TX to FL and north to DE. Used in traditional herbal medicine, a poultice from its leaves treats pain and inflammation.

Hymenopappus artemisiifolius DC. var. *artemisiifolius*

WOOLLYWHITE

From a taproot, this perennial herb produces a solitary stem up to 1 m tall. The alternately arranged simple or pinnately lobed leaves are densely woolly on their abaxial surfaces. Arranged in open panicles, the campanulate heads bear disk florets with whitish corollas that are tinged with rose or purple. Phyllaries are elliptic to broadly ovate, greenish white, and membranous. Fruits are obpyramidal achenes with pubescence on the angles. Blooming from spring to summer, woollywhite inhabits pine and oak woods in eastern TX, western LA, and southwestern AR. *H. scabiosaeus* L.' Hér., Carolina woolly white, has completely white disk florets. This species inhabits open woods, and its range extends from TX to southeastern NE and eastward to northern FL and southern SC.

Krigia cespitosa (Raf.) Chambers var. *cespitosa*

DWARF DANDELION

Iva annua L.

ANNUAL MARSH ELDER

From a taproot, this annual herb produces a freely branching, pubescent stem up to 2 m tall. The oppositely arranged leaves are petiolate with ovate or lanceolate blades and toothed margins. Hemispheric heads of yellow disk florets are arranged in terminal spikes. The green phyllaries are mostly obovate with stiff glandular white hairs. Fruits are brown, ovoid achenes with a few resinous punctae. Blooming from summer to fall, annual marsh elder inhabits stream banks, wet woods, and disturbed areas throughout much of the eastern U.S. *I frutescens* L., Jesult's bark, is a bushy perennial up to 3.5 m tall with glabrous phyllaries. This species inhabits brackish marshes, and its range extends from southeastern TX to FL and north to ME.

From fibrous roots, this annual herb produces erect or decumbent, freely branching stems up to 4 dm tall. The lower leaves are linear, lanceolate, or elliptic and sessile or clasping. The upper leaves are reduced and subopposite. Heads of yellow or orange ray florets terminate simple or branching axillary stems. Arranged in two series, the lanceolate phyllaries remain erect in fruit. Fruits are reddish brown, oblong, ribbed achenes. Blooming from spring to summer, dwarf dandelion inhabits wet woods, fields, pastures, roadsides, and disturbed sites from eastern TX to southeastern NE and east to the Atlantic coastal states as far north as southern VA. *K. dandelion* (L.) Nutt., potato dwarf dandeliuon, is a perennial with phyllaries that become reflexed in fruit. This species inhabits open woods, fields, roadsides, and disturbed sites, and its range extends from eastern TX to IA and east to the Atlantic coastal states as far north as NJ.

Lactuca floridana (L.) Gaertn.

WOODLAND LETTUCE

From a taproot, this annual or biennial herb produces a solitary branching stem up to 2 m tall. Entire or pinnately lobed, the alternately arranged
leaves are oblong, ovate, or elliptic with
entire or minutely toothed margins.
Cylindric heads of blue or white ray florets are arranged in a pyramid-shaped
panicle. The imbricate phyllaries are
green with purplish apices. Fruits are
brown, fusiform, ribbed achenes with
white pappi. Blooming from summer to fall, woodland lettuce inhabits
open woods, roadsides, and disturbed
sites throughout much of the eastern
half of the U.S. *L. graminifolia* Michx.,
grassleaf lettuce, has spathulate, lanceolate, or linear leaves. It inhabits fields
and disturbed sites, and its range extends from AZ to FL and north to NC.

Liatris acidota Engelm. & Gray

SHARP BLAZING STAR

From a cormlike rhizome, this perennial herb produces a slender, glabrous
stem up to 8 dm tall. Linear or lanceolate on the lower part of the stem,
the leaves become wholly linear and
reduced distally. Purple disk florets are
arranged in cylindrical-shaped heads.
The two series of involucral bracts are
green and suffused with purple. The
fruits are obconic glandular achenes.
Blooming from summer to fall, sharp
blazing star inhabits bogs, wet savannas, pinelands, and ditches from eastern
TX to LA. Up to 1.5 m tall, *L. tenuifolia* Nutt., pine-needle gayfeather, has
linear or lanceolate leaves and glabrous phyllaries with purple margins.
This species inhabits open woods and
pinelands, and its range extends from
AL to FL and north to GA and SC.

Liatris aspera Michx.

TALL BLAZING STAR

From a rounded corm, this perennial herb produces one to several stems, each up to 2 m long. Lower stem leaves are petiolate and narrowly elliptic; upper stem leaves are sessile and lanceolate or linear. The lavender florets are borne in a hemispheric head. Phyllaries are spathulate and somewhat puckered. Fruits are pubescent achenes. Blooming from summer to fall, tall blazing star inhabits open, sandy wood margins and pinelands throughout much of the eastern U.S. *L. squarrulosa* Michx., southern gayfeather, has campanulate heads and nonpuckered phyllaries. This species inhabits open woods, sandhills, prairies, and roadsides, and its range extends throughout much of the Southeast and the lower Midwest.

Liatris elegans (Walt.) Michx. var. *elegans*

PINKSCALE BLAZING STAR

From a globose corm, this perennial herb produces a solitary stem up to 1.2 m tall. The alternately arranged leaves are oblanceolate or linear and punctate. Turban-shaped heads of white disk florets are densely arranged in an elongated spike. The recurved, petal-like phyllaries are lavender or pink with hyaline margins. Fruits are achenes with plumose pappi. Blooming from summer to fall, pinkscale blazing star inhabits dry open woods, dunes, and sandhills from eastern TX and OK to northern FL and north to SC. *L. elegans* var. *kralii* Mayfield has white or yellowish phyllaries. This species inhabits wet savannas, dunes, stream banks, and open woods, and its range extends from MS to FL and GA.

Liatris punctata Hook. var. *mexicana* Gaiser

MEXICAN BLAZING STAR

From a corm or rhizome, this perennial herb produces one to several erect stems, each up to 8.5 dm tall. The alternately arranged leaves are linear and conspicuously punctate. Cylindrical heads, each bearing up to six purple or lavender florets, are loosely arranged along a glabrous rachis. The green, glabrous phyllaries are oblong or obovate and neither petaloid nor hyaline-margined. Fruits are pubescent, ribbed achenes. Blooming from summer to fall, Mexican blazing star inhabits prairies, pinelands, and savannas from NM to southwestern LA. With each head bearing up to fourteen florets, *L. bracteata* Gaiser, South Texas gayfeather, inhabits coastal prairies and roadsides in southeastern TX.

Liatris pycnostachya Michx. var. *pycnostachya*

PRAIRIE BLAZING STAR

From a globose corm or an elongated rhizome, this perennial herb produces one to several stout stems, each up to 1.8 m tall. The linear leaves are densely arranged, punctate, and gradually reduced to bracts distally. Cylindrical-shaped heads of purple disk florets are densely arranged in a terminal spike. Phyllaries are green to purplish and reflexed with acute tips. Fruits are brown, obconic achenes. Blooming from summer to fall, prairie blazing star inhabits bogs, pinelands, savannas, and prairies from eastern TX to MS and north to Canada and from NJ to MA. *L. spicata* (L.) Willd., marsh gayfeather, has obtuse-tipped phyllaries that are not reflexed. This species inhabits fields, bogs, swamps, prairies, and roadsides, and its range extends from LA, AR, and MO to FL and north to MA.

Lygodesmia aphylla (Nutt.) DC.

ROSE RUSH

From a slender, branching rhizome, this perennial herb produces a solitary wiry stem up to 8 dm tall. Often absent at flowering, leaves of the basal rosette are linear; those along the stem are reduced and scalelike. Arranged in corymbs, cylindrical-shaped heads bearing pink or lavender ray florets are subtended by thin, membranous phyllaries. Fruits are ribbed achenes. Blooming from spring to fall, rose rush inhabits dry sandy pinelands and disturbed sites from FL to southern GA.

Liatris squarrosa (L.) Michx. var. *squarrosa*

SCALY BLAZING STAR

From a rounded corm, this perennial herb produces one to several stems, each up to 1 m tall. The alternately arranged leaves are linear, rigid, and punctate. Cylindrical heads of purple disk florets are arranged in spikes or racemes. Greenish purple phyllaries with ciliated margins have acuminate tips that are held at right angles. Fruits are pubescent, plumose achenes. Blooming from summer to fall, scaly blazing star inhabits pinelands, savannas, and open woods throughout much of the eastern U.S. excluding the Northeast. This species is endangered in MD.

Marshallia caespitosa Nutt. ex DC.
PUFFBALLS

From a short rhizome, this perennial herb produces a simple, erect stem up to 4 dm tall. Basally disposed, the alternately arranged leaves are obovate, spathulate, or oblanceolate with winged petioles. Solitary hemispheric heads of white florets are subtended by green, herbaceous phyllaries with hyaline margins. Fruits are ribbed achenes beset with resin dots. Blooming from spring to summer, puffballs inhabits wet pinelands, savannas, and roadsides from eastern TX to western LA and north to southern KS and southwestern MO. *M. ramosa* Beadle & F.E. Boynt, southern Barbara's buttons, has several heads per stem. This species inhabits hardwood forests and savannas and occurs in southeast GA and north FL.

Marshallia graminifolia (Walt.) Small
GRASSLEAF BARBARA'S BUTTONS

From a fibrous-rooted caudex, this perennial herb produces a single simple or branching stem up to 8 dm tall. Forming a basal rosette, the lower leaves are petiolate with spathulate blades. Leaves along the stem are sessile and mostly linear. Arranged in branching cymes, the hemispheric heads of pink, lavender, or purple disk florets are subtended by reddish, punctate bracts. Fruits are five-angled, pubescent, punctate achenes. Blooming from summer to fall, grassleaf Barbara's buttons inhabits wet pinelands, savannas, and bogs from eastern TX to FL and north to southeastern NC. *M. trinerva* (Walt.) Trel., broadleaf Barbara's buttons, has ovate stem leaves. This species inhabits hardwood forests, stream banks, and disturbed sites; its range extends from LA to GA and north to NC and TN.

Mikania cordifolia (L. f.) Willd.
HEMPWEED

This is a perennial climbing or trailing vine with angled, pubescent stems. The oppositely arranged leaves are ovate or deltoid with cordate bases. Terminating axillary stems, the cylindrical heads are arranged in aggregated corymbs. Subtended by an outer series of one and an inner series of four elliptic, involucral bracts, each head bears four white disk florets. Fruits are brown, five-angled, glandular achenes. Blooming from fall to winter, hempweed inhabits wet woods and disturbed areas from eastern TX to FL and southern GA. *M. scandens* (L.) Willd., climbing hempweed, has florets that are pinkish or bluish. This species inhabits swamps, lake margins, and stream banks, and its range extends throughout much of the eastern U.S.

Packera glabella (Poir.) C. Jeffrey
BUTTERWEED

This is a glabrous annual herb with hollow stems up to 1 m tall. The basal leaves are petiolate and often absent at flowering. The alternately arranged stem leaves are pinnately lobed and often bear rounded teeth on their margins. Some floral heads bear both ray and disk florets, whereas others bear only disk florets. Arranged in cymes, cylindrical heads are subtended by narrowly lanceolate phyllaries with acute tips. The ellipsoid achenes are brown and prominently ribbed. Blooming from spring to summer, butterweed inhabits wet woods, swamps, and ditches throughout much of the Southeast and lower Midwest. A perennial, *P. obovata* (Muhl. ex Willd.) W.A. Weber & A. Löve, roundleaf ragwort, has rounded basal leaves. This species inhabits deciduous woods, stream banks, and ditches; its range extends throughout much of the eastern U.S.

Parthenium hysterophorus L.

FEVERFEW

From a taproot, this annual herb produces a solitary hirsute stem up to 1 m tall. The alternately arranged punctate leaves are deeply pinnately lobed. Numerous hemispheric heads of white ray and disk florets are arranged in a branching panicle. The phyllaries bear coarse white hairs. Fruits are flattened achenes with ribbed margins. Blooming from spring to fall, feverfew inhabits fields, roadsides, and disturbed sites from eastern TX, southern OK and eastern KS to FL and from VA to MA. *P. integrifolium* L., wild quinine, has a flat-topped corymb and entire leaves. This species inhabits pine barrens, prairies, and disturbed sites, and its range extends throughout much of the eastern U.S. excluding FL.

Pityopsis graminifolia (Michx.) Nutt. var. *graminifolia*

SILKGRASS

From a rhizome, this silvery, pubescent perennial herb produces one to several stems, each up to 8 dm tall. Present at flowering, the basal leaves are ascending and grasslike. Leaves along the stem are alternately arranged and also grasslike. Campanulate heads of yellow disk and ray florets are arranged in corymbs. Phyllaries are linear with hyaline margins and stipitate glands near their apices. Fruits are fusiform achenes. Blooming in fall, silkgrass inhabits open woods, wood margins, fields, and roadsides on the outer coastal plain from LA to FL and north to NC. *P. graminifolia* var. *tenuifolia* (Torr.) Semple & Bowers has phyllary apices that typically are not glandular. This species inhabits open woods and roadsides, and its range extends from eastern TX and OK to FL and north to southeastern NC.

Pluchea baccharis (Miller) Pruski

ROSY CAMPHORWEED

From a short woody crown, this aromatic perennial herb produces one to several stems, each up to 1 m long. Alternately arranged, pubescent, sessile leaves are elliptic or oblong with toothed margins. Arranged in compact corymbs, the campanulate heads bear pink disk florets and are subtended by ovate-lanceolate involucral bracts. Fruits are black, pubescent achenes. Blooming in summer, rosy camphorweed inhabits wet pinelands, savannas, prairies, and lake margins from eastern TX to FL and north to NC. *P. foetida* (L.) DC., stinking camphorweed, has white florets. This species inhabits swamps, lake margins, and ditches; its range extends from southeastern TX, AR, and OK to FL and north to MO.

Pluchea odorata (L.) Cass. var. *odorata*

STINKWEED

This annual herb produces branching stems, each up to 1.5 m tall. The alternately arranged leaves are lanceolate, ovate, or elliptic with cuneate bases and toothed margins. Subtended by purplish phyllaries bearing a few punctae, the campanulate-shaped floral heads are arranged in a flat-topped cyme. Corollas are pink or rose colored. Fruits are brown achenes with pubescent ridges. Blooming from spring to fall, stinkweed inhabits fresh and brackish marshes, wet pinelands, and prairies from CA to FL and north to ME. *P. camphorata* (L.) DC., plowman's wort, has a paniculate inflorescence and copiously punctate phyllaries. This species inhabits wet pinelands and prairies, and its range extends from TX, OK, and KS east to the Atlantic coastal states as far north as NJ.

Pyrrhopappus carolinianus (Walt.) DC.

FALSE DANDELION

From a turnip-shaped taproot, this annual or biennial herb produces stems up to 1 m tall. Basal leaves are petiolate and often absent at flowering. Leaves along the stem are alternate, sessile, oblanceolate, or narrowly elliptic and often with a single lobe on one or both margins. Arranged in corymbs, cylindrical-shaped heads bear yellow ray florets. Phyllaries are cleft at their apices. Fruits are grooved, fusiform achenes. Blooming from spring to summer, false dandelion inhabits open woods, fields, roadsides, and disturbed sites throughout much of the Southeast and lower Midwest. *P. pauciflorus* (D. Don) DC., smallflower desert chicory, has stem leaves that bear several marginal lobes. This species inhabits prairies and disturbed sites, and its range extends from AZ to FL.

Rayjacksonia phyllocephala (DC.) R.L. Hartman & M.A. Lane

CAMPHOR DAISY

This is a freely branching, suffruticose, aromatic annual or perennial herb. The alternate succulent leaves are obovate or oblanceolate with lobed or toothed margins. Bearing yellow disk and ray florets, each hemispheric head is subtended by phyllaries up to 1.7 mm broad. Cylindrical achenes bear white, fuzzy pubescence. Blooming from summer to winter, camphor daisy inhabits dunes and beaches along the coast in TX, LA, and FL. *R. aurea* (Gray) R.L. Hartman & M.A. Lane, Houston camphor weed, has phyllaries that are about 1 mm wide. This species inhabits fields and pastures and occurs in the vicinity of Houston, TX.

Rudbeckia hirta L. var. *angustifolia* (T.V. Moore) Perdue

BLACKEYED SUSAN

Rudbeckia amplexicaulis (Vahl) Cass.

CLASPING CONEFLOWER

From a solitary stem, this annual herb branches near its midstem. The alternately arranged glaucous leaves are clasping and obscurely serrate. Blades are lanceolate, ovate, or spathulate and the bases are mostly cordate. Arranged in a conical receptacle, the disk florets are brown and the ray ligules are yellow and often marked with reddish brown or purple near their bases. The outer phyllaries, about twice as long as the inner ones, are leaflike. Fruits are wrinkled, brownish purple achenes. Blooming from spring to summer, clasping coneflower inhabits wet prairies, ditches, and stream banks from TX to IL and east to northern FL. This easily grown, showy species is planted as a garden ornamental.

From a mass of fibrous roots, this roughly pubescent annual or short-lived perennial produces one to several stems, each up to 1 m tall. Leaves are ovate, elliptic, or lanceolate with entire or obscurely toothed margins. Solitary or arranged in loose corymbs, hemispheric heads of purple disk florets terminate peduncles that are at least one-half the overall length of the plant. Blooming from spring to summer, blackeyed Susan inhabits open woods, pastures, fields, and roadsides from eastern TX to FL and north to SC. *R. hirta* var. *pulcherrima* Farwell has peduncles that are only about one-third the length of the overall plant. This species inhabits prairies and roadsides, and its range extends throughout much of the U.S.

Rudbeckia texana (Perdue) P. Cox & Urbatsch

TEXAS CONEFLOWER

From a branching caudex, this perennial herb produces one to several simple or branching stems, each up to 1.2 m tall. The alternately arranged, lustrous leaves are lanceolate, ovate, or oblong with entire, undulate, or toothed margins. Petiolate on the lower portion of the stem, the leaves become sessile distally. Solitary conical heads bear yellow rays that are toothed apically and purple disk florets. Arranged in several series, the greenish phyllaries are lanceolate, ovate, or spathulate with ciliated margins. Fruits are purplish achenes with a crown of purplish pappus. Blooming from spring to fall, Texas coneflower inhabits wet pinelands, savannas, and prairies in southeastern TX and western LA. *R. maxima* Nutt., great cabbage coneflower, has glaucous leaves and stems up to 3 m tall. This species inhabits swamps and marshes, and it occurs in eastern TX, OK, LA, and southwestern AR.

Silphium radula Nut. var. *gracile* (Gray) J.A. Clevinger

ROSINWEED

From a stout woody rhizome, this perennial herb produces a solitary erect stem up to 6 dm tall. Crowded near the base, the shallowly toothed, elliptic, or ovate scabrous leaves are reduced distally. Each head of yellow ray and disk florets is subtended by an involucre of ovate or elliptic bracts. Fruits are broadly winged achenes. Blooming in summer, rosinweed inhabits pinelands and wood margins from southeastern TX to FL and GA. *S. integrifolium* Michx., whole-leaf rosinweed, has a branching inflorescence and broadly elliptic leaves. This species inhabits prairies and roadsides, and its range extends from NM to MS and north to MI, MN, and WI.

Smallanthus uvedalia (L.)
Mackenzie ex Small

BEAR'S FOOT

From fibrous tuberous roots, this perennial herb produces stout stems up to 3
m tall. Oppositely arranged leaves are
sessile, broadly ovate, and palmately
lobed. Hemispheric heads bearing yellow ray and disk florets are solitary.
Arranged in two series, the phyllaries
are broadly ovate or deltoid. Fruits are
ovate and somewhat flattened black
achenes. Blooming from summer to
fall, bear's foot inhabits moist woods,
pastures, and roadsides throughout
much of the eastern U.S. This species is endangered in NJ and NY.

Solidago altissima L. ssp. *altissima*

LATE GOLDENROD

From a creeping rhizome, this perennial herb produces one to several stems,
each up to 2 m tall. The roughly pubescent leaves are lanceolate or oblanceolate
with toothed margins. Campanulate
heads of yellow ray and disk florets are
arranged in secund, paniculate arrays.
Arranged in three series, the lanceolate phyllaries are unequal in length.
Fruits are obconic achenes. Blooming
from summer to fall, late goldenrod
inhabits open woods, fields, and roadsides throughout much of the eastern
half of the U.S. *S. tortifolia* Ell., twist-
leaf goldenrod, has lanceolate or linear
leaves that are often twisted. This species inhabits pinelands and savannas,
and its range extends from eastern TX
to FL and north to southeastern VA.

Solidago nitida Torr. & Gray

SHINY GOLDENROD

From a rhizome, this perennial herb produces a glabrous stem up to 1.2 m tall. The alternately arranged leaves are linear or lanceolate and glabrous. Cylindrical-shaped heads of yellow florets are arranged in a flat-topped corymb. Phyllaries are yellowish and oblong. Fruits are pubescent achenes. Blooming from summer to fall, shiny goldenrod inhabits pinelands and savannas from eastern TX and OK to southern MS. *Oligoneuron rigidum* (L.) Small, stiff goldenrod, is a similar appearing species, but it has pubescent stems and leaves. It inhabits open woods and prairies, and its range extends throughout much of the eastern U.S., excluding FL.

Solidago caesia L. var. *caesia*

WREATH GOLDENROD

From a short rhizome, this perennial herb produces bluish, glaucous, arching stems. The alternately arranged leaves are lanceolate or elliptic with cuneate bases and toothed margins. Arranged in short axillary racemes, the floral heads bear yellow ray florets. Fruits are pubescent achenes. Blooming from summer to fall, wreath goldenrod inhabits rich, moist woodlands throughout much of the eastern half of the U.S. *S. hispida* Muhl. ex Willd., hairy goldenrod, has densely hairy, greenish stems. This species inhabits open woods, fields, and roadsides, and its range extends from northern LA to northwestern GA and north to Canada.

Solidago rugosa P. Mill. var.
celtidifolia (Small) Fernald

WRINKLELEAF GOLDENROD

From a slender, creeping rhizome, this
perennial herb produces a pubescent
stem up to 1.5 m tall. Reduced distally,
the principal stem leaves are alternate,
sessile, or elliptic, with toothed margins; their adaxial surfaces bear short,
stiff hairs. Arranged in arching panicles,
the heads are arranged along one side
of the floral axis. The phyllaries are linear or oblong with hyaline margins.
Fruits are obconic, pubescent achenes.
Blooming in fall, wrinkleleaf goldenrod inhabits open wet woods and bogs
from TX and OK to FL and north to
VA. *S. rugosa* var. *aspera* (Ait.) Fernald
has leaves that are not reduced distally.
This species inhabits open woods, fields,
roadsides, and ditches; its range extends
throughout much of the eastern U.S.

Solidago odora Ait. ssp. *odora*

ANISE-SCENTED GOLDENROD

From a short rhizome, this perennial
herb produces an erect stem up to 1.5 m
tall. The alternately arranged leaves
are sessile and mostly lanceolate. Arranged in panicles, the floral heads of
yellow florets are arrayed along one
side of the floral axis. Phyllaries are oblong with hyaline margins. Fruits are
pubescent achenes. Blooming from
summer to fall, anise-scented goldenrod inhabits savannas and pinelands
from eastern TX, OK, and southeastern
MO east to the Atlantic coastal states
as far north as NH. Its leaves emit a
strong scent of anise when crushed.

Sonchus asper (L.) Hill.

Solidago sempervirens L. ssp. *mexicana* (L.) Semple
SEASIDE GOLDENROD

From an extensive branching rhizome, this perennial herb produces stems up to 2 m tall. From the previous year's basal rosette, the proximal portion of the flowering stem bears oblong, linear, or elliptic leaves with winged petioles. The distal leaves are reduced, linear, and sessile. Cylindrical heads bearing yellow disk florets are arranged in erect or arching panicles. Phyllaries are mostly oblong or linear with acute or obtuse apices. Blooming from fall to winter, seaside goldenrod inhabits brackish marshes from southeastern TX to FL and north to MA. *S. stricta* Ait., wand goldenrod, has a racemose, wandlike inflorescence. It inhabits wet pinelands, savannas, and sandhills from southeastern TX to FL and north to southern NJ.

From a taproot, this introduced annual herb produces hollow stems up to 2 m tall. The alternately arranged leaves are pinnately lobed with spiny margins and rounded auricles. Obconic heads bearing yellow florets are arranged in corymbs. The phyllaries are greenish and lanceolate with glandular hairs. Fruits are reddish brown, compressed, ellipsoid achenes that are broadest near the middle. Blooming from spring to summer, spiny sowthistle inhabits disturbed sites throughout much of the U.S. *S. oleraceus* L., common sowthistle, has achenes that are widest above the middle and leaves that have acute auricles. It also occurs in disturbed sites throughout much of the U.S.

Stokesia laevis (Hill) Greene

STOKE'S ASTER

From a stout rhizome, this perennial herb produces one to several erect stems, each up to 5 dm tall. The alternately arranged leaves are somewhat thickened and punctate. Lower leaves are petiolate and mostly spathulate; the upper leaves are linear or lanceolate and sessile. Hemispheric heads of blue or purple ray and disk florets are arranged in long-peduncled corymbs. Leaflike phyllaries bear spines on their margins. Fruits are four-angled, greenish white, glabrous achenes. Blooming from summer to fall, Stoke's aster inhabits wet pinelands, savannas, and bogs from LA to northern FL and north to eastern SC. Several cultivars are commercially available for ornamental plantings.

Symphyotrichum praealtum (Poir.) Nesom

WILLOWLEAF ASTER

From a long, fleshy rhizome, this colonial perennial herb produces an erect or arching pubescent stem up to 1.5 m long. The alternately arranged and somewhat thickened leaves are linear, lanceolate, or narrowly elliptic with entire margins. Hemispheric heads bearing blue, white, or violet ray florets and yellow disk florets are arranged in leafy, elongated panicles. Phyllaries are oblong, lanceolate, or linear with hyaline margins. Fruits are obovoid, tan to purplish, pubescent achenes. Blooming from summer to fall, willowleaf aster inhabits low woods, marshes, pinelands, savannas, and roadsides throughout much of the eastern U.S. *S. lateriflorum* (L.) A. & D. Löve, calico flower, has thin membranous leaves with toothed margins. This species inhabits deciduous woods, swamps, and pinelands, and its range also extends throughout much of the eastern half of the U.S.

Symphyotrichum subulatum
(Michx.) Nesom var. *ligulatum*
S.D. Sundberg

SALTMARSH ASTER

From a taproot, this annual herb produces a single, freely branching stem up
to 1.5 m tall. Typically absent at flowering, the basal leaves are ovate or oblanceolate. Becoming reduced distally, the
stem leaves are lanceolate. Turbinate
heads are arranged in open panicles. The
ray florets are lavender or blue; the disk
florets are yellow and number up to fifty
per head. Purple-tinged phyllaries are
lanceolate with hyaline margins. Fruits
are brownish purple, fusiform, pubescent
achenes. Blooming from summer to fall,
saltmarsh aster inhabits fresh and brackish marshes, ditches, wood margins,
and fields from TX to NE and eastward to TN and AL. *S. subulatum* var.
subulatum (Michx.) Nesom has white,
pink, or lavender ray florets and disk
florets that number less than twenty-
three per head. This species inhabits
saline marshes, and its range extends
throughout much of the eastern U.S.

Taraxacum officinale Wiggers ssp.
officinale

DANDELION

From a stout taproot, this introduced
biennial or perennial herb produces
a basal rosette of oblanceolate, pinnately lobed leaves. A cylindrical head
of bright yellow ray florets terminates
each hollow scape. The outer series of
phyllaries are reflexed and shorter than
the inner series. Fruits are fusiform,
wind-dispersed achenes with white,
feathery pappus. Blooming throughout
the year, dandelion inhabits pastures,
roadsides, fields, lawns, and disturbed
sites throughout much of the U.S.
and is native to Eurasia. Its leaves are
used in potherbs and salads, its flowers are fermented to make wine, and its
roots provide a substitute for coffee.

Tetragonotheca helianthoides L.

This perennial herb produces erect, villous stems up to 1 m tall. The oppositely arranged leaves are coarsely toothed and are lanceolate, ovate, or rhombic. Large, showy heads of yellow disk and ray florets are subtended by an outer series of broad, leaflike bracts and an inner series of narrow bracts. Fruits are thickened, angled achenes. Blooming from spring to summer, pineland ginseng inhabits dry, open woodlands from southern MS to FL and north to southeastern VA. *T. ludoviciana* (Torr. & Gray) Gray & Hall, Louisiana nerveray, has sparsely pubescent or glabrous stems. This species inhabits scrub oak forests, and its range extends from eastern TX and western LA to southwestern AR.

Thymophylla tenuiloba (DC.) Small var. *tenuiloba*

DAHLBERG DAISY

From a taproot, this annual or short-lived perennial produces an erect or spreading branching stem up to 3 dm tall. The alternately arranged leaves are entire or dissected into linear lobes. On long peduncles, yellow or orange ray and disk florets are borne in a campanulate head. The membraneous phyllaries are yellowish and glandular. Fruits are slender, glabrous, awned achenes. Blooming from spring to fall, Dahlberg daisy inhabits open woods and roadsides from southern TX to FL and north to SC. *T. tenuiloba* var. *wrightii* (Gray) Strother has entire spathulate leaves. This species inhabits savannas and roadsides and occurs in southeastern TX.

Verbesina virginica L.

CROWNBEARD

From a rhizome, this perennial herb produces stout, pubescent stems up to 2 m tall. The coarsely toothed, alternately arranged leaves are ovate or lanceolate. Wings of the petioles extend down the stem. Densely arranged in corymbs, each turbinate head bears about three ray and ten disk florets. The phyllaries are spathulate. Fruits are dark brown, pubescent achenes. Blooming from summer to fall, crownbeard inhabits wet woods, wood margins, and disturbed areas from eastern TX, OK, and KS east to the Atlantic coastal states as far north as MD. *V. microptera* DC., Texas crownbeard, has heads that bear about ten ray and twenty disk florets each. This species inhabits disturbed sites and occurs in southeastern TX.

Vernonia missurica Raf.

MISSOURI IRONWEED

From a short rhizome, this perennial herb produces a stout, pubescent stem up to 1.5 m tall. The alternately arranged leaves are lanceolate or narrowly elliptic and often toothed. Campanulate heads of purple disk florets are arranged in corymbs. Phyllaries are purplish green with acute or obtuse tips. Fruits are pale yellow, ribbed, pubescent achenes. Blooming from summer to fall, Missouri ironweed inhabits wet woods, swamps, prairies, ditches, and roadsides from eastern TX to northwestern FL and north to southeastern NE, western IA, and southern MI. *V. angustifolia* Michx., tall ironweed, has acuminate phyllaries. This species inhabits open woods and pine barrens, and its range extends from southern MS to FL and north to southeastern NC.

Youngia japonica (L.) DC.

FALSE HAWKSBEARD

Up to 8 dm tall, this is a sparingly branched, taprooted annual herb. Forming a basal rosette, the principal leaves are oblanceolate and pinnately lobed. Leaves along the stem are few, alternate, and much reduced. Arranged in corymbs or panicles, the cylindrical or campanulate heads bear yellow ray florets. Phyllaries of the inner series are narrowly lanceolate or oblong, and those of the outer series are ovate. Fruits are fusiform, ribbed achenes. Blooming throughout the year, false hawksbeard inhabits lawns, gardens, and disturbed sites from eastern TX and southern AR to FL and north to PA. Introduced from Asia, this species has become an invasive weed throughout much of the Southeast.

Bataceae

Batis maritima L.

SALTWORT

This is a dioecious species with thickened roots. Herbaceous, erect stems of the season emerge from old prostrate woody stems. The oppositely arranged leaves are light green or yellowish, clavate, and succulent. Inconspicuous flowers are arranged in axillary spikes. Each staminate flower has a two-lobed, cup-shaped calyx and no corolla. The carpellate flowers have no perianth. Fruits are spike-shaped aggregates of berries. Blooming in summer, saltwort inhabits saline marshes from southeastern TX to FL and northward to SC. All parts of the plant are edible. The fruits are highly nutritious.

Berberidaceae

Podophyllum peltatum L.

MAYAPPLE

This is a colonial, rhizomatous perennial herb. Mature plants produce two oppositely arranged, peltate, orbicular lobed leaves. A solitary nodding, fragrant white flower is borne on a peduncle that emerges between the two leaf petioles. The fruits are ovoid berries with many small seeds. Blooming in spring, mayapple inhabits wet or mesic deciduous woods throughout much of the eastern U.S. excluding peninsular FL. Although the ripe berry is edible, all other parts of the plant are considered toxic. Native Americans used the plant as an insecticide and a cathartic.

Bignoniaceae

Bignonia capreolata L.

CROSS VINE

An evergreen perennial herb, this high-climbing vine may grow up to 20 m long. The oppositely arranged compound leaves are divided into two elliptic leaflets with cordate bases. Between the leaflets is a tendril with branches terminated by small discs. Arranged in axillary cymes, showy bilabiate flowers are red-orange without and yellowish within. Fruits are linear capsules with winged seeds. Blooming in spring, cross vine inhabits wet woods throughout much of the Southeast and lower Midwest. Native Americans used an infusion of the leaves to cleanse the blood.

Boraginaceae

Campsis radicans (L.) Seem. ex Bureau

TRUMPET VINE

This robust perennial vine produces stems up to 12 m long. The oppositely arranged leaves are pinnately compound. Individual leaflets are ovate with serrated margins. Large, bilabiate flowers are orange or red. Fruits are oblong, cylindrical capsules with winged seeds. Blooming from spring to fall, trumpet vine grows on trees, utility poles, and fences in open woods, roadsides, and disturbed sites throughout much of the U.S. east of the Rocky Mountains. Several cultivars are commercially available for ornamental plantings. Contact with the leaves can irritate the skin.

Cynoglossum virginianum L. var. *virginianum*

WILD COMFREY

From a thickened taproot, this densely hairy, perennial herb produces a solitary stem up to 8 dm tall. The lower leaves are elliptic or oblong with long petioles; the upper leaves are reduced, sessile, and clasping. Pale blue or whitish funnel-form flowers are arranged in one to several terminal scorpioid cymes. Fruits are schizocarps that divide into four bristly, globose mericarps. Blooming in spring, wild comfrey inhabits rich woods from eastern TX to southern IL and east to the Atlantic coastal states as far north as CN. A native of Asia, *C. furcatum* Wallich ex Roxb., Ceylon hound's tongue, is an occasional escape from eastern TX to southern FL.

Heliotropium curassavicum L. var. *curassavicum*

SEASIDE HELIOTROPE

From a deep rhizome, this perennial herb produces prostrate or weakly ascending glabrous stems that give the plant an overall matlike appearance. The alternately arranged leaves are succulent and mostly oblanceolate. The flowers are arranged in terminal and axillary scorpioid cymes. Five-lobed, tubular corollas are white or tinged with blue. Fruits are buoyant mericarps adapted for water dispersal. Blooming throughout the year, seaside heliotrope occurs in fresh and brackish marshes, salt flats, beaches, and lake margins throughout much of the U.S. excluding the upper Midwest, KY, and TN. *H. tenellum* (Nutt.) Torr., pasture heliotrope, is a gray-pubescent species with small white flowers that inhabits open rocky areas. Its range extends from the Gulf States to the lower Midwest.

Heliotropium indicum L.

TURNSOLE

This is a branching, introduced annual herb up to 1 m tall. The alternately arranged leaves are ovate or elliptic with prominently undulated margins. Flowers are arranged in an elongated, scorpioid cyme. The salverform corollas are purplish blue. Fruits are schizocarps that split into two mericarps. Blooming from summer to fall, turnsole inhabits creek banks, ditches, roadsides, and swamps from eastern TX, OK, and NE to the Atlantic coastal states as far north as CT. *H. europaeum* L., European heliotrope, is also an introduced species but has white flowers. It inhabits fields, roadsides, and disturbed sites; its range extends from eastern TX to northwestern FL and north to CT.

Lithospermum caroliniense (Walt. ex J.F. Gmel.) MacM. var. *caroliniense*

CAROLINA PUCCOON

From a deep taproot, these long-lived perennial herbs produce stems up to 8 dm tall. The alternately arranged leaves are coarsely hairy and may be linear, lanceolate, or oblong. Bright yellow or orange funnel-shaped flowers are arranged in densely packed cymes. Fruits are hard nutlets. Blooming from spring to summer, Carolina puccoon inhabits dry sandy woods, pine barrens, and sand dunes from eastern TX, OK, and MO to northwestern FL and north to southeastern VA. *L. canescens* (Michx.) Lehm., hairy puccoon, has softly pubescent leaves. This species inhabits open woods and prairies, and its range extends throughout much of the eastern half of the U.S. excluding LA and FL. Root extracts from these plants have been used as dyes and medicine. The name *puccoon* is an Algonquian derivative that refers to any plant that yields a dye.

Cakile geniculata (B.L. Robins.) Millsp.

GULF SEAROCKET

From a taproot, this fleshy, glabrous, annual herb produces several stems, each up to 4 dm long. The alternately arranged leaves are linear or oblanceolate with entire or coarsely toothed margins. Small, lavender, four-petaled flowers are arranged in terminal racemes. Fruits are two-jointed terete siliques. The infrutescence is strongly zigzagged. Blooming throughout the year, Gulf searocket inhabits beaches and dunes near the coast from southeastern TX to southern LA. *C. constricta* Rodman, Gulf Coast searocket, has an infrutescence that is not zigzagged. This species inhabits coastal beaches and dunes, and its range extends from southeastern TX to FL.

Cakile lanceolata (Willd.)
O.E. Schultz

COASTAL SEAROCKET

This is a fleshy, glabrous annual herb
with decumbent stems up to 7 dm long.
The alternately arranged leaves are
oblanceolate or elliptic with pinnately
lobed or entire margins. Arranged in
elongated racemes, the four-petaled
flowers are typically white but sometimes violet. Fruits are two-jointed
siliques with oblong seeds. The infrutescence is typically greater than 2 dm
long. Blooming throughout the year,
coastal searocket inhabits coastal dunes
in southeastern TX and peninsular FL.
C. edentula (Bigelow) Hook., American searocket, has an infrutescence that
is typically shorter than 2 dm and is
straight or wavy. This species inhabits
dunes and beaches, and its range extends
from southeastern LA to FL and northward into ME.

Cardamine bulbosa (Schreb.
ex Muhl.) B.S.P.

BITTERCRESS

From a short tuber, this perennial herb
produces one to several stems, each up to
6 dm tall. The alternately arranged leaves
are ovate and glabrous with undulate
margins. White, four-petaled flowers
are arranged in terminal racemes. Fruits
are long, slender siliques. Blooming in
spring, bittercress inhabits lake margins,
wet woods, and meadows throughout
much of the U.S. east of the Rocky
Mountains. *C. concatenata* (Michx.)
Sw., cutleaf toothwort, bears a single
whorl of three deeply toothed leaves
on its stem. This species inhabits wet
woods, and its range extends throughout much of the eastern half of the U.S.

Cardamine hirsuta L.

HAIRY BITTERCRESS

From a taproot, this introduced annual
herb produces one to several glabrous
stems, each up to 3 dm tall. Leaves
of the basal rosette are deeply pinnately lobed; the divisions are elliptic
or reniform with shallowly toothed
margins. The stem leaves are similarly
shaped but smaller. Arranged in terminal racemes, the four-petaled flowers
are white and bear four stamens each.
Fruits are beaked siliques with brown
seeds. Blooming in spring, hairy bittercress inhabits fields, roadsides, gardens,
and disturbed sites from eastern TX
to MI and east to the Atlantic coastal
states as far north as MA. A native
herb, *C. parviflora* L., sand bittercress,
has flowers with six stamens each. This
species inhabits roadsides, fields, and
gardens; its range extends throughout
much of the eastern half of the U.S.

Cardamine pensylvanica Muhl.
ex Willd.

PENNSYLVANIA BITTERCRESS

From a taproot, this biennial or short-
lived perennial herb produces several
green or purplish branching stems. The
alternately arranged stem leaves are pinnately compound; the oblong or oblanceolate leaflets are entire or lobed. The
basal rosette typically is absent at flowering. Arranged in terminal racemes,
each white, four-petaled flower bears
six stamens. Fruits are slightly beaked
siliques with many small seeds. Blooming in spring, Pennsylvania bittercress
inhabits wet woods, swamps, ditches,
lawns, and gardens throughout much
of the U.S. Its edible leaves are said to
have a flavor similar to watercress.

Coronopus didymus (L.) Sm.

SWINECRESS

From a long taproot, this European introduction produces prostrate or decumbent stems up to 4 dm long. Leaves are pinnately divided into toothed lobes. Those of the basal rosette are petiolate, whereas those of the stems are short-petiolate or sessile. Small white or greenish flowers are arranged in racemes that are positioned opposite to the alternately arranged leaves. Fruits are globose siliques. Blooming in spring, swinecress inhabits fields, roadsides, and disturbed sites throughout much of the U.S. excluding the Plains and Rocky Mountain states. Also introduced from Europe, *C. squamatus* (Forssk.) Aschers, greater swinecress, is a larger plant with stems up to 1 m long. This species inhabits fields and coastal prairies, and it occurs sporadically on the coastal plain from TX to FL.

Lepidium virginicum L. var. *virginicum*

VIRGINIA PEPPERWEED

This is a freely branching annual herb up to 7 dm tall. Typically absent at flowering, the basal leaves are pinnately compound or deeply dissected. The alternately arranged leaves along the stem are oblanceolate with coarsely toothed or entire margins. Racemes of small, white, four-petaled flowers terminate the upper branches. Fruits are apically notched, orbicular silicles with redbrown seeds. Blooming from spring to summer, Virginia pepperweed inhabits open woods, roadsides, and disturbed sites throughout much of the eastern U.S. *L. densiflorum* Schrad., common pepperweed, has obovate silicles. This species inhabits fields, pastures, and roadsides, and its range extends throughout much of the U.S.

Bromeliaceae

Tillandsia fasciculata Sw. var.
densispica Mez

WILD PINE

This is a clustering perennial herb that
is epiphytic on various trees. Densely arranged on a short stem, the coriaceous,
gray-green leaves are narrowly triangular and evenly tapered distally. Subtended by red, yellow, or green bracts,
tubular violet flowers are arranged in
palmately or pinnately branched spikes.
Fruits are cylindrical capsules with comose seeds. Blooming in summer, wild
pine inhabits wet forests in peninsular
FL. *T. utriculata* L., spreading airplant,
is a larger plant with a spike of white
flowers on a scape up to 2 m tall. Also
epiphytic, it occurs in peninsular FL.

Tillandsia simulata Small

MANATEE RIVER AIRPLANT

Up to 4 dm long, this is a solitary or
clustering, urn-shaped perennial herb.
The erect to spreading, gray-green,
coriaceous leaves are linear with triangular and somewhat inflated bases.
Solitary or palmately arranged spikes of
violet tubular flowers terminate a foliaceous scape. The imbricated floral bracts
are greenish or rose colored. Fruits are
cylindric capsules with comose seeds.
Blooming in spring, Manatee River airplant is epiphytic on various tree species
in swamps, hammocks, and riverbanks
in central FL. *T. bartramii* Ell., Bartram's
airplant, has uniformly red or pink floral
bracts. This species is also an epiphyte,
with a range extending from peninsular
FL to southeastern GA. *T. setacea* Sw.,
southern needleleaf, is a densely clustering species with leaves that are often
reddish. Its range also extends from
peninsular FL to southeastern GA.

Buddlejaceae

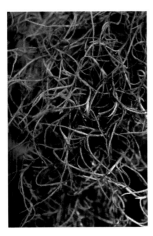

Polypremum procumbens L.
JUNIPER LEAF

Tillandsia usneoides (L.) L.
SPANISH MOSS

This is a rootless, epiphytic perennial herb with wiry, pendant stems up to several meters long. The alternately arranged leaves are gray, scurfy, filiform, and curly. Small, bright yellow-green flowers are sessile in the leaf axils. Fruits are cylindrical capsules with numerous comose seeds. Blooming in spring, Spanish moss attaches to trees, fences, and wires in wet woods, swamps, and maritime forests from eastern TX to FL and northward to MD. *T. recurvata* (L.) L., ballmoss, has a stem that is formed into a sphere. It is also an epiphyte, its range extending from AZ to FL and southeastern GA.

From a crown, this annual or perennial herb produces several freely branching, angled stems, each up to 1.2 dm long. The oppositely arranged linear leaves may be green, orange, or reddish. Flowers are solitary or arranged in leafy cymes. The small, four-lobed corollas are rotate and densely bearded within. Fruits are ovoid, flattened, two-chambered capsules with numerous small amber-colored seeds. Blooming from spring to fall, juniper leaf inhabits open woods, fields, dunes, roadsides, and disturbed sites from eastern TX to southern IL and east to the Atlantic coastal states as far north as NY. Introduced in many warmer regions of the world, this species has become invasive.

Burmanniaceae

Apteria aphylla (Nutt.) Barnhart ex Small

NODDING NIXIE

From filiform roots, this perennial herb produces a simple or sparingly branched stem up to 1 dm tall. Stems and scalelike leaves are purplish. Solitary or arranged in racemose cymes, the nodding or erect tubular flowers are white or purplish and marked with darker stripes from within. The three outer perianth lobes are broader than the inner three. Capsules are ellipsoid with minute seeds. Blooming from summer to fall, nodding nixie inhabits moist woods, sphagnum bogs, and stream banks from eastern TX to FL and southern GA. This species is nonphotosynthetic and obtains its nutrients by parasitizing a fungus.

Burmannia capitata (J.F. Gmel.) Mart.

SOUTHERN BLUETHREAD

From threadlike roots this annual herb produces a solitary simple, erect stem up to 2.4 dm tall. The alternately arranged leaves are minute and bractlike. Greenish white or cream-colored tubular flowers, often tinged with blue, are arranged in a terminal headlike cyme. The three-angled perianth is wingless and six-lobed. Fruits are three-chambered capsules with numerous tiny, yellowish seeds. Blooming from summer to fall, southern bluestem inhabits wet pinelands, savannas, bogs, pond margins, creek banks, and seeps from eastern TX and OK to FL and north to southeastern NC. *B. biflora* L., northern bluethread, has violet, three-winged corollas. This species inhabits wet pinelands, savannas, and bogs, and its range extends from eastern TX to FL and north to southeastern VA.

Buxaceae

Pachysandra procumbens Michx.

ALLEGHENY SPURGE

From a knotty rhizome, this woody, semi-evergreen, stoloniferous, monoecious vine produces trailing stems, each up to 2 dm long. Mottled with whitish splotches, the alternately arranged, thickened leaves are ovate or broadly elliptic with coarsely toothed margins. Densely arranged in spikes, the carpellate flowers are positioned on the proximal portion of the inflorescence and the staminate flowers on the distal portion. Sepals are whitish and the corolla is absent. Fruits are three-chambered, horned capsules. Blooming in spring, Allegheny spurge inhabits rich wooded slopes from southeastern LA to northwestern FL and north to NC, TN, KY, and southern IN. Native to Asia and grown as an ornamental, *P. terminalis* Sieb. & Zucc., Japanese pachysandra, has evergreen leaves.

Cabombaceae

Brasenia schreberi J. F. Gemel.

WATER SHIELD

This aquatic perennial herb produces long, creeping rhizomes. The oval-shaped, floating leaf blades are peltate. Solitary on axillary stems, the red-maroon flowers are held above the water's surface. The three or four petals are slightly longer than the sepals. Fruits are fusiform capsules with ovoid seeds. Blooming in summer, water shield inhabits lakes, sluggish streams, marshes, and canals throughout much of the eastern U.S. This species is noteworthy for the thick mucilage that coats its submerged vegetative parts.

Cabomba caroliniana Gray
FANWORT

From a rhizome, this aquatic perennial herb produces numerous elongated,
freely branching stems. The submersed
leaves are oppositely arranged, fan-
shaped, and dichotomously dissected
into linear segments. The floating leaves
are inconspicuous, elliptic, and subtend
the flowers. Borne singly in the leaf axils,
each flower is composed of three white
or purplish petals, a yellow, ear-shaped
nectary gland, and three petal-like
sepals. Each of several leathery, nutlike
fruits contains three seeds. Blooming
from spring to fall, fanwort inhabits marshes, lakes, canals, and ditches
from eastern TX, southeastern OK, and
southern IL east to the Atlantic coastal
states as far north as NH. This species
is sold as an aquarium plant and is a
food source for waterfowl and fish.

Opuntia X *alata* Griffiths
PRICKLYPEAR

This is a branched erect shrub that produces glabrous flattened stems called
pads. Along the pads are rounded depressions called areoles from which yellow spines and yellow barbed bristles
called glochids are borne. Showy yellow flowers, sometimes tinged with
light orange, appear on the pad margins. Numerous stamens are yellow and
the stigmatic lobes are light green. The
red-purple obovoid fruit is fleshy and
juicy. Blooming from spring to summer, pricklypear appears near the coast
on dunes and cheniers from southeastern TX to southwestern LA. This
plant is apparently a hybrid between *O.
stricta* (Haw.) Haw. and *O. engelman-
nii* Salm-Dyck ex Engelm. var. *lindheimeri* (Engelm.) Parfitt & Pinkava.

Opuntia humifusa (Raf.) Raf. var. *humifusa*

EASTERN PRICKLYPEAR

This is an erect or prostrate shrub up to 5 dm high. The pads are glabrous and often tuberculate. One to several white or brown spines extend from the aeroles. Glochids are yellow or reddish brown. The pale or bright yellow flowers have yellow or orange stamens and white stigmatic lobes. Mature fruits become elongated and are pale yellow or reddish brown. Blooming from spring to summer, eastern pricklypear inhabits open woods, dunes, and pinelands throughout much of the eastern U.S. *O. humifusa* var. *ammophila* (Small) L.D. Benson may become treelike with a height up to 2 m. Inhabiting scrub woodlands and dunes, it occurs sporadically in FL.

Lobelia appendiculata A. DC.

PALE LOBELIA

From a taproot, this annual or biennial herb produces an erect simple or branching stem up to 9 dm tall. Often absent at flowering, the basal leaves are lanceolate, oblanceolate, or elliptic and petiolate. Leaves on the stem are oblong or oblanceolate and sessile or clasping with toothed margins. Arranged in a secund raceme, the bilabiate flowers are violet. Each calyx lobe has prominent basal auricles and bristly-toothed margins. Fruits are hemispheric capsules that are nodding or held horizontally. Blooming from spring to summer, pale lobelia inhabits wet pinelands, fields, prairies, and roadsides from eastern TX to KS and east to AL, TN, and KY. Native Americans used this and other species of *Lobelia* to treat respiratory ailments.

Lobelia cardinalis L.

CARDINAL FLOWER

From a taproot, this perennial herb produces a simple or branching stem up to 1.5 m tall. Alternately arranged lanceolate leaves have finely toothed margins. Few to many flowers are arranged in a terminal raceme. Each corolla is bilabiate and brilliant red. Five connate stamens form a tube that surrounds the style. Fruits are capsules with many small seeds. Blooming from summer to fall, cardinal flower inhabits wet woods and stream banks throughout much of the U.S. excluding the Northwest. Although the plant is toxic, its flowers, leaves, and roots have been used in traditional medicine to treat numerous ailments.

Lobelia flaccidifolia Small

FOLDEAR LOBELIA

This is an annual herb with simple or sparingly branched stems each up to 1 m tall. The alternately arranged leaves are lanceolate or oblanceolate with minute teeth. Bilabiate flowers are borne in a loose terminal raceme. Corollas are lavender or blue and marked with white on the lower lip. Each calyx lobe is sagittate with a pair of prominent basal auricles. Fruits are hemispheric capsules. Blooming from summer to fall, foldear lobelia inhabits wet pinelands, savannas, prairies, and swamps from southeastern TX to northwestern LA and east to southern GA. *L. siphilitica* L., great blue lobelia, is a robust species with dark blue flowers each subtended by a leaf-like bract. Its range extends throughout much of the eastern U.S. excluding FL.

Lobelia puberula Michx. var. *pauci-flora* Bush

DOWNY LOBELIA

From an erect caudex, this pubescent perennial herb produces a solitary stem up to 1.5 m tall. The alternately arranged leaves are toothed with lanceolate, elliptic, or ovate blades. Arranged in terminal racemes, the bilabiate flowers are blue or purple and marked with white near their bases. Each calyx lobe base bears a dense tuft of hair. Fruits are hemispheric capsules with glossy brown reticulate seeds. Blooming from summer to fall, downy lobelia inhabits wet woods, savannas, prairies, and roadsides from eastern TX to western LA. *L. puberula* Michx. var. *puberula* has calyx lobes that are devoid of hair tufts. Its range extends from eastern TX and OK east to the Atlantic coastal states as far north as southern NJ.

Sphenoclea zeylanica Gaertn.

CHICKEN SPIKE

Up to 1.5 m tall, this is a fibrous-rooted, hollow-stemmed, and freely branching introduced annual herb. The alternately arranged leaves are elliptic and petiolate with entire margins. Small white flowers are densely arranged in a terminal spike. Fruits are circumscissle capsules with numerous small tan seeds. Blooming from summer to fall, chicken spike inhabits wet woods, ditches, and rice fields from eastern TX, OK, and southeastern MO to FL and north to eastern NC. Native to tropical Asia, this species has become widespread in many warmer regions of the world.

Cannaceae

Triodanis perfoliata (L.) Nieuwl.

VENUS' LOOKING-GLASS

From fibrous roots, this annual herb produces a simple or branching stem up to 1 m tall. The alternately arranged leaves are ovate and clasping with toothed margins. Solitary or arranged in cymules, the blue or purple flowers are terminal and axillary. Inconspicuous self-fertile flowers are also produced and are borne in the lower leaf axils. Fruits are two-chambered capsules with brown ellipsoid seeds. Blooming from spring to summer, Venus' looking-glass inhabits roadsides, fields, gardens, and disturbed sites throughout much of the U.S. *T. biflora* (Ruiz & Pavón) Greene, small Venus' looking-glass, has nonclasping sessile leaves. Inhabiting open woods, prairies, fields, roadsides, and disturbed sites, its range extends from CA to FL and north to NY.

Canna flaccida Salisb.

GOLDEN CANNA

From a large rhizome, this glaucous perennial herb produces a stem up to 2 m tall. The large alternate leaves are ovate or elliptic with entire margins. Up to five showy yellow flowers are borne on a simple raceme. The three free sepals are strongly reflexed and the three petals are basally connate. Three staminodes are petal-like and the anterior one is designated a labellum. Only one stamen is fertile. The single style is also petal-like. Fruits are ellipsoid capsules that become fimbriate at maturity and contain hard seeds. Blooming from spring to summer, golden canna inhabits swamps and marshes from southeastern TX to southwestern LA and from FL to southeastern SC. *Canna glauca* L., maraca amarilla, produces a branching inflorescences with up to ten flowers. It occurs in coastal marshes from southeastern TX to southern LA, northeastern FL, and eastern SC.

Caprifoliaceae

Lonicera japonica Thunb.

JAPANESE HONEYSUCKLE

Lonicera sempervirens L.

CORAL HONEYSUCKLE

This is a trailing or climbing, woody evergreen vine that is native to eastern Asia. The oppositely arranged leaves are elliptic with entire margins. Early leaves may be toothed. Tubular, bilabiate flowers are borne in axillary pairs. The white corollas turn yellow with age. Fruits are glossy black berries. Blooming from spring to fall, Japanese honeysuckle inhabits open woods, roadsides, fencerows, and disturbed sites throughout much of the eastern and southwestern U.S. Thoroughly naturalized, this species is an invasive weed in some areas.

This evergreen perennial vine produces long, twining stems. The oppositely arranged, elliptic or obovate leaves are glabrous. The distal one or two pairs are connate at their bases, forming a cup shape. One to several whorls of fan-shaped floral spikes terminate each stem. Red or orange from without, the tubular corollas are yellowish from within. Fruits are glossy, red-orange berries. Blooming from spring to summer, coral honeysuckle inhabits open woods, thickets, and fencerows throughout much of the eastern U.S. Hummingbirds pollinate its brightly colored tubular flowers. Several cultivars are commercially available for ornamental plantings.

Sambucus nigra L. ssp. *caerulea*
(Raf.) R. Bolli

ELDERBERRY

This is a slightly woody colonial shrub
with branches up to 4 m tall. The oppositely arranged leaves are pinnately
compound; the leaflets are oblong or
lanceolate with toothed margins. Small,
fragrant flowers are arranged in terminal compound cymes. The white corollas are rotate. Fruits are dark purple,
berrylike drupes with several stonelike
seeds. Blooming from spring to summer, elderberry inhabits open woods,
swamps, roadsides, and disturbed sites
throughout much of the U.S. excluding the Northwest. Fruits are used
to make jelly, jam, pie, and wine.

Cerastium glomeratum Thuill.

STICKY CHICKWEED

Introduced from Eurasia, this fibrous-
rooted, glandular-pubescent annual
produces erect or decumbent stems,
each up to 3 dm long. The oppositely
arranged leaves are sessile and ovate, elliptic, or obovate. Flowers are arranged
in compact terminal cymes. The white
corollas are tubular with five notched
lobes. The sepals bear glandular hairs
that extend beyond their apices. Fruits
are slender capsules with tiny brown
seeds. Blooming in spring, sticky chickweed inhabits fields, roadsides, gardens, and disturbed sites throughout
much of the U.S. *C. fontanum* Baumg.,
big chickweed, is devoid of glandular hairs on its sepals. This species is
also an introduction, and its range extends throughout much of the U.S.

Paronychia erecta (Chapman)
Shinners

SQUAREFLOWER

From a taproot, this mat-forming perennial herb produces prostrate or
ascending, branching stems. The oppositely arranged leaves are linear or
spathulate and somewhat coriaceous.
Subtended by leaflike bracts, the small
ellipsoid-shaped flowers are arranged
in congested terminal cymes that are
grouped to form square-shaped clusters.
Flowers are apetalous; the sepals are
white and petal-like. Fruits are ovoid
or ellipsoid utricles with brown seeds.
Blooming in summer, squareflower inhabits dunes and scrub woods from
southeastern LA to northern FL. *P. rugelii* (Chapman) Shuttlw. ex Chapman,
Rugel's nailwort, is an annual that is not
mat-forming. It inhabits open woods,
roadsides, fields, and disturbed sites; its
range extends from FL to southern GA.

Stellaria media (L.) Vill.

CHICKWEED

Native to Eurasia, this naturalized annual herb produces trailing, matted
stems. The oppositely arranged, petiolate
leaves are elliptic, ovate, or rhombic with
cuneate bases. Small white flowers are
borne in terminal cymes and are solitary
in the upper leaf axils. The five corolla
lobes are so deeply divided that they
appear as ten. Fruits are ovoid capsules
with tuberculate seeds. Blooming from
winter to spring, chickweed inhabits wet
woods, roadsides, and disturbed sites
throughout much of the U.S. *S. pallida*
(Dumort.) Crépin, lesser chickweed,
is an introduced prostrate annual herb
with flowers that are typically devoid of
petals. This species inhabits dunes, roadsides, and disturbed sites, and its range
extends from TX to MI and east to the
Atlantic coastal states as far north as VA.

Celestraceae

Euonymus americana L.

BURSTING HEART

This is a green-stemmed, deciduous shrub up to 2 m tall. The oppositely arranged, sessile leaves are lanceolate or ovate with small teeth. One to several flowers terminate axillary peduncles. Corollas are composed of five purplish green petals. Fruits are coriaceous, ellipsoid, warty capsules with scarlet seeds. Blooming from spring to summer, bursting heart inhabits deciduous woods and swamps from eastern TX to southeastern MO and east to the Atlantic coastal states as far north as NY. *E. atropurpurea* Jacq., burningbush, has dark maroon, four-lobed corollas. It inhabits wet woods throughout much of the eastern half of the U.S.

Chenopodiaceae

Salicornia bigelovii Torr.

GLASSWORT

This fleshy annual herb produces a simple or branching, green or reddish stem up to 6 dm tall. The oppositely arranged leaves are sessile and scale-like with acute apices. Flowers are arranged in terminal, jointed, cylindrical spikes. Each joint bears two opposite, axillary, three-flowered cymes. Fruits are utricles with ellipsoid, yellowish, hairy seeds. Blooming from summer to fall, glasswort inhabits saline marshes and low dunes along the coast from TX to FL and north to ME. *S. depressa* Standley, Virginia glasswort, has leaves with obtuse apices. This species inhabits saline marshes, and its range extends along the coast from GA to ME.

Chrysobalanaceae

Licania michauxii Prance

GOPHER APPLE

From subterranean horizontal stems, this colonial evergreen subshrub produces aerial shoots. The alternately arranged glossy leaves are spathulate with undulate margins. Inconspicuous, creamy white, five-petaled flowers are arranged in terminal clusters. Fruits are ellipsoid drupes with a single seed. Blooming from spring to summer, gopher apple inhabits dunes, pinelands, and scrub oak forests from southeastern LA to FL and north to southeastern SC. Fruits are eaten by gopher tortoises and small mammals.

Cistaceae

Helianthemum arenicola Chapman

GULF ROCKROSE

This is an erect perennial herb with reddish brown stems clothed in stellate hairs. The alternately arranged gray-green leaves are oblong, petiolate, and densely covered by stellate hairs. Arranged in terminal and axillary cymes, the flowers are bright yellow with numerous stamens. Two of the three sepals bear a linear lobe along one margin. Fruits are capsules with brownish seeds. Blooming from spring to summer, Gulf rockrose inhabits coastal dunes from southern MS to northwestern FL. *H. carolinianum* (Walt.) Michx., Carolina frostweed, has elliptic or obovate leaves in a basal rosette. This species inhabits open woods, pinelands, savannas, fields, and roadsides; its range extends from eastern TX and southern AR to FL and north to southeastern NC.

Clethraceae

Clethra alnifolia L.

SWEET PEPPER BUSH

Up to 3 m tall, this is a deciduous woody shrub with erect branches. The alternately arranged leaves are oblanceolate, obovate, or elliptic with cuneate bases and toothed margins. White, fragrant flowers are densely arranged in erect terminal and axillary racemes. Fruits are pubescent, ovoid capsules. Blooming from spring to summer, sweet pepper bush inhabits wet pinelands, savannas, lake margins, and swamps from southeastern TX to northern FL and north into ME. Flowers of this attractive shrub attract butterflies, bees, and hummingbirds. Several cultivars are commercially available for ornamental plantings.

Clusiaceae

Hypericum brachyphyllum (Spach) Steud.

COASTAL PLAIN ST. JOHNSWORT

This freely branching subshrub produces erect stems up to 1.5 m tall. The alternately arranged leaves are strongly revolute and needlelike. Smaller leaves are clustered on short axillary branchlets. An abundance of bright yellow flowers with leaflike sepals and numerous stamens are arranged in leafy cymes. Fruits are conical capsules with dark brown seeds. Blooming from spring to summer, coastal plain St. Johnswort inhabits wet pinelands, savannas, lake margins, and ditches from LA to FL and north to SC. *H. reductum* (Svens.) P. Adams, Atlantic St. Johnswort has decumbent, mat-forming branches. This species inhabits pinelands, oak scrub, and sandhills; its range extends from AL to FL and north to NC.

Hypericum crux-andreae (L.) Crantz

ST. PETERSWORT

This is a branching perennial subshrub with stems up to 8 dm tall. The oppositely arranged leaves are oblong, ovate, or oblanceolate and somewhat coriaceous. Showy, bright yellow flowers are solitary or in small terminal and axillary cymes. Sepals and petals number four each; the outer two sepals are much broader than the inner two. Each flower is composed of numerous stamens and three styles. Fruits are ovoid capsules with brown reticulate seeds. Blooming from spring to summer, St. Peterswort inhabits wet woods, pinelands, and savannas from eastern TX to the Atlantic coastal states as far north as Long Island, NY. *H. hypericoides* (L.) Crantz, St. Andrew's cross, has two styles and black seeds. This species inhabits wet woods, sandhills, pinelands, and hammocks, and its range extends from eastern TX, eastern OK, and southeastern KS east to the Atlantic coastal states as far north as southeastern MA.

Triadenum walteri (J.G. Gmel.) Gleason

GREATER MARSH ST. JOHNSWORT

From a rhizome, this glabrous perennial herb produces a simple or branching stem up to 1 m tall. The oppositely arranged leaves are oblong or elliptic with short petioles and cuneate bases. The lower surfaces are punctate. Arranged in terminal and axillary cymes, the pinkish flowers bear conspicuous orange staminodal glands. Fruits are ellipsoid capsules with glossy, dark brown, pitted seeds. Blooming from summer to fall, greater marsh St. Johnswort inhabits wet woods, swamps, stream banks, and pond margins from eastern TX to southern IL and east to the Atlantic coastal states as far north as southern NJ. *T. virginicum* (L.) Raf., Virginia marsh St. Johnswort, has sessile or clasping leaves with cordate bases. It inhabits swamps, bogs, and marshes; its range extends throughout much of the eastern half of the U.S.

Colchicaceae

Uvularia perfoliata L.

BELLWORT

From a rhizome, this perennial herb produces a solitary simple or once-branched stem up to 4 dm tall. The alternately arranged leaves are glaucous, elliptic, and perfoliate. Solitary yellow, nodding flowers are terminal. Each pedicel bears a leaflike, perfoliate bract. Fruits are three-angled, ovoid capsules with brown, turgid seeds. Blooming in spring, bellwort inhabits mesic woods from eastern TX to northern FL and north to ME. *U. sessilifolia* L., sessileleaf bellwort, has sessile leaves and bractless pedicels. Its range extends from northern LA to northwestern FL and north to Canada. *U. floridana* Chapman, Florida bellwort, has sessile leaves and each of its pedicels is subtended by a leaflike sessile bract. Its range extends from southern MS to northern FL and north to southeastern SC.

Commelinaceae

Commelina erecta L.

DAYFLOWER

From fleshy roots, this perennial herb produces tufts of erect stems. The alternately arranged, sheathing leaves are linear or lanceolate. Enclosed in a pouchlike spathe, each inflorescence is composed of one fertile and one vestigial cyme. In each flower, the two distal petals are blue and the proximal one is white or translucent. Fruits are capsules with brown seeds. Blooming from spring to fall, dayflower occurs in scrub forests, pinelands, and disturbed sites throughout much of the Southeast and lower Midwest. *C. virginica* L., Virginia dayflower, has three blue petals. This species inhabits wet woods, and its range extends throughout much of the Southeast excluding peninsular FL.

Tradescantia hirsutiflora Bush
HAIRY SPIDERWORT

From fleshy roots, this perennial herb produces hairy stems up to 5 dm tall. The alternately arranged leaves are narrowly lanceolate with clasping sheaths. Arranged in a terminal cyme, the flowers are subtended by leaflike bracts. Corolla lobes are white, pink, or blue. The stamens are free and prominently bearded. Blooming in spring, hairy spiderwort inhabits wet woods, roadsides, and disturbed sites from eastern TX to northwestern FL. *T. virginiana* L., Virginia spiderwort, is a shorter plant with each stem up to 3 dm tall. This species inhabits open woods, roadsides, and disturbed sites; its range extends throughout much of the eastern half of the U.S. excluding FL.

Tradescantia ohiensis Raf.
OHIO SPIDERWORT

From slender, fleshy roots, this perennial herb produces glaucous stems up to 1.5 m tall. The alternately arranged leaves are narrowly lanceolate with clasping sheaths. Arranged in terminal umbellate cymes, the blue, violet, or white flowers are subtended by leaflike bracts. The sepals are glabrous or bear tufts of hairs on their tips. Fruits are ellipsoid capsules with gray, flattened seeds. Blooming from spring to fall, Ohio spiderwort inhabits open woods, prairies, roadsides, and disturbed sites throughout much of the eastern half of the U.S. *T. reverchonii* Bush, Reverchon's spiderwort, has glandular and nonglandular hairs. It inhabits open, rocky woods, and its range extends from eastern TX to western LA and southwestern AR.

Convolvulaceae

Calystegia sepium (L.) Br.

HEDGE BINDWEED

From a large, creeping rhizome, this perennial herb produces trailing and twining stems, each up to 4 m long. Alternately arranged leaves are sagittate with acuminate tips. Solitary or arranged in pairs, the white, funnelform flowers are axillary. Two overlapping floral bracts completely conceal the calyx. Fruits are capsules containing up to four seeds. Blooming from spring to fall, hedge bindweed inhabits open woods, fields, and coastal glades throughout much of the U.S. *C. silvatica* (Kit.) Griseb., shortstalk false bindweed, also has white flowers but is an introduced species that has become weedy throughout much of the U.S. east of the Rocky Mountains.

Cuscuta pentagona Engelm. var. *pentagona*

FIVE-ANGLED DODDER

This is an achlorophyllous vine that is parasitic on various plant species. Reduced leaves are scalelike on twining orange stems. The small white flowers are arranged in headlike cymes. Several seeds are produced in circumscissle capsules. Blooming from summer to fall, five-angle dodder occurs throughout much of the U.S. After germination of the seeds in the soil, plants quickly parasitize a compatible host. Specialized structures called haustoria penetrate the vascular system of the host to obtain water and nutrients. As its roots atrophy, the parasite becomes completely dependent on the host. There are several dodder species native to the coastal plain, and they are difficult to distinguish.

Dichondra carolinensis Michx.

PONY FOOT

This is a stoloniferous, mat-forming, prostrate perennial herb. Leaf blades are orbicular or reniform with cordate bases. Solitary or paired, the minute flowers are borne in leaf axils. Corollas are light green or white and funnelform. Fruits are two-lobed capsules; each lobe bears a single brown, pubescent seed. Blooming from spring to summer, pony foot inhabits pinelands, roadsides, lawns, and gardens from eastern TX, southeastern OK and MO east to the Atlantic coastal states as far north as PA. This species is used commercially as a landscape ground cover.

Ipomoea cordatotriloba Dennst. var. *cordatotriloba*

TIEVINE

This is an herbaceous, trailing or climbing, pubescent perennial vine. The alternately arranged leaves are ovate with cordate bases. The blades may be entire or deeply lobed. One to several flowers are borne on each axillary peduncle. The funnelform corollas are lavender or rarely white. Fruits are globose capsules with asymmetrically angled, blackish seeds. Blooming from summer to fall, tievine inhabits fields, roadsides, dunes, and disturbed sites from eastern TX to FL and north to southeastern NC. Native to India, *I. wrightii* Gray, Wright's morning glory, has palmately compound leaves. This species inhabits wet woods and ditches, and its range extends from TX and OK to FL and north to VA.

Ipomoea imperati (Vahl) Griseb.

BEACH MORNING GLORY

This is a trailing perennial vine with stems up to 5 m long. The alternately arranged leaves are ovate, oblong, or pandurate and somewhat succulent. Solitary or in clusters, flowers are borne in the leaf axils. The funnelform corollas are white with a yellow center. Fruits are globose capsules with several seeds. Blooming from spring to fall, beach morning glory inhabits dunes and beaches from TX to FL and north to southeastern NC. *I. hederacea* Jacq., ivyleaf morning glory, has a twining habit and cordate leaves. It inhabits fields, roadsides, and disturbed sites, and its range extends throughout much of the eastern U.S.

Ipomoea lacunosa L.

WHITESTAR

From a taproot, this annual herb produces twining, branching stems. The alternately arranged leaves are ovate or pandurate with cordate bases; the margins are entire or bear one or two coarse teeth. Typically white but sometimes purplish, the funnelform flowers are borne in the leaf axils. Fruits are subglobose capsules. Blooming from summer to fall, whitestar inhabits stream banks, marsh margins, ditches, and roadsides from eastern TX to IA and east to the Atlantic coastal states as far north as MA. The night-blooming *I. macrorhiza* Michx., largeroot morning glory, has prominently veined leaves and white flowers with pinkish centers. This species inhabits dunes, beaches, and shell middens, and its range extends from MS to FL and north to NC.

Ipomoea pandurata (L.)
G.F.W. Mey.

MAN OF THE EARTH

From a large, tuberous root, this herbaceous perennial vine produces trailing or climbing stems, each up to 5 m long. The alternately arranged leaves are ovate or pandurate. Flowers are clustered in axillary cymes. The funnelform corollas are white with a reddish center. Fruits are ovoid capsules with dark brown, angled seeds. Blooming in summer, man of the earth inhabits mesic or xeric woods, fields, and disturbed sites throughout much of the eastern U.S. Its starchy roots were roasted and eaten by Native Americans.

Ipomoea pes-caprae (L.) R. Br.

RAILROAD VINE

From a massive rhizome up to 3 m long, this evergreen perennial vine produces stems up to 30 m long. The branching stems are prostrate and freely rooting at the nodes. The somewhat succulent leaves are ovate, oblong, or orbicular with a deep notch in the apex. The lavender or purple flowers are arranged in axillary clusters. Fruits are globose capsules with several brown, pubescent seeds. Blooming from spring to fall, railroad vine inhabits dunes, beaches, and disturbed sites near the coast from eastern TX to FL and north to SC. This is a cosmopolitan species that occurs along warm beaches throughout much of the world. Its extensive root system helps stabilize beaches and dunes.

Ipomoea quamoclit L.

CYPRESS VINE

Introduced from tropical America, this is a trailing or climbing, glabrous annual vine. The alternately arranged leaves are ovate and pinnately divided into linear segments. One to several flowers are clustered on axillary peduncles. The salverform corollas are bright scarlet. Fruits are globose capsules with asymmetrical, angular seeds. Blooming from spring to fall, cypress vine inhabits fields, roadsides, and disturbed sites from TX, OK, and KS east to the Atlantic coastal states as far north as NY. *I. coccinea* L., red-star, has scarlet flowers and simple ovate leaves. It inhabits fields, roadsides, and disturbed sites, and its range extends from TX to MI and east to the Atlantic coastal states as far north as MA.

Ipomoea sagittata Poir.

SALTMARSH MORNING GLORY

This is a glabrous perennial herb with a low-climbing habit. The alternately arranged leaves are narrowly sagittate. Axillary on one-flowered peduncles, the funnelform flowers are bright pink or reddish purple. Blooming from spring to fall, saltmarsh morning glory inhabits beaches, dunes, and brackish and freshwater marshes along the outer coastal plain from TX to NC. Native Americans made a decoction from the root to detoxify the blood.

Jacquemontia tamnifolia (L.) Griseb.

HAIRY CLUSTER VINE

This herbaceous, trailing annual vine produces several stems, each up to 2 m long. The alternately arranged leaves are ovate or elliptic with cordate bases. Headlike cymes are subtended by leaflike bracts. Corollas are blue and funnelform. Fruits are subglobose capsules, each containing four brown, glabrous seeds. Blooming from spring to summer, hairy cluster vine inhabits disturbed sites from eastern TX and OK to FL and north to southeastern VA. An aggressive colonizer of disturbed soil, this species rapidly can become invasive.

Stylisma humistrata (Walt.) Chapman

DAWNFLOWER

From slender roots, this herbaceous perennial vine produces several prostrate stems. The alternately arranged leaves are elliptic or lanceolate with cordate bases. Each axillary cluster of flowers is borne on a peduncle that exceeds the length of the subtending leaf. Corollas are white and campanulate. Each style is divided into two branches. Fruits are two-chambered, papery capsules. Blooming from spring to fall, dawnflower inhabits open woods, sandhills, roadsides, stream banks, and disturbed sites from eastern TX and AR to northern FL and north to eastern VA. *S. aquatica* (Walt.) Raf., water dawnflower, has lavender flowers and oblong leaves. This species inhabits wet pinelands, and its range extends from eastern TX to northwestern FL and north to southeastern NC.

Cucurbitaceae

Melothria pendula L. var. *pendula*

CREEPING CUCUMBER

Cucumis melo L.

CANTALOUPE

This is an introduced or escaped, trailing or climbing annual vine. The shallowly lobed leaves are scabrous and broadly ovate or orbicular with toothed margins. Climbing tendrils are borne opposite the leaves. Clustered in the leaf axils, the tubular yellow flowers are unisexual. The fruit is an ellipsoid pepo with numerous seeds. Blooming from spring to summer, cantaloupe inhabits fields, roadsides, and other disturbed areas throughout much of the U.S. excluding the upper Midwest and the Northwest. The garden cucumber, *C. sativus* L., is a close relative.

This is a slender, climbing or creeping annual vine. The alternately arranged leaves are palmately lobed and basally cordate with irregularly toothed margins. Simple tendrils are axillary. Staminate flowers are borne in axillary clusters; carpellate and perfect flowers are solitary in the leaf axils. The small yellow corollas are campanulate. Fruits are smooth green or black juicy berries with numerous small white seeds. Blooming from spring to fall, creeping cucumber inhabits wet woods, marsh margins, hammocks, and fencerows from TX, OK, and southern KS east to the Atlantic coastal states as far north as MD. Fruits are nutritious and pleasant tasting.

Cyperaceae

Rhynchospora latifolia (Bald.) Thomas

WHITE-TOP SEDGE

From a scaly rhizome, this perennial herb produces one to several scapes each up to 1 m tall. The linear leaves are held erect or arching. Spikelets of inconspicuous white flowers are densely arranged in a terminal head. Becoming green distally, several white, spreading, involucral bracts subtend the inflorescence. The largest of these bracts is typically greater than 5 mm at its base. Fruits are biconvex achenes. Blooming from spring to summer, white-top sedge occurs in wet pinelands, savannas, and bogs from southeastern TX to FL and north to NC. *R. colorata* (L.) H. Pfeiffer, sandswamp white-top, is a shorter plant with smaller involucral bracts. This species inhabits wet pinelands, savannas, bogs, and ditches, and its range extends from eastern TX to FL and north to VA.

Droseraceae

Dionaea muscipula Ellis

VENUS FLYTRAP

From a short rhizome, this insectivorous perennial herb produces leaves in a basal rosette. Green or red reniform leaf blades are hinged in the middle and bear sharp teeth on their margins. The petioles are prominently winged. An umbelliform cyme of white flowers terminates a solitary scape up to 3 dm tall. Fruits are ovoid capsules with numerous black seeds. Blooming in spring, Venus flytrap inhabits wet pinelands, savannas, bogs, and ditches in northeastern SC and southeastern NC. Three trigger hairs are positioned near the middle of each of the two leaf lobes. Stimulation of these hairs by an insect springs the trap. Nitrogen is the primary nutrient absorbed from the insect after it is digested by enzymes.

Drosera brevifolia Pursh
SUNDEW

This is an annual or short-lived perennial insectivorous herb. Arranged in
a basal rosette, the spathulate leaves
bear sticky, glandular hairs that trap
and digest small insects. Arranged in
a drooping, one-sided, glandular-hairy
raceme, the white or pink flowers open
in sequence as the scape becomes erect.
Numerous minute, pitted seeds are contained in an obovoid capsule. Blooming
in spring and summer, sundew inhabits
wet savannas, pinelands, and sphagnum bogs from TX, OK, and KS east
to FL and VA. *D. intermedia* Hayne,
swampleaf sundew, is a larger plant
with a glabrous scape. It inhabits bogs
and pond margins, and its range extend
throughout much of the eastern U.S.

Drosera tracyi Macfarlane
DEWTHREADS

This is a stemless, insectivorous perennial herb. The expanded petioles of
the alternately arranged filiform leaves
form a cormlike structure. Uncoiling
from the top like a fern, the leaves are
beset with tentaclelike, glandular hairs.
Arranged along one side of a drooping raceme, the rose-purple flowers
bloom sequentially. The raceme gradually becomes erect so that the flower
in bloom is held uppermost. Fruits are
capsules with numerous minute black
seeds. Blooming in spring, dewthreads
inhabits wet pinelands and savannas
from southeastern LA to northwestern FL and southern GA. *D. filiformis*
Raf., threadleaf sundew, has leaves that
are up to 2.5 dm tall and bear purple
glandular hairs. This species inhabits
wet pinelands and savannas, and it occurs in northwestern FL, southeastern
NC, and also from DE to eastern MA.

Ericaceae

Bejaria racemosa Vent.

TAR FLOWER

Growing up to 2.5 m tall, this slender evergreen shrub produces erect, pubescent branches. The alternately arranged leaves are sessile with elliptic or ovate blades and cuneate bases. Borne in terminal racemes, the showy, fragrant flowers secrete a gluelike exudate that traps bees and flies. Composed of seven lobes, the corollas are white and tinged with pink. Fruits are woody, globose capsules with numerous yellow, falcate seeds. Blooming in summer, tar flower inhabits scrub woods and pinelands from peninsular FL to southeastern GA. Plants are used as garden ornamentals in the Southeast.

Conradina canescens Gray

FALSE ROSEMARY

This is a small evergreen shrub up to 5 dm tall. The oppositely arranged aromatic leaves are linear with both surfaces densely clothed in gray pubescence. Flowers appear on the new growth of the season. The corollas are bilabiate and pale lavender with purplish spots. Fruits are small nutlets. Blooming from spring to summer, false rosemary inhabits coastal dunes, sandhills, and pinelands from southern MS to northwestern and central FL. *C. glabra* Shinners, Apalachicola false rosemary, has leaves that are gray-pubescent below and nearly glabrous above. This species inhabits pinelands and oak scrub, and its range is restricted to northwestern FL.

Epigaea repens L.

TRAILING ARBUTUS

This is a small, prostrate evergreen shrub with spreading, pubescent branches. The alternately arranged leaves are elliptic or ovate and somewhat coriaceous. The fragrant pink or white flowers are arranged in congested terminal racemes. Corollas are salverform with tubes that are densely pubescent within. Fruits are globose capsules with numerous red-brown seeds. Blooming in spring, trailing arbutus inhabits sandy mesic or xeric woods from MS to northern FL and north to Canada. This, the state flower of Massachusetts, is endangered in FL.

Kalmia hirsuta Walt.

HAIRY WICKY

This low evergreen shrub produces several stems up to 6 dm long. The alternately arranged leaves are ovate, elliptic, or oblanceolate and sessile. One to three campanulate pink flowers are borne in the leaf axils. The epipetalous stamens are borne in red-colored pockets. Fruits are globose capsules with numerous hard seeds. Blooming from spring to summer, hairy wicky inhabits wet pinelands, savannas, and bogs from southern AL to central FL and north to southeastern SC. Up to 1.5 m tall, *K. cuneata* Michx., white wicky, is a larger plant and is deciduous. It inhabits upland sandhill swamps, and its range extends from northeastern SC to southeastern NC.

Rhododendron austrinum (Small) Rehd.

FLORIDA AZALEA

Monotropa uniflora L.

INDIANPIPE

This glabrous perennial herb is white or pinkish with a waxy texture. Leaves along the scape are reduced to scale-like, sessile bracts. Solitary nodding, fragrant flowers terminate each scape. As the flowers mature they become erect. Fruits are ovoid capsules with many small seeds. Blooming from summer to fall, Indianpipe inhabits mesic woods and sandy pinelands throughout much of the U.S. excluding the Rocky Mountains and the desert Southwest. This non-green species obtains its nutrients by parasitizing a fungal host. *M. hypopithys* L., pinesap, is a pubescent species with several flowers per raceme. Individuals are typically yellow or red. This species inhabits rich deciduous woods, and its range extends throughout much of the U.S.

This is a deciduous shrub up to 3 m tall. The alternately arranged leaves are obovate or elliptic with ciliated margins. Arranged in terminal clusters, the showy, fragrant flowers bloom before the new shoots unfurl their leaves. Corollas are yellow or orange and sometimes suffused with red. Fruits are oblong brown capsules. Blooming in spring, Florida azalea inhabits open acidic woods from southern MS to northern FL and southern GA. This attractive shrub is used in southern landscaping.

Rhododendron canescens (Michx.) Sweet

PINXTER AZALEA

This is a freely branching, deciduous shrub up to 5 m tall. The alternately arranged leaves are pubescent with ciliated margins and oblanceolate or elliptic blades. Arranged in whorled clusters, the sweetly fragrant bilabiate flowers are pink or nearly white. Prominent stamens extend well beyond the glandular, hairy corolla tube. Fruits are densely hairy, sickle-shaped capsules. Blooming in spring, Pinxter azalea inhabits wet woods, pinelands, and stream banks from TX and OK to FL and north to VA. Planted as an ornamental, this showy species attracts hummingbirds and butterflies with its flowers.

Rhododendron chapmanii Gray

CHAPMAN'S RHODODENDRON

This is an evergreen shrub up to 2.5 m tall. The alternately arranged leaves are elliptic and leathery with revolute margins. Arranged in terminal clusters, the showy flowers bloom before the new leafy shoots appear. The funnelform corollas are rose colored and marked with orange spots. Fruits are urceolate capsules with many seeds. Blooming in spring, Chapman's rhododendron inhabits wet pinelands and bog margins in a few locations in the Florida Panhandle. This species is listed as federally endangered.

Rhododendron viscosum (L.) Torr.

SWAMP AZALEA

This is a woody deciduous shrub up to 2 m tall. The alternately arranged simple leaves are obovate or elliptic and somewhat leathery. Arranged in whorled clusters, the white fragrant flowers are glandular, hairy, and appear before the leaves have emerged. Elongated capsules are covered with stiff, glandular hairs. Blooming in spring, swamp azalea inhabits wet woods and stream banks from eastern TX and OK to FL and north to ME.

Eriocaulon decangulare L.

PIPEWORT

From a short, branching rhizome, this perennial herb produces a basal cluster of linear leaves. Terminating a scape up to 1 m tall, a hard globose head of small unisexual flowers is subtended by narrowly ovate or lanceolate bracts. Both male and female flowers have two sepals and two petals. The male flower has four stamens. Fruits are capsules with pale brown seeds. Blooming from spring to summer, pipewort inhabits wet pinelands, savannas, lake margins, and ditches along the outer coastal plain from eastern TX to FL and north to NJ. *E. compressum* Lam., flattened pipewort, has soft floral heads and dark brown seeds. This species inhabits wet pinelands, savannas, bogs, and ditches, and its range extends along the outer coastal plain from southeastern TX to FL and north to NJ.

Acalypha ostryifolia Riddell

THREE-SEEDED MERCURY

Lachnocaulon anceps (Walt.) Morong

BOG BUTTON

With fibrous, branching roots and a short rhizome, this monoecious perennial herb forms dense clumps. The bright green, linear leaves are arranged in a basal rosette. Up to 3 dm tall, the solitary hairy, twisted scape bears a basal sheath. Unisexual whitish flowers are densely arranged in a globose head that is subtended by brownish bracts. Male flowers are composed of three brown sepals and three stamens. The female flowers are composed of three sepals and a three-chambered ovary. Fruits are capsules with brown, ribbed seeds. Blooming from spring to summer, bog button inhabits wet pinelands, savannas, bogs, and pond margins from southeastern TX to FL and north to southeastern VA. *L. digynum* Koern., pineland bog button, has a pale brown floral head and a smooth scape. It inhabits pinelands, savannas, and ditches; its range extends from southeastern TX to northwestern FL.

From a taproot this monoecious annual herb produces an erect, branching, hairy stem up to 1 m tall. The alternately arranged petiolate leaves are ovate or rhombic with cordate bases and toothed margins. Staminate flowers are arranged in axillary spikes, and carpellate flowers are arranged in terminal spikes. Fruits are prickly capsules with tuberculate seeds. Blooming in summer, three-seeded Mercury inhabits open woods, roadsides, and disturbed sites throughout the Southeast and the lower Midwest. *A. rhomboidea* Raf., common three-seeded Mercury, has both carpellate and staminate flowers borne in the same spike. It inhabits open sandy sites, and its range extends throughout much of the eastern U.S.

Chamaesyce hirta (L.) Millsp.

PILLPOD SANDMAT

From a slender taproot, this annual herb produces erect to decumbent stems, each up to 6 dm long with soft, straight, yellowish hairs. The oppositely arranged leaves are lanceolate, ovate, or rhombic with sharp or rounded teeth on the margins. Borne in the upper leaf axils, cyathia are densely arranged in stalked, leafless cymes. Each cyathium bears several staminate flowers, a single carpellate flower, and five small glands. Clothed in short, appressed hairs, fruits are three-angled capsules with four-angled brown seeds. Blooming from summer to winter, pillpod sandmat inhabits roadsides, gardens, and disturbed sites from CA to FL and north to NY. *C. hypericifolia* (L.) Millsp., graceful sandmat, is an erect branching annual up to 5 dm tall with glabrous capsules. This species inhabits disturbed sites, and its range extends from CA to FL and north to SC.

Caperonia palustris (L.) St.-Hil.

TEXASWEED

From a taproot, this sparingly branching annual herb produces a solitary stem up to 1 m tall. The alternately arranged, broadly lanceolate leaves are prominently veined and coarsely pubescent with serrated margins. Small white flowers are unisexual. Both male and female flowers are borne in the same spike. The three-chambered fruits contain small brown seeds. Blooming from summer to fall, Texasweed inhabits wet woods and marshes in eastern TX, LA, and AR and southern FL. This species has become an invasive weed in rice and soybean fields.

Cnidoscolus texanus (Muell.-Arg.) Small

TEXAS BULLNETTLE

From an extensive root system, this perennial herb produces several branching stems, each up to 1 m long. The alternately arranged leaves are palmately lobed; the lobes are coarsely toothed. Both stems and leaves bear stinging hairs that contain several compounds including seratonin. Cymes of fragrant white flowers are arranged in a branching terminal inflorescence. Flowers are unisexual with both male and female flowers in the same cyme. Bearing long, white hairs, fruits are oblong capsules, each with three brownish white seeds. Blooming from spring to summer, Texas bullnettle inhabits open woods, pastures, roadsides, and disturbed sites from TX to KS and east to AR and western LA.

Cnidoscolus urens (L.) Arthur var. *stimulosus* (Michx.) Govaerts

BULLNETTLE

This monoecious perennial herb is clothed in stinging hairs. The alternately arranged leaves are palmately lobed with toothed margins. The inflorescence is a terminal compound cyme bearing both carpellate and staminate flowers. Each white calyx is salverform and showy; the corolla is absent. Fruits are three-chambered capsules; each chamber bears a single dark brown seed. Blooming from spring to summer, bullnettle inhabits open woods, fields, and dunes from southeastern LA to FL and north to southeastern VA. Steeped in whiskey or gin, the sap of this plant has been used in traditional herbal medicine as a potency aid for men.

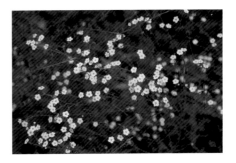

Euphorbia corollata L.

FLOWERING SPURGE

Croton capitatus Michx. var. *lindheimeri* (Engelm. & Gray) Muell.-Arg.

HOGWORT

From a taproot, this freely branching, monoecious annual produces a stem up to 1.2 m tall. All vegetative parts of the plant are densely stellate pubescent. The alternately arranged leaves are ovate or lanceolate. Flowers are arranged in a terminal raceme. Apetalous female flowers bearing seven sepals each occupy the basal part of the raceme, whereas the male flowers, bearing five sepals and five petals each, occupy the distal portion. Fruits are three-chambered capsules with glossy brown seeds. Blooming from summer to fall, hogwort inhabits fields, roadsides, pastures, and wood margins from eastern TX to FL and north to eastern KS, southern MO, and southern IN. *C. punctatus* Jacq., Gulf croton, has apetalous, dioecious male flowers. It inhabits coastal dunes from eastern TX to FL and north to NC.

From a stout rhizome, this monoecious perennial herb produces one to several stems, each up to 8 dm tall. The alternately arranged leaves are linear, oblong, or elliptic and somewhat revolute. Leaves subtending the inflorescence branches are whorled. Each cyathium, composed of five glands and five white petal-like lobes, bears several staminate and a solitary carpellate flower. Fruits are glabrous capsules with smooth, ovoid seeds. Blooming from spring to fall, flowering spurge inhabits open woods, pinelands, savannas, and disturbed sites throughout much of the eastern U.S. Native Americans used the plant to treat a variety of ailments including toothache, urinary infections, and worms.

Euphorbia cyathophora Murr.

WILD POINSETTIA

From a taproot, this annual herb produces a glabrous, branching stem up to 7 dm tall. The leaves are mostly opposite and may be lanceolate, obovate, or pandurate. Those subtending the inflorescences are often marked with red near their bases. Each cyathium bears a cup-shaped nectar gland. Several cyathia are irregularly clustered at the terminus of each stem. Fruits are capsules with dark brown, ovoid seeds. Blooming from summer to fall, wild poinsettia inhabits disturbed areas throughout much of the eastern U.S. excluding the Northeast. Grown as an ornamental, plants may persist around old home sites.

Euphorbia dentata Michx. var. *dentata*

SUMMER POINSETTIA

From a taproot, this annual herb produces a freely branching, pubescent stem up to 6 dm tall. The mostly opposite leaves are lanceolate or ovate and toothed. Those subtending the inflorescences are solid green and marked with reddish spots or suffused with white. Each cyathium bears a cup-shaped nectar gland. Several cyathia are irregularly clustered at the terminus of each stem. Fruits are green capsules with dark brown, glabrous seeds. Blooming from spring to fall, summer poinsettia inhabits prairies and disturbed sites from TX, OK, and KS to the Atlantic coastal states as far north as NJ but excluding FL. Stems and leaves contain milky latex that may be a skin irritant.

Fabaceae

Apios americana Medik.
GROUNDNUT

Stillingia sylvatica L. ssp. *sylvatica*
QUEEN'S DELIGHT

From a thick, woody crown, this monoecious perennial herb produces one to several stems, each up to 5 dm tall. The alternately arranged leaves are lanceolate or narrowly elliptic with toothed margins. Unisexual flowers are arranged in a terminal spike with a few carpellate flowers below and numerous staminate flowers above. The calyx lobes are yellow and the corolla is absent. Fruits are ovoid, three-lobed capsules with gray seeds. Blooming from spring to summer, queen's delight inhabits sandy open woods, pinelands, and savannas from eastern NM, TX, OK, and southern KS east to the Atlantic coastal states as far north as southeastern VA. *S. aquatica* Chapman, water toothleaf, has a woody stem. This species inhabits wet pinelands, and its range extends from southern MS to FL, southern GA, and southeastern SC.

From fleshy, tuberous rhizomes, this perennial herb produces trailing or climbing stems up to 3 m long. The alternately arranged leaves are pinnately compound. The leaflets are mostly ovate with acuminate tips. Brown-red flowers are densely arranged in axillary racemes. Fruits are somewhat flattened, linear legumes. Blooming from summer to fall, groundnut inhabits wet woods and riverbanks throughout much of the eastern U.S. The federally threatened *A. priceana* B.L. Robins., traveler's delight, has pink flowers. It inhabits mesic woods often along stream banks, and its range extends from eastern MS and adjacent AL to western KY and southern IL.

Baptisia bracteata Muhl. ex Ell. var.
laevicaulis (Grey ex Canby) Isley
CREAM WILD INDIGO

Baptisia alba (L.) Vent. var.
macrophylla (Larisey) Isely
WHITE WILD INDIGO

From a stout rhizome, this perennial herb produces a solitary branching stem up to 2 m tall. The alternately arranged leaves are trifoliate; the leaflets are elliptic, oblanceolate, or obovate. Flowers are laxly arranged on an elongated slender raceme. Corollas are white; the standard petal is splotched with purple. Fruits are light brown, cylindric, inflated legumes. Blooming in spring, white wild indigo inhabits open woods, prairies, and roadsides from eastern TX to MS and north to southern MI and NY. Having smaller leaves, *B. alba* (L.) Vent. var. *alba* has a range that extends from MS to FL and north to eastern VA.

From a taproot, this perennial herb produces a solitary branching stem up to 7 dm tall. Alternately arranged, blue-green leaves are trifoliate with two prominent, persisting stipules. Creamy white or yellowish flowers are borne on long, drooping racemes. The prominently beaked legumes are black and contain large, hard seeds. Blooming in spring, cream wild indigo inhabits open woods, prairies, and pinelands from eastern TX to LA and north to MO and OK. This species is planted as a garden ornamental, and its dried seedpods are used in floral arrangements.

Baptisia lanceolata (Walt.) Ell. var. *lanceolata*

GOPHERWEED

This is a bushy-branching perennial herb up to 9 dm tall. The alternately arranged leaves are trifoliate and divided into spathulate or oblanceolate leaflets. Bright yellow flowers are solitary in the upper leaf axils and arranged in short, terminal racemes. Fruits are beaked, globose or ovoid legumes. Blooming in summer, gopherweed inhabits sandhills, pinelands, and oak scrub from southern AL to FL and north to SC. Beginning in late fall, the dried plants break at ground level and are pushed along as tumbleweeds. This action provides an effective mechanism for seed dispersal.

Baptisia nuttalliana Small

NUTTALL'S WILD INDIGO

From a stout rhizome, this perennial herb produces a solitary, bushy-branching stem up to 1.2 m tall. The alternately arranged leaves are trifoliate and divided into obovate, mucronate leaflets. Yellow flowers are solitary in the upper leaf axils and on short, terminal racemes. Fruits are ovoid legumes, each with a recurved beak. Blooming in spring, Nuttall's wild indigo inhabits open woods and roadsides from eastern TX and OK to MS. The showy flowers are highly attractive to bees and butterflies.

Baptisia sphareocarpa Nutt.

YELLOW WILD INDIGO

From a large rhizome, this shrubby perennial herb produces a single branching stem up to 1 m tall. The blue-green leaves are mostly palmately compound and divided into oblanceolate, obovate, or elliptic leaflets. The lower leaves are mostly divided into three leaflets; the upper leaves are simple or divided into two leaflets. Bright yellow flowers are arranged in erect racemes. Fruits are spherical legumes with glossy brown seeds. Blooming in spring, yellow wild indigo inhabits open woods and roadsides from eastern TX to southern MS and north to MO. This species may have been introduced in part of its present range.

Canavalia rosea (Sw.) DC.

BAY BEAN

This is a robust perennial herb with trailing or twining stems, each up to 6 m long. The alternately arranged leaves are trifoliate and coriaceous; the leaflets are orbicular. Lavender and pinkish flowers are borne in axillary racemes. Fruits are flattened, woody legumes with marbled brown seeds. Blooming throughout the year, bay bean inhabits sandy beaches in southern TX and FL. It is found throughout much of the world's warm beaches, and its extensive roots help prevent beach erosion.

Centrosema virginianum (L.) Benth.

BUTTERFLY PEA

This trailing or twining herbaceous, perennial vine produces stems up to 1.6 m long. The alternately arranged leaves are trifoliate; the leaflets are linear or ovate. On pedicels bearing a pair of membranous bracts, the axillary purple, blue-violet, or lavender flowers are solitary or paired. Each tubular calyx is deeply cleft into five linear lobes. Fruits are long, linear legumes with numerous seeds. Blooming from spring to summer, butterfly pea inhabits open woods, fields, and roadsides from TX and OK to FL and north to NJ. *Clitoria mariana* L., Atlantic pigeonwings, has similar flowers but can be distinguished by its deltoid calyx lobes. This species inhabits open woods and disturbed sites, and its range extends throughout much of the U.S. east of the Rocky Mountains.

Chamaecrista fasciculata (Michx.) Greene var. *fasciculata*

PARTRIDGE PEA

From a taproot, this annual herb produces sparingly branching stems up to 1 m tall. The alternately arranged leaves are pinnately compound with a sessile gland on each petiole. Leaflets are narrowly oblong. Four of the five yellow corolla lobes are marked with red near their bases. The red, sickle-shaped anthers are laterally swept to either side of the flower. Fruits are linear, hairy legumes with dark brown seeds. Blooming from summer to fall, partridge pea inhabits open woods, fields, and roadsides throughout much of the eastern U.S. From central FL, *C. rotundifolia* (Pers.) Greene, roundleaf sensitive pea, is an annual with compound leaves divided into two broadly ovate leaflets.

Chamaecrista nictitans (L.) Moench
ssp. *nictitans* var. *nictitans*

SENSITIVE PEA

From a taproot, this annual herb produces spreading, pubescent stems up
to 5 dm tall. The alternately arranged
leaves are pinnately compound with
narrow, oblong leaflets and persistent
linear stipules. A peltate gland is situated slightly below the most proximal
pair of leaflets. The yellow flowers are
solitary or clustered in the leaf axils.
Fruits are erect, pubescent, oblong legumes with black seeds. Blooming from
spring to summer, sensitive pea inhabits
wood margins, fields, and disturbed sites
throughout much of the U.S. Its sensitive leaves rapidly wilt when touched.

Crotalaria spectabilis Roth

SHOWY RATTLEBOX

From a woody taproot, this introduced
annual herb produces a stout, purplish,
branching stem up to 2 m tall. The
simple, alternately arranged leaves are
obovate with conspicuous persistent
stipules. Bright yellow flowers are arranged in terminal and axillary racemes.
Fruits are elongate legumes with several seeds. Blooming from summer
to fall, showy rattlebox inhabits fields,
roadsides and disturbed sites from
eastern TX to FL and north to eastern VA. Also introduced, *C. ochroleuca*
G. Don, slender leaf rattlebox, has
trifoliate leaves. This species inhabits
fields, roadsides, and disturbed sites,
and its range extends from southeastern LA to FL and north to NC.

Desmanthus illinoensis (Michx.)
Macm. ex B.L. Robins. & Fern.

ILLINOIS BUNDLEFLOWER

From a crown, this perennial herb produces several stems, each up to 1 m
long. The alternately arranged leaves
are bipinnately compound; the ultimate
divisions are linear. A head of greenish
white flowers terminates each axillary
peduncle. Each flower bears five stamens. Densely arranged in heads, fruits
are flattened, falcate legumes. Blooming
from spring to summer, Illinois bundleflower inhabits fields, prairies, dunes,
roadsides, and disturbed sites throughout much of the eastern half of the U.S.
excluding New England. *D. tatuhyen-
sis* Hoehne, dwarf bundleflower, has
straight legumes and each of its flowers
bears ten stamens. This species inhabits coastal dunes, and its range extends
from eastern TX to southwestern LA.

Desmodium paniculatum (L.) DC.

TICK TREFOIL

From an elongated, branching taproot,
this perennial herb produces erect, ascending, or reclining stems, each up to
1 m long. The alternately arranged leaves
are trifoliate; the leaflets are lanceolate,
ovate, or oblong with ciliated margins.
Arranged in terminal and axillary panicles, each of the pink flowers is marked
with two yellow spots near the base of
the standard petal. Clothed with hooked
hairs, the fruits are loments. Blooming
from summer to fall, tick trefoil inhabits
woods, prairies, roadsides, and riverbanks throughout much of the eastern
half of the U.S. *D. glabellum* (Michx.)
DC., Dillenius' tick trefoil, has coriaceous leaflets with prominent reticulate
veins. It inhabits dry woods, and its
range extends throughout much of the
eastern half of the U.S.

Galactia volubilis (L.) Britt.

MILKPEA

Erythrina herbacea L.

CORAL BEAN

From a woody caudex, this prickly, deciduous subshrub produces stems up to
3 m long. The alternately arranged leaves
are trifoliate with long petioles. Leaflets
are hastate or deltoid. One to several
scapes are terminated by a raceme of
showy scarlet flowers. Fruits are blackish legumes with bright scarlet seeds.
Blooming in spring, coral bean inhabits
open woods along the outer coastal plain
from southeastern TX and OK to FL
and north to southeastern NC. Seeds
contain toxic alkaloids that are purgative
and narcotic.

This perennial herb produces trailing or
climbing hairy stems, each up to 1.5 m
long. The alternately arranged leaves
are trifoliate. Leaflets vary from ovate
to elliptic. Pink flowers are arranged in
axillary racemes. The standard petal is
marked with yellow near its base. Fruits
are straight, pubescent legumes with
several seeds. Blooming in summer,
milkpea inhabits open woods, fencerows,
and disturbed sites from eastern TX,
OK, and KS east to the Atlantic coastal
states as far north as Long Island, NY.
G. regularis (L.) B.S.P., eastern milkpea,
has a trailing habit. This species inhabits
open woods and fields, and its range extends from eastern TX, OK, and KS east
to the Atlantic coastal states as far north
as southern NJ.

Indigofera hendecaphylla Jacq.
TRAILING INDIGO

From a taproot, this annual or perennial introduced herb produces prostrate stems up to 8 dm long. The alternately arranged leaves are pinnately compound; the leaflets are obovate or elliptic with shallowly lobed margins. Pink or salmon-colored flowers are arranged on elongated axillary racemes. Fruits are narrowly oblong legumes with yellowish, glossy seeds. Blooming throughout the year, trailing indigo inhabits pastures, fields, and coastal dunes in FL. A native perennial, *I. miniata* Ortega, coastal indigo, inhabits open woods and prairies from TX to KS and east to FL and southeastern GA.

Lathyrus venosus Muhl. ex Willd.
VEINY PEA

From a rhizome, this perennial herb produces erect or sprawling stems up to 1 m long. Each of the alternately arranged leaves is pinnately compound with a branched terminal tendril; the leaflets are ovate or elliptic. Blue, purple, or pink flowers are arranged in pedunculate axillary racemes. Fruits are flattened legumes. Blooming from spring to summer, veiny pea inhabits open woods, stream banks, and roadsides throughout much of the eastern half of the U.S. excluding MS and FL. Native Americans used a decoction of the root as a tonic and stimulant and for the treatment of wounds and convulsions.

Lespedeza cuneata (Dum.-Cours.) G. Don

SERICEA

From a branched taproot, this perennial herb produces several erect, simple or branching stems, each up to 2 m tall. The alternately arranged leaves are trifoliate. The gray-green or silvery leaflets are cuneate with short, appressed pubescence on both surfaces. Borne in the leaf axils, the white or cream-colored flowers are solitary or arranged in short racemes. Each standard petal is marked with a purplish splotch. Fruits are oblong legumes with a single seed. Blooming from summer to fall, sericea inhabits fields, pastures, roadsides, and disturbed sites from eastern TX to southern MI and east to the Atlantic coastal states as far north as MA. Introduced from Asia for forage and erosion control, this species has become an aggressive, noxious weed in parts of its range.

Lespedeza virginica (L.) Britt.

SLENDER LESPEDEZA

This is an erect perennial herb with stems up to 1.6 m tall. The alternately arranged leaves are trifoliate; the leaflets are linear or oblong and mostly over four times as long as wide. Flowers are arranged in few-flowered axillary racemes. The corollas are pink or purple. Fruits are flattened, reticulate legumes that are elliptic, ovate, or orbicular in outline. Blooming from spring to summer, slender lespedeza inhabits open woods, roadsides, and fields throughout much of the eastern half of the U.S. *L. stuevei* Nutt., tall lespedeza, has elliptic or oblong leaflets that are mostly less than 3.5 times as long as wide. This species inhabits open woods, roadsides, and fields, and its range extends from eastern TX to southeastern KS and east to the Atlantic coastal states as far north as MA.

Lupinus diffusus Nutt.

OAK RIDGE LUPINE

Lupinus texensis Hook.

TEXAS BLUEBONNET

From a woody taproot, this clumping perennial herb produces short, pubescent, decumbent stems. The simple leaves are elliptic or oblong and silky pubescent. The blue flowers are densely arranged in a raceme up to 3 dm tall. The standard petal is conspicuously marked by a cream-colored spot. Fruits are linear legumes covered with short, appressed hairs. Blooming in spring, oak ridge lupine inhabits dry open woods, pinelands, and sandhills from MS to FL and north to NC. *L. perennis* L., sundial lupine, has palmately divided leaves. It inhabits open woods, sandhills, and roadsides; its range extends throughout much of the eastern U.S. excluding MO, AR, and TN.

This is an annual herb with a branching, decumbent stem. The palmately lobed leaves are silky pubescent. Densely arranged in a terminal raceme, the flowers are blue with a white spot on each standard petal. Fruits are legumes containing four or five large seeds. Blooming in spring, Texas bluebonnet inhabits prairies and roadsides from eastern TX to western LA. This is one of several similar species that has been designated the state flower of Texas. It is commonly seeded along highways for beautification and erosion control.

Medicago arabica (L.) Huds
SPOTTED MEDIC

From a taproot, this annual herb produces erect or decumbent stems up to
6 dm long. The alternately arranged
leaves are trifoliate. The leaflets are
obovate or obcordate with toothed
margins and are marked by a dark, reddish purple, V-shaped splotch. Axillary peduncles bear headlike racemes
of bright yellow flowers. Fruits are
subglobose, coiled legumes bearing
two rows of recurved prickles. Blooming in spring, spotted medic inhabits
fields, roadsides, lawns, and disturbed
sites from eastern TX to southern IL
and east to the Atlantic coastal states
as far north as ME. A native of the
Mediterranean region, this introduction
has become thoroughly naturalized.

Medicago minima (L.) L.
LITTLE BURCLOVER

From a taproot, this introduced annual
herb produces several pubescent, decumbent or ascending stems, each up
to 3 dm long. The alternately arranged
leaves are petiolate and trifoliate. Leaflets are obovate or oblong with finely
toothed margins. Bright yellow flowers are densely arranged in axillary and
terminal headlike racemes. Fruits are
coiled, globose legumes with hooked
prickles. Blooming from winter to
spring, little burclover inhabits lawns,
fields, roadsides, and disturbed sites
from TX to eastern KS and east to the
Atlantic coastal states as far north as
MA. Also an introduced annual, *M. lu-
pulina* L., black medic, has blackened,
glabrous, reniform legumes. This species
inhabits fields, roadsides, and disturbed
sites; its range extends throughout much
of the U.S.

Medicago polymorpha L.

BURCLOVER

From a taproot, this introduced annual
herb produces several decumbent or
ascending stems, each up to 5 dm long.
The alternately arranged leaves are petiolate and trifoliate. Leaflets are obovate
or obcordate with finely toothed margins. The persistent stipules are deeply
lobed. Yellow flowers are arranged in
headlike axillary racemes. Fruits are
coiled legumes with hook-tipped prickles. Blooming from winter to summer,
burclover inhabits pastures, lawns, fields,
roadsides, and disturbed sites throughout much of the U.S. excluding the upper Midwest. Native to Eurasia, this
species is planted as a cover crop in
orchards and vineyards and as a forage
crop for cattle.

Melilotus indicus (L.) All.

ANNUAL YELLOW SWEETCLOVER

From a taproot, this introduced annual
from Eurasia produces several branching
stems, each up to 5 dm tall. The alternately arranged leaves are trifoliate. The
leaflets are lanceolate, oblanceolate, or
oblong with sharply toothed margins
and truncate tips. Flowers are arranged
in spikelike axillary racemes. The yellow
corollas are mostly less than 3 mm long.
Fruits are flattened, orbicular, yellow or
reddish legumes. Blooming in spring,
annual yellow sweetclover inhabits
pastures, roadsides, and disturbed sites
from TX and OK to FL and north to
ME. Also an introduction, *M. officinalis* (L.) Lam., yellow sweetclover, is a
taller plant with longer corollas that are
yellow or white. This species inhabits
pastures and roadsides, and its range
extends throughout much of the U.S.

Mimosa hystricina (Small ex Britt. & Rose) B.L. Turner

SENSITIVE PLANT

This perennial herb produces prickly, prostrate stems up to 4 m long. The alternately arranged leaves are twice pinnately compound and quickly wilt when touched. Small flowers with long, pink filaments are densely arranged in axillary heads. Fruits are prickly legumes. Blooming from spring to fall, sensitive plant inhabits open woods and disturbed sites from eastern TX to LA. *M. strigillosa* Torr. & Gray, porcupine mimosa, has stems that are not prickly but bear long, bristlelike hairs. This species inhabits open woods, and its range extends from eastern TX to FL and GA.

Neptunia lutea (Leavenworth) Benth.

YELLOW PUFF

From an orange, woody taproot, this perennial herb produces one to several prostrate stems. The alternately arranged leaves are twice pinnately compound. The leaflets are narrow and oblong. Small yellow flowers are densely arranged in a cylindrical-shaped head. The peduncles are axillary and bear several minute, lanceolate bracts. Fruits are flattened legumes with several seeds. Blooming from spring to summer, yellow puff inhabits pinelands, savannas, prairies, and dunes from eastern TX and OK to southwestern AL. *N. pubescens* Benth., tropical puff, has some flowers in the lower portion of the floral head that bear petaloid staminodes. This species inhabits coastal prairies, and its range extends from eastern TX to FL.

Orbexilum simplex (Nutt. ex Torr. & Gray) Rydb.

LEATHER ROOT

From a fusiform root, this hirsute perennial herb produces one to several erect stems, each up to 9 dm tall. The alternately arranged, trifoliate leaves are punctate and divided into narrowly lanceolate leaflets. Dark purple flowers, subtended by lanceolate floral bracts, are arranged in terminal and axillary racemes. The flat, papery pods are beaked and contain smooth brown seeds. Blooming in spring, leather root inhabits moist woods and pinelands throughout much of the Southeast and Midwest. *O. pedunculatum* (P. Mil.) Rydb., Sampson's snakeroot, has ovate floral bracts and inhabits dry open woods throughout the Southeast and Midwest.

Pueraria montana (Lour.) Merr.

KUDZU

From a massive taproot, this semiwoody vine produces several hairy, climbing or trailing stems, each up to 30 m long. The alternately arranged leaves are trifoliate; the leaflets are ovate or rhombic with entire or lobed margins. Purplish red flowers are arranged in axillary racemes; a conspicuous yellow patch marks the standard petal. Fruits are linear, flattened legumes with several hard seeds. Blooming in summer, kudzu inhabits wood margins, fields, roadsides, and disturbed sites throughout much of the eastern half of the U.S. Originally introduced to reduce erosion, this prolific Asian native is a noxious weed.

Rhynchosia latifolia Nutt. ex T. & G.

SNOUTBEAN

This is a trailing or twining, herbaceous perennial vine. The alternately arranged trifoliate leaves bear resinous punctae; leaflets are broadly ovate and pubescent. Flowers are arranged in elongated axillary racemes. Corollas are yellow with the standard petals often marked with purplish brown. Fruits are flattened, pubescent legumes, each with one or two seeds and a persisting calyx. Blooming from spring to summer, snoutbean inhabits open woods from eastern TX to MS and north to OK, southern MO, and western TN. *R. tomentosa* (L.) Hook. & Arn., twining snoutbean, has an erect growth habit and prominently reticulate leaves. This species inhabits open woods, and its range extends from eastern TX to northern FL and north to DE.

Rhynchosia minima (L.) DC.

LEAST SNOUTBEAN

From a woody rhizome, this perennial herb produces several trailing or climbing stems, each up to 2 m long. The alternately arranged leaves are trifoliate. Individual leaflets are rhombic or broadly ovate with ciliated margins and glandular punctae. Small flowers are borne in erect axillary racemes. Corollas are yellow and often tinged with brown or red. Fruits are pubescent, falcate legumes with reniform seeds. Blooming from spring to fall, least snoutbean inhabits wood margins, pastures, roadsides, and disturbed sites from southeastern TX and AR to FL and north to southeastern GA. *R. reniformis* DC., dollarleaf, has simple reniform or broadly ovate leaves. This species inhabits pinelands, and its range extends from southeastern TX to FL and north to southeastern NC.

Senna obtusifolia (L.) Irwin & Barneby

SICKLE POD

This is a freely branching annual herb up to 1.5 m tall. The alternately arranged leaves are pinnately compound. Leaflets are obovate with broadly rounded apices. An elongated petiole gland is situated between the lower leaflet pair. One to several yellow flowers are clustered on an axillary peduncle. Fruits are elongated, thin, curved legumes with numerous dark brown seeds. Blooming in summer, sickle pod inhabits wood margins, roadsides, pasture, and disturbed sites from eastern TX to NE and east to the Atlantic coastal states as far north as CT. *S. occidentalis* (L.) Link, septicweed, has ovate leaves and a gland positioned near the base of each petiole. This species inhabits roadsides and disturbed sites, and its range extends from southeastern TX to IA and east to the Atlantic coastal states as far north as CT.

Sesbania drummondii (Rydb.) Cory

POISON BEAN

This is a suffruticose species with stems up to 3 m tall. The alternately arranged leaves are pinnately compound; the leaflets are oblong and mucronate. Yellow flowers, often marked with reddish lines and splotches, are arranged in many-flowered, pendulous racemes. Fruits are four-angled, winged legumes with reddish brown seeds. Blooming in summer, poison bean inhabits fresh and brackish marshes, beaches, wood margins, and disturbed sites from eastern TX to northwestern FL and north to SC. *S. herbacea* (P. Mill.) McVaugh, bigpod sesbania, is a robust annual with few-flowered racemes of yellow flowers and linear wingless legumes. This species inhabits riverbanks and marsh margins; its range extends from TX, OK, and KS east to the Atlantic coastal states as far north as MA.

Sesbania punicea (Cav.) Benth.

RATTLEBOX

This is an introduced suffruticose species with stems up to 2 m tall. The alternately arranged leaves are pinnately compound; the leaflets are narrowly oblong. Red-orange flowers are arranged in drooping axillary racemes. Fruits are reddish brown, four-winged pods with numerous reniform seeds. Blooming from spring to summer, rattlebox inhabits wet woods, ditches, and marshes from TX and AR to FL and north to VA. *S. vesicaria* (Jacq.) Ell., bagpod, is an annual that produces few-flowered racemes of yellow or red flowers and has flat pods that typically bear two seeds each. This species inhabits marsh margins, fields, and roadsides; its range extends from eastern TX and OK to FL and north to NC.

Strophostyles helvola (L.) Elliott

AMBERIQUE BEAN

This trailing annual herb produces stems up to 2 m long. The alternately arranged leaves are trifoliate with persistent stipules. Pink, lavender, or cream-colored flowers with prominently twisted keel petals are arranged in short axillary racemes. Each flower is subtended by an obtuse bract. Fruits are short-beaked legumes with pubescent seeds. Blooming from summer to fall, amberique bean inhabits open woods, pinelands, savannas, and beaches throughout much of the eastern U.S. *S. umbellata* (Muhl. ex Willd.) Britt., pink fuzzybean, has acute floral bracts. This species inhabits open woods and stream banks, and its range extends throughout much of the eastern U.S. excluding New England.

Stylosanthes biflora (L.) B.S.P.
PENCIL FLOWER

From a vertical rhizome, this perennial herb produces one to several erect or prostrate, pubescent stems, each up to 5 dm long. The alternately arranged leaves are trifoliate; the leaflets are lanceolate or elliptic and conspicuously veined. Yellow-orange flowers are solitary in the distal leaf axils. Fruits are pubescent, flattened loments that break off into one-seeded segments at maturity. Blooming from spring to fall, pencil flower inhabits open woods, wood margins, and disturbed sites from eastern TX, OK, and eastern KS east to the Atlantic coastal states as far north as Long Island, NY. An infusion of its roots was used by Native Americans to treat a variety of female ailments.

Tephrosia onobrychoides Nutt.
HOARY PEA

From a woody caudex, this pubescent perennial herb produces one to several decumbent or reclining stems each up to 7 dm long. The alternately arranged leaves are pinnately compound; the leaflets are linear oblanceolate to narrowly elliptic. Arranged in elongate racemes, white flowers become reddened with age. Fruits are straight legumes, each with up to ten seeds. Blooming from spring to summer, hoary pea inhabits pinelands and savannas from eastern TX and OK to AL. The taprooted *T. florida* (F.G. Dietr.) C.E. Wood, Florida hoary pea, also has white flowers that become reddened. This species inhabits open woods and savannas, and its range extends from LA to FL and north to southeastern NC.

Tephrosia virginiana (L.) Pers.

GOAT'S RUE

From a caudex, this perennial herb produces several hairy stems, each up to 7 dm tall. The alternately arranged leaves are pinnately compound; the leaflets are elliptic or oblong. Arranged in a compact terminal raceme, each flower has rose-colored wing and keel petals and a cream-colored standard petal. Fruits are straight or falcate, hairy legumes. Blooming in spring, goat's rue inhabits open woods, prairies, and roadsides throughout much of the eastern half of the U.S. The toxic compound rotenone is present in all parts of the plant.

Trifolium incarnatum L.

CRIMSON CLOVER

Introduced from Europe, this annual herb produces erect, silky pubescent stems up to 4 dm tall. The alternately arranged leaves are trifoliate; the leaflets are obovate or orbicular with finely toothed margins. Bright red flowers are densely arranged in elongated racemes. Fruits are ovoid legumes, each bearing a single seed. Blooming in spring, crimson clover inhabits fields, pastures, roadsides, and disturbed sites throughout much of the U.S. Used as a cover crop to enrich the soil and as a forage crop for cattle, this species is also planted along highways for erosion control and beautification.

Trifolium repens L.

WHITE CLOVER

Trifolium pratense L.

RED CLOVER

From fibrous roots, this biennial or perennial herb produces several decumbent, branching stems, each up to 7 dm long. The alternately arranged leaves are trifoliate; the leaflets are ovate or elliptic and marked with a whitish, V-shaped splotch near the middle. Arranged in ovoid heads, the flowers are pink or purplish. Fruits are oblong legumes with one or two seeds. Blooming from spring to summer, red clover inhabits roadsides, pastures, fields, and disturbed sites throughout much of the U.S. A native of Europe, this species is grown for pasturage and used in traditional medicine to treat a wide variety of ailments.

With creeping stems rooting at the nodes, this is a mat-forming introduced perennial herb. The alternately arranged leaves are petiolate and trifoliate. The broadly ovate leaflets are marked with a white V-shaped pattern. On peduncles up to 2 dm tall, the flowers are densely arranged in headlike racemes. Corollas are white and often suffused with pink. Fruits are linear legumes with several seeds. Blooming from fall to spring, white clover inhabits lawns, fields, roadsides, and disturbed sites throughout much of the U.S. A common escape from cultivation, *T. hybridum* L., alsike clover, has stems that do not root at the nodes. Its range also extends throughout much of the U.S.

Trifolium resupinatum L.

PERSIAN CLOVER

This annual herb produces decumbent or ascending stems, each up to 4 dm long. The alternately arranged leaves are trifoliate; the leaflets are obovate or oblanceolate with finely toothed margins. Pinkish or lavender flowers are arranged in hemispheric, headlike racemes. The corollas are resupinate as the standard petal is lowermost. Fruits are oblong or ovoid capsules that are enclosed in their bladder-shaped, persistent calyx. Blooming in spring, Persian clover inhabits fields, roadsides, lawns, and disturbed sites throughout much of the eastern half of the U.S. Introduced from Eurasia, this species is planted as a soil-enriching cover crop and for fodder.

Vicia ludoviciana Nutt. ssp. *ludoviciana*

LOUISIANA VETCH

This is an annual herb with trailing or climbing stems. The alternately arranged leaves are pinnately compound on a rachis that is terminated by a branching tendril. The leaflets are oblong or elliptic. One to several lavender-blue flowers are arranged in each axillary raceme. Fruits are flattened, oblong legumes with several seeds. Blooming in spring, Louisiana vetch inhabits wood margins, fields, pastures, and disturbed sites from CA and OR to FL. The legumes are eaten by quail, turkey, deer, and other wild animals.

Vicia sativa L.
GARDEN VETCH

From a taproot, this annual herb produces hollow trailing or climbing stems, each up to 1 m long. The alternately arranged leaves are pinnately compound with a terminal branched tendril; leaflets are oblong, elliptic, or ovate with ciliated margins and truncated mucronate apices. Coarsely toothed stipules bear two purplish nectaries. One or two violet, rose, or white flowers are borne in the leaf axils. Fruits are cylindric or flattened brown legumes with about a dozen seeds. Blooming in spring, garden vetch inhabits fields, roadsides, and disturbed sites throughout much of the U.S. This European native is widely naturalized and can become invasive.

Vicia villosa Roth ssp. *varia* (Host) Corb.
WINTER VETCH

From a taproot, this introduced annual, biennial, or perennial herb produces trailing or climbing stems, each up to 1 m long. The alternately arranged leaves are pinnately compound with a terminal branching tendril. The leaflets are oblong, lanceolate, or linear with acute or mucronate apices. Violet or purple flowers are densely arranged along one side of each axillary raceme. The lowest lobe of each tubular calyx bears short pubescence or is glabrous. Fruits are oblong, beaked, compressed legumes. Blooming in spring, winter vetch inhabits roadsides, fields, and disturbed sites throughout much of the U.S. east of the Rocky Mountains. *V. villosa* Roth ssp. *villosa* bears long, shaggy hairs on its lowest calyx lobe. This species inhabits fields, roadsides, and disturbed sites, and its range extends throughout much of the U.S.

Vigna luteola (Jacq.) Benth.

COW PEA

This is a trailing or twining perennial vine with each stem up to 3 m long. The compound leaves are trifoliate; the leaflets are ovate or narrowly lanceolate. On long peduncles, the sparsely flowered racemes of yellow flowers are borne in the leaf axils. Fruits are reflexed, plump legumes with brown seeds. Blooming from spring to fall, cow pea inhabits tidal marshes, shores, and roadsides from southeastern TX to FL and north to southeastern NC. Blackeyed pea, *V. unguiculata* (L.) Walp., is a close relative.

Wisteria frutescens (L.) Poir.

AMERICAN WISTERIA

This is a high-climbing or twining vine with an extensive network of woody roots. The alternately arranged leaves are pinnately compound with persistent lanceolate stipules. The leaflets are ovate, elliptic, or oblong. Showy bluish, purple, or lilac flowers are borne in terminal and axillary racemes. Fruits are glabrous, linear, flattened legumes with brown reniform seeds. Blooming from spring to summer, American wisteria inhabits wet woods, lake margins, and riverbanks from eastern TX to southern MI and east to the Atlantic coastal states as far north as MA. A native of Asia, *W. sinensis* (Sims) DC., Chinese wisteria, has pubescent legumes. An occasional escape from cultivation, it has a range extending from eastern TX to MI and east to the Atlantic coastal states as far north as VT.

Fumariaceae

Corydalis micrantha (Engelm. ex Gray) ssp. *australis* (Chapman) G.B. Ownbey

FUMEWORT

From a taproot, this annual herb produces one to several erect or decumbent stems, each up to 4 dm long. The alternately arranged leaves are pinnately lobed with pinnately dissected leaflets. Yellow flowers are borne in terminal racemes. The two outer petals are hooded and crested, and one is elongated into a nectar spur. The two inner petals are connate apically. Fruits are slender, erect capsules with many glossy black seeds. Blooming in spring, fumewort inhabits roadsides, fields, open woods, and disturbed sites from eastern TX to southern IL and east to the Atlantic coastal states as far north as NC. *C. micrantha* ssp. *micrantha* has a globose-tipped nectar spur. This species inhabits open woods and riverbanks, and its range extends from TX and LA north to southern MN and WI.

Gentianaceae

Centaurium pulchellum (Sw.) Drucc

BRANCHED CENTAURY

From fibrous roots, this annual Eurasian introduction produces several branching stems, each up to 3 dm tall. The oppositely arranged leaves are oblong and sessile with entire margins. Solitary or in small clusters, the flowers are axillary and terminal. The salverform corollas are pink with a white center. Fruits are single-chambered capsules. Blooming from spring to summer, branched centaury inhabits roadsides and disturbed sites from eastern TX to MS and from eastern VA to ME and across the upper Midwest. The flowers of this species have been used in traditional folk medicine to treat a wide variety of ailments.

Gentiana saponaria L. var. *saponaria*

SOAPWORT GENTIAN

Eustoma exaltatum (L.) Salisb. ex
G. Don ssp. *exaltatum*

SEASIDE GENTIAN

Up to 1 m tall, this is a glabrous, branching annual or short-lived perennial. Leaves are glaucous and somewhat succulent. The basal leaves are obovate, and the stem leaves are lanceolate or elliptic. Arranged in cymes, the erect, tubular flowers are white or lavender and marked with purple and white on their throats. Fruits are ellipsoid capsules with many seeds. Blooming from spring to summer, seaside gentian inhabits prairies and marshes from TX to FL. Several cultivars are commercially available for ornamental plantings.

From a stout caudex this perennial herb produces weak, glabrous stems up to 8 dm long. The oppositely arranged leaves are lanceolate or elliptic. Brilliant blue tubular flowers are arranged in a dichasium that is subtended by leaflike bracts. Between each corolla lobe is a toothed, pleated structure called a plait. Fruits are ellipsoid capsules with many seeds. Blooming in fall, soapwort gentian inhabits wet woods and swamps from eastern TX and OK to northern FL and north to NY and MI. *G. catesbaei* Walt., Elliott's gentian, has reddish, scabrous hair on its stems. This species inhabits pine barrens, savannas, and upland sandhill swamps, and its range extends from southern AL to northern FL and north to NJ.

Sabatia bartramii Wilbur

BARTRAM'S ROSE GENTIAN

Obolaria virginica L.

PENNYWORT

From fleshy, brittle roots, this glabrous perennial herb produces a simple or branching stem up to 1.5 dm tall. The oppositely arranged leaves along the lower stem are bractlike; those above are obovate, sessile, and green or purplish. Flowers are arranged in terminal and axillary cymes. The campanulate corollas are white or purplish. Fruits are globose capsules with translucent yellowish seeds. Blooming in spring, pennywort inhabits rich mesic woods from eastern TX to southeastern MO and east to the Altantic coastal states as far north as NJ. This species obtains part of its nutrients by parasitizing an underground fungus.

From a slender rhizome, this perennial herb produces a solitary stem up to 1.5 m tall. Leaves on the lower part of the stem are oblanceolate or spathulate. The distal leaves are linear, appressed, and narrower than the width of the stem that bears them. Showy flowers terminate each of several alternately arranged inflorescence branches. The corolla is rotate with pink or magenta lobes that are marked with yellow and edged with red near their bases. Fruits are capsules with numerous pitted seeds. Blooming from spring to summer, Bartram's rose gentian inhabits wet pinelands, savannahs, and ditches from southern MS to FL and north to southeastern SC. The upper leaves of *S. kennedyana* Fern., Plymouth rose gentian, are wider than the stem that bears them. This species inhabits savannas, and its range extends from northeastern SC to southeastern VA and also from RI to southeastern MA.

Sabatia campestris Nutt.

TEXAS STAR

Sabatia gentianoides Ell.

ROSE GENTIAN

From a single erect stem up to 5 dm tall, this annual herb is freely branching above. The oppositely arranged elliptic leaves are membranous and clasping. Each showy rotate pink or white flower is marked with a yellow center. The lateral veins on the calyx lobes are more prominent than is the midvein. Fruits are capsules. Blooming from spring to summer, Texas star inhabits fields and marsh edges from eastern TX to MS and north to IA and IL. *S. calycina* (Lam.) Heller, coastal rose gentian, has calyx lobes with midveins that are more prominent than are the lateral veins. This species inhabits swamps and riverbanks, and its range extends from TX to FL and north to VA.

This annual herb produces a simple stem up to 5 dm tall. Basal leaves are oblong or spathulate; those on the stem are linear and held erect. Two leaflike bracts subtend terminal and axillary clusters of pink or rose-colored rotate flowers. Fruits are ovoid capsules. Blooming from spring to summer, rose gentian inhabits wet pinelands and savannas from southeastern TX to FL and north to NC. *S. dodecandra* (L.) B.S.P., marsh rose gentian, has long-peduncled flowers that are not subtended by bracts. This species inhabits savannas and marshes; its range extends from TX to FL and north to NY and CT.

Sabatia macrophylla Hook. var. *macrophylla*

LARGE-LEAF ROSE GENTIAN

From a branched rhizome, this perennial herb produces an erect, glaucous, branching, terete stem. The oppositely arranged, clasping leaves are lanceolate, oblong, or ovate and somewhat succulent. Flowers are arranged in flat-topped or slightly convex terminal cymes. The rotate corollas are white or cream colored. Fruits are capsules with numerous seeds. Blooming from spring to summer, large-leaf rose gentian inhabits wet pinelands, savannas, bogs, and ditches from eastern LA to northern FL and southern GA. *S. difformis* (L.) Druce, lanceleaf rose gentian, has leaves that are not glaucous and an upper stem that is angled. This species inhabits wet pinelands, savannas, bogs, and ditches, and its range extends from southern MS to FL and north to southern NJ.

Geranium carolinianum L. var. *carolinianum*

CAROLINA GERANIUM

From a taproot, this annual or biennial herb produces densely pubescent branching stems. Arranged in a basal rosette and along the stems, the leaves are orbicular or reniform and palmately lobed. Typically paired, the pale pink or whitish flowers terminate the stems. The branched styles are yellow. Fruits are elongated schizocarps that divide into one-seeded mericarps. Blooming in spring, Carolina geranium inhabits fields, roadsides, lawns, and gardens throughout much of the U.S. *G. dissectum* L., cutleaf geranium, has reddish pink flowers with purple stylar branches. This species inhabits fields, roadsides, and disturbed sites; its range extends from eastern TX to IL and east to the Atlantic coastal states as far north as MA.

Grossulariaceae

Itea virginica L.
VIRGINIA SWEETSPIRE

This small, deciduous woody shrub produces slender, arching branches up to 2.5
m tall. The alternately arranged elliptic
leaves bear small teeth on their margins.
Racemes of small, white, fragrant flowers terminate the branches. Corolla lobes
are linear or narrowly lanceolate and
connate at their bases; the calyx is cup-
shaped. Fruits are grooved, pubescent
capsules with golden seeds. Blooming
in spring, Virginia sweetspire inhabits
wet woods, swamps, and stream banks
throughout much of the Southeast and
lower Midwest. This showy species is
planted as a garden ornamental.

Haemodoraceae

Lachnanthes caroliniana (Lam.)
Dandy
REDROOT

From reddish rhizomes with fibrous
roots, this perennial herb produces
an erect stem up to 1 m tall. Disposed
near the base of the stem are several
linear, sword-shaped leaves. Branches
of the inflorescence are arranged in
corymbs; the ultimate branches are
helicoid cymes of yellow flowers, each
subtended by a conspicuous bract.
Much of the inflorescence is densely
and conspicuously tomentose. Fruits are
globose capsules with brownish, disk-
shaped seeds. Blooming in summer,
redroot inhabits wet pinelands, savannas, bogs, swamps, and ditches from
southeastern LA to FL and north to
southeastern MA. Native Americans
used the rhizome as a narcotic and for
the treatment of cough and pneumonia.

Haloragaceae

Proserpinaca pectinata Lam.

MERMAIDWEED

Myriophyllum aquaticum (Vell.) Verdc.

PARROT FEATHER

From a rhizome, this introduced aquatic, monoecious perennial herb produces several stems, each up to 2 m long. The lower stem portion typically is submergent, and the upper portion is emergent. Arranged in whorls, each leaf is dissected into linear or filiform divisions. Minute flowers are borne in the axils of the emergent leaves. Mature fruits split into four one-seeded nutlets. Blooming in summer, parrot feather inhabits ponds, ditches, canals, and sluggish streams from CA to FL and north to Long Island, NY. A native of Eurasia, *M. spicatum* L., Eurasian watermilfoil, has flowers that are borne in whorls on an emergent spike. This species inhabits swamps, marshes, and lakes, and its range extends throughout much of the U.S.

From a rhizome, this perennial herb produces stems up to 5 dm long. The lower stem is creeping and often bears adventitious roots; the upper stem is ascending. The alternately arranged ovate leaves are pinnately dissected. Small flowers are solitary in the upper leaf axils. The calyx lobes are white and the corolla is absent. Fruits are three-angled nutlets. Blooming from spring to summer, mermaidweed inhabits wet pinelands, savannas, swamps, and ditches from southeastern TX to FL and north to ME. *P. palustris* L., marsh mermaidweed, has pinnately dissected leaves on the lower stem and toothed ones on the upper stem. This species inhabits wet pinelands, savannas, and swamps; its range extends throughout much of the eastern U.S.

Hippocastanaceae

Aesculus pavia L. var. *pavia*
RED BUCKEYE

This is a single-stemmed deciduous shrub up to 10 m tall. The oppositely arranged, palmately compound leaves are prominently veined. Pale pink or bright red tubular flowers are arranged in terminal panicles. Fruits are globose capsules with several large, glossy brown, poisonous seeds. Blooming in spring, red buckeye inhabits mesic to wet woods often near streams throughout much of the Southeast. The seeds were carried by Native Americans for good luck and made into a poultice for the treatment of sprains, tumors, and infections.

Hyacinthaceae

Schoenolirion croceum (Michx.) Wood
SUNNYBELLS

From a large bulb, this perennial herb produces a scape up to 4 dm tall. The several linear leaves are basally disposed and prominently veined. With each perianth composed of six bright yellow, free tepals, the flowers are arranged in a solitary terminal raceme. Fruits are three-lobed capsules with shiny black seeds. Blooming in spring, sunnybells inhabits wet pinelands and savannas from eastern TX to FL and north to TN and NC. *S. albiflorum* (Raf.) R.R. Gates, white sunnybells, has white tepals and a branched inflorescence. This species inhabits wet pinelands and cypress swamps, and its range extends from FL to southeastern GA.

Hydrocharitaceae

Egeria densa Planch.

BRAZILIAN WATERWEED

Limnobium spongia (Bosc) L.C. Rich. ex Steud.

FROGBIT

From fibrous roots or free floating, this introduced dioecious perennial herb produces simple or sparingly branching stems, each up to 2 m long. Up to 3 cm long, the whorled leaves are linear with finely toothed margins. One to several small white flowers emerge from each axillary fusiform spathe. Fruits are translucent achenes. Blooming from spring to fall, Brazilian waterweed inhabits streams, ponds, and marshes throughout much of the U.S. excluding the upper Midwest and the upper Rocky Mountain states. Similar in appearance, *Elodea canadensis* Michx., Canadian waterweed, has leaves that typically do not exceed 1.5 cm in length. This species inhabits lakes, ponds, and streams; its range extends throughout much of the U.S. excluding TX, LA, and GA.

This aquatic, monoecious perennial herb may be free floating or rooted in substrate. The thickened leaves are orbicular, cordate, or reniform. Floating leaves have an elevated layer of reddish tissue on the abaxial surface that is absent on the emergent leaves. Each carpellate flower produces up to nine prominent styles, and each staminate flower bears up to twelve basally connate filaments. The ellipsoid, berrylike fruits are positioned under water at the time the echinate seeds are released. Blooming from spring to fall, frogbit inhabits lakes and sluggish streams from southeastern TX to southern IL and east to the Atlantic coastal states as far north as NY.

Ottelia alismoides (L.) Pers.

DUCK LETTUCE

This aquatic perennial herb produces a submerged basal rosette of prominently veined lanceolate or ovate leaves. Each white or pinkish flower is borne in a strongly winged spathe and held just above the water's surface on an elongate peduncle. The fragrant flowers are unisexual or hermaphroditic. Corolla lobes are pinkish with yellow bases. Fruits are oblong, strongly ribbed capsules with numerous seeds. Blooming from spring to summer, duck lettuce inhabits shallow water in lakes, bayous, canals, and marshes from southeastern TX to southern LA. One population is reported in northwestern FL. This species is native to the warmer areas of eastern Asia and Australia, where it is often a pest in irrigation canals and rice patties. It has been suggested that this plant arrived in North America with rice seed.

Hydrolea ovata Nutt. ex Choisy

FALSE FIDDLELEAF

This showy perennial herb forms dense stands through extensive rhizome development. The alternately arranged leaves are hairy with ovate or lanceolate blades. Sharp spines are borne in the leaf axils. Blue tubular flowers are arranged in terminal cymes. Fruits are spherical, glandular capsules. Blooming in summer, false fiddleleaf occurs in swamps, lake margins, and ditches from eastern TX, OK, and southern MO east to southern GA and northwestern FL. *H. corymbosa* J. Macbr. ex Ell., skyflower, is devoid of axillary spines. This species inhabits wet woods, marshes, and ditches; its range extends from northwestern FL to southern GA.

Phacelia hirsuta Nutt.

FUZZY PHACELIA

From a taproot, this densely pubescent annual herb produces simple or branching stems, each up to 3 dm long. The alternately arranged leaves are oblong and pinnately lobed. Flowers are arranged in scorpioid cymes. The campanulate corollas are bluish lavender with whitish centers marked with dark purple spots. Fruits are globose capsules with several seeds. Blooming in spring, fuzzy phacelia inhabits open woods and roadsides from eastern TX to LA and north to southeastern KS and southern MO. *P. strictiflora* (Engelm. & Gray) Gray, prairie phacelia, has a conspicuous rosette of leaves. This species inhabits open woods and fields, and its range extends from eastern TX and OK to AL.

Hypoxis hirsuta (L.) Coville

YELLOW STAR-GRASS

From a corm, this perennial herb produces basal linear leaves. Terminating a scape up to 2.5 dm tall, bright yellow flowers are arranged in an irregular umbel. Fruits are orbicular capsules with rough-surfaced black seeds. Blooming from spring to summer, yellow star-grass inhabits woodlands meadows, pinelands, savannas, and bogs throughout much of the eastern U.S. excluding FL. *H. juncea* Smith, fringed yellow star-grass, has filiform leaves. This species inhabits wet pinelands, savannas, and ditches; its range extends from southeastern AL to FL and north to southern VA.

Illiciaceae

Illicium floridanum Ellis

FLORIDA ANISE

This is an open-branched evergreen shrub up to 3 m tall. The alternately arranged, anise-scented coriaceous leaves are glossy above and glandular-punctate below. Solitary in the leaf axils, the showy, reddish maroon flowers are somewhat nodding with a fishlike aroma. Fruits are star-shaped aggregates of follicles. Each follicle bears an ellipsoid, glossy brown seed. Blooming from spring to summer, Florida anise inhabits low wet woods from southeastern LA to northwestern FL and southwestern GA. *I. parviflorum* Michx. ex Vent., yellow anisetree, is a larger shrub with small, greenish yellow flowers. This species inhabits wet woods, and its range extends from central FL to central GA.

Iridaceae

Alophia drummondii (Graham) R.C. Foster

PINEWOOD LILY

From a dark brown bulb, this perennial herb produces a solitary wiry scape up to 7.5 dm tall. The narrowly lanceolate leaves are basal and pleated. Borne within terminal spathes, the secund flowers bloom in succession over a period of several days. Depressed at their bases and forming an overall cup shape, the tepals are bluish or purplish and flecked with red-brown or dark purple. Fruits are ellipsoid capsules with many seeds. Blooming from spring to summer, pinewood lily inhabits open woods, pinelands, and savannas from eastern TX, OK, and southern AR to southern MS.

Belamcanda chinensis (L.) DC.

BLACKBERRY LILY

From an orange rhizome, this perennial herb produces a solitary stem up to
1 m tall. The alternately arranged leaves
are lanceolate and glaucous. Flowers
are arranged in a terminal, fan-shaped
cyme. The orange or reddish tepals are
marked with darker spots. Fruits are
ovoid capsules with black seeds. Blooming from summer to fall, blackberry lily
inhabits pastures, fields, and roadsides
throughout much of the eastern half
of the U.S. An escape from cultivation,
this introduction is native to Asia.

Herbertia lauhue (Molina) Goldblatt

PRAIRIE NYMPH

From an ovoid bulb, this perennial herb
produces one to three stems, each up
to 1.5 dm tall. The mostly basal leaves
are linear and pleated. Enclosed by
two unequal spathes, flowers bloom in
succession. The spreading, broadly lanceolate sepals are lavender and marked
with white and purple on the claws.
Lavender and purple petals are spreading and smaller than the sepals. Ovoid
capsules are apically truncate with many
brown seeds. Blooming in spring, prairie
nymph inhabits open woods, prairies,
and roadsides along the outer coastal
plain from southeastern TX to MS.

Iris giganticaerulea Small

GIANT BLUE IRIS

Iris fulva Ker-Gawl.

COPPER IRIS

From a short, branching rhizome, this perennial herb produces basal linear leaves. The blades are equitant in that they are folded lengthwise and closely appressed. Up to 1 m tall, the flowering stem is simple or branching. The perianth is copper-orange. The sepals are clawed, arching, and beardless; the petals are arching or descending and obscurely clawed. Hexagonal in transverse section, the fruits are elliptic green capsules with corky, flattened seeds. Blooming in spring, copper iris inhabits swamps, marshes, and ditches from LA and western MS to southern IL. Planted as a garden ornamental, it attracts hummingbirds and butterflies with its showy flowers.

From a branching, green rhizome, this perennial herb produces several basal sword-shaped leaves. Up to 1.5 m tall, the flowering stem is simple or branching. Blue or purplish flowers are subtended by leaflike spathes. On each clawed sepal, white streaks surround the yellow, pubescent signal patch. The spathulate petals are erect or spreading. Fruits are drooping, ellipsoid capsules, each with six broad, rounded lobes. Blooming in spring, giant blue iris inhabits swamps, marshes, and ditches from western and southern LA to southern MS and western AL. This, the tallest iris on the coastal plain, is the state flower of Louisiana. *I. hexagona* Walt., Dixie iris, has capsules, each with three plain and three ridged faces. This species inhabits marshes and ditches, and it occurs in northern FL and in eastern SC.

Iris virginica L.

BLUE FLAG

Iris pseudacorus L.

YELLOW FLAG

From a stout rhizome, this perennial herb produces erect or arching, sword-shaped basal leaves. A floral stalk up to 1.2 m tall bears one or two leaflike bracts. Subtended by two spathes, one or two bright yellow flowers terminate the stalk. Additionally, a solitary flower emerges from each of the floral bracts. Sepals are beardless and marked with brown near their bases. Fruits are three-angled, ellipsoid capsules with brown corky seeds. Blooming in spring, yellow flag inhabits marshes, ditches, and stream banks throughout much of the eastern half of the U.S. Planted as an ornamental, this introduction from Eurasia can become invasive.

This is a rhizomatous, clumping perennial herb. Linear leaves are equitant and arranged in a fan-shaped basal cluster. The floral stalk is often branched, and each branch is terminated by an inflorescence consisting of one to three blue or rarely white flowers. Arching, clawed sepals are marked with yellow and dark veins, and each bears a finely pubescent signal patch. Petals are clawed and held erect. Petaloid styles are closely appressed to the sepals. Fruits are three-angled capsules with pitted, corky seeds. Blooming in spring, blue flag inhabits swamps, marshes, and lake margins throughout much of the Southeast and the Midwest. *I. brevicaulis* Raf., zigzag iris, has hexagonal or rounded capsules with six equally positioned ribs and a sharply zigzagged stem. This species inhabits wet woods, and its range extends from LA to northwestern FL and north to southeastern OK, AR, MO, TN, KY, IL, and IN.

Sisyrinchium atlanticum Bickn.

EASTERN BLUE-EYED GRASS

From a small rhizome, this perennial herb produces glabrous, winged stems up to 6 dm tall. The alternately arranged leaves are linear and equitant. The inflorescence is a fan-shaped cyme subtended by two greenish spathes. Corollas are blue or purple with yellow bases. Fruits are blackish, globose capsules with many seeds. Blooming in spring, eastern blue-eyed grass inhabits open woods, marshes, fields, and disturbed sites from southeastern TX to central WI and east to the Atlantic coastal states as far north as ME. *S. fuscatum* Bickn., coastal plain blue-eyed grass, has leaf bases that persist as fibrous tufts. This species inhabits open woods, fields, and savannas; its range extends from southern MS to FL and north to MA.

Sisyrinchium rosulatum Bickn.

ANNUAL BLUE-EYED GRASS

From fibrous roots, this annual or perennial herb produces branching stems up to 3.6 dm tall. The alternately arranged leaves are linear and grasslike. Campanulate flowers are arranged in cymes that are subtended by green spathes. Tepals may be maroon, yellow, lavender, rose, or whitish. Each tepal is marked by a purplish line near its base. Fruits are brownish, globose capsules. Blooming in spring, annual blue-eyed grass inhabits wet pinelands, savannas, fields, roadsides, and disturbed sites from eastern TX to FL and north to NC. *S. minus* Engelm. & Gray, dwarf blue-eyed grass, has turbinate capsules. This species inhabits open woods, and its range extends from eastern TX to southwestern MS.

Juncaceae

Juncus effusus L.

COMMON RUSH

From a short, thickened rhizome, this densely clumping perennial herb produces erect, leafless, terete stems up to 1.5 m tall. The numerous brownish flowers are arranged in a freely branching terminal inflorescence. The single involucral bract is erect and appears to be a continuation of the stem. Fruits are three-angled capsules with glossy brown seeds. Blooming in summer, common rush inhabits marshes, lake margins, and ditches throughout much of the eastern half of the U.S. This species is an important source of food and nesting material for wetland wildlife.

Lamiaceae

Hyptis alata (Raf.) Shinners

BUSH MINT

From a woody caudex, this perennial herb produces a quadrangular stem up to 2 m tall. Oppositely arranged ovate or lanceolate leaves are irregularly toothed. Flowers are arranged in axillary hemispheric heads subtended by bracts. The bilabiate corollas are white with lavender spots. Fruits are smooth, oblong, dull black nutlets. Blooming from summer to fall, bush mint inhabits marshes, swamps, wet woods, savannas, pinelands, and ditches from southeastern TX to FL and north to NC. Naturalized from tropical America, *H. mutabilis* (A. Rich.) Briq., tropical bush mint, has flower heads that are about 1 cm wide and broadly ovate leaves. This species inhabits wet woods, stream banks, and lake margins; its range extends along the outer coastal plain from southeastern LA to FL.

Lamium amplexicaule L.
HENBIT

From a taproot, this introduced annual or biennial herb produces branching stems up to 4.5 dm long. The oppositely arranged leaves are ovate, orbicular, or reniform with coarsely toothed margins. The lower leaves are petiolate, whereas the upper leaves are sessile or clasping. Flowers are whorled in terminal and axillary clusters. The lavender or pink corollas are bilabiate. The upper lip is hooded and densely hairy; the lower lip is inflated with two small lobes at the apex, each bearing purple splotches. Fruits are shiny brown nutlets. Blooming from winter to spring, henbit inhabits pastures, roadsides, lawns, and gardens throughout much of the U.S. All leaves of *L. purpureum* L., purple deadnettle, are petiolate; those subtending the infloresence are purplish. This species inhabits fields and disturbed sites; its range extends throughout much of the eastern half of the U.S.

Lycopus rubellus Moench
WATER HOREHOUND

From a small rhizome, this stoloniferous perennial herb produces a solitary simple stem up to 1.2 m tall. The oppositely arranged punctate leaves are lanceolate, elliptic, or ovate with toothed margins. Bilabiate flowers are densely arranged in axillary glomerules. The campanulate corollas are white and often mottled with purple; the calyx lobe apices are acuminate. Fruits are three-angled nutlets with several corky teeth. Blooming from summer to fall, water horehound inhabits wet pinelands, savannas, marshes, swamps, and bogs throughout much of the eastern U.S. *L. virginicus* L., Virginia water horehound, has acute or obtuse calyx lobe apices and purplish leaves. Its range also extends throughout much of the eastern U.S.

Monarda fistulosa L. ssp. *fistulosa*

WILD BERGAMOT

From a slender rhizome, this perennial herb produces simple or branching hollow stems, each up to 1.5 m tall. The oppositely arranged leaves are grayish green, ovate, or lanceolate with toothed margins. Headlike terminal cymes of bilabiate lavender flowers are subtended by leaflike, reflexed bracts. Fruits are oblong, smooth, glossy nutlets. Blooming in summer, wild bergamot inhabits open woods, prairies, fields, and roadsides throughout much of the U.S. excluding FL. *M. lindheimeri* Engelm. & Gray ex Gray, Lindheimer's beebalm, has creamy white flowers. This species inhabits open woods and fields, and its range extends from eastern TX to southwestern LA.

Monarda punctata L. ssp. *punctata* var. *punctata*

SPOTTED BEEBALM

This annual, biennial, or perennial herb produces quadrangular stems, each up to 1 m long. The oppositely arranged leaves are lanceolate or narrowly elliptic with toothed margins. Flowers are arranged in several interrupted pairs of cymes along a central axis. Leafy bracts, suffused with white, yellow, or purple, subtend each pair of cymes. The bilabiate corollas are white or yellow and spotted with maroon. Fruits are olive-colored schizocarps. Blooming from spring to fall, spotted beebalm inhabits open woods, fields, and roadsides from eastern TX to FL and north to NJ. *M. citriodora* Cerv. ex Lag., lemon beebalm, has pink, purplish, or white flowers with dark spots. This species inhabits prairies and savannas, and its range extends throughout much of the southern half of the U.S.

Physostegia digitalis Small
FINGER FALSE DRAGONHEAD

Physostegia longisepala Cantino
LONGSEPAL FALSE DRAGONHEAD

From a vertical rhizome, this perennial herb produces a quadrangular stem up to 2 m tall. The oppositely arranged leaves are oblanceolate, obovate, or elliptic with entire or irregularly toothed margins. The bases are often auriculate and clasping. Flowers are arranged in erect or ascending paniculate racemes. The tubular, bilabiate corollas are lavender or pink and marked with purplish spots. Fruits are smooth, three-sided nutlets. Blooming in summer, finger false dragonhead inhabits wet pinelands, prairies, and ditches in eastern TX, western LA, and southwestern AR. *P. correlii* (Lundell) Shinners, Correll's false dragonhead, bears conspicuous glandular punctae on its upper leaf surfaces. This species inhabits wet pinelands and swamps, and its range extends from southern TX to southern LA.

From a branching rhizome, this perennial herb produces a branching stem up to 1 m tall. The lower leaves are elliptic, oblong, or oblanceolate and petiolate with blunt teeth. The upper leaves are elliptic or lanceolate and sessile. The tubular, bilabiate flowers are arranged in terminal racemes. Corollas are dark lavender or reddish and spotted or streaked with purple. Fruits are smooth nutlets. Blooming in summer, longsepal false dragonhead inhabits wet woods and ditches from eastern TX to western LA. *P. angustifolia* Fern., narrowleaf false dragonhead, has pale lavender or white flowers and its leaf margins are sharply toothed. This species inhabits stream banks, roadsides, and fields; its range extends from eastern TX to IL and east to southwestern GA.

Prunella vulgaris L. ssp. *lanceolata* (W. Bart.) Hultén

SELFHEAL

Physostegia virginiana (L.) Benth. ssp. *praemorsa* (Shinners) Cantino

OBEDIENT PLANT

From a long, slender rhizome, this colonial perennial herb produces one to several stems, each up to 1.5 m long. The oppositely arranged leaves are elliptic or lanceolate and sessile with sharply toothed margins. Showy flowers are arranged in terminal racemes. The pink or purple bilabiate corollas are marked with dark purple spots. Fruits are three-angled, ovoid, olive-brown nutlets. Blooming from spring to summer, obedient plant inhabits wet woods, stream banks, and prairies throughout much of the eastern half of the U.S. excluding the Northeast. When one of the flowers is repositioned, it obediently stays in the new position. *P. purpurea* (Walt.) Blake, eastern false dragonhead, has leaves with rounded teeth. This species inhabits wet pinelands, savannas, prairies, and ditches; its range extends from FL to eastern NC.

From a slender rhizome, this perennial herb produces one to several four-angled, winged stems, each up to 6 dm tall. The oppositely arranged leaves are narrowly elliptic or lanceolate with entire or toothed margins. Lavender flowers are densely arranged in a leafy spike. Corollas are bilabiate; the upper lip is hooded and the lower lip is cleft. Fruits are tan nutlets. Blooming in spring, selfheal inhabits fields, pastures, open woods, and roadsides throughout much of the U.S. This species has a wide array of biological activity including antifungal and antiviral properties. An extract is used in some herpes medicines.

Pycnanthemum albescens Torr. & Gray

WHITELEAF MOUNTAINMINT

From fibrous roots, this freely branching perennial herb produces square stems up to 1.5 m tall. The oppositely arranged leaves are ovate or lanceolate with a few marginal teeth and acute apices. Heads of flowers are arranged in terminal and axillary branching cymes that are subtended by densely white, tomentose, leaflike bracts. Bilabiate corollas are white or pinkish with purple spots. Fruits are brown, ellipsoid nutlets. Blooming from summer to fall, whiteleaf mountainmint inhabits wet to dry woods, pinelands, and savannas from eastern TX to southern IL and east to northwestern FL. *P. flexuosum* (Walt.) B.S.P., Appalachian mountainmint, has lanceolate or elliptic leaves with blunt apices. This species inhabits wet pinelands, bogs, and ditches; its range extends from northern MS to northern FL and north to southeastern VA.

Pycnanthemum tenuifolium Schrad.

NARROWLEAF MOUNTAINMINT

From a slender rhizome, this perennial herb produces one to several erect stems, each up to 8 dm tall. Up to 5 cm long, the oppositely arranged leaves are linear or lanceolate, glabrous, and punctate with entire margins. Marked with purple sploches, the white or pinkish bilabiate flowers are arranged in sparingly branched cymes that are subtended by white, powdery, pubescent bracts. Fruits are oblong, purplish black, granular nutlets. Blooming from summer to fall, narrowleaf mountainmint inhabits open woods, prairies, fields, pastures, and roadsides throughout much of the eastern half of the U.S. *P. nudum* Nutt., coastal plain mountainmint, has leaves that are no more than 2 cm long. This species inhabits wet pinelands, savannas, and bogs; its range extends from southern AL to northern FL and north to southeastern SC.

Salvia azurea Michx. ex Lam.

BLUE SAGE

From a stout rhizome, this perennial herb produces one to several four-angled stems, each up to 1.5 m tall. The oppositely arranged, toothed leaves are mostly lanceolate on the lower part of the stem but become linear distally. The bilabiate blue flowers are arranged in spikes. The upper lips are broad and entire; the lower lips are three-lobed and marked with white. Fruits are olive-brown, glandular, punctate, ellipsoid nutlets. Blooming from summer to fall, blue sage inhabits prairies, pinelands, and savannas throughout much of the eastern U.S. but is absent from VA to ME. This showy species is planted as a garden ornamental.

Salvia coccinea P.J. Buchoz ex Ettinger

BLOOD SAGE

This perennial herb produces a branching stem up to 1 m tall. The oppositely arranged leaves are ovate, petiolate, prominently veined, and toothed. Scarlet flowers are arranged in a lax raceme. Corollas are bilabiate; the lower lip is two-lobed. Fruits are dark brown, smooth, ellipsoid nutlets. Blooming from summer to fall, blood sage inhabits open woods and disturbed sites from eastern TX to FL and north to eastern SC. A showy species, it is grown as a garden ornamental.

Salvia lyrata L.

LYRELEAF SAGE

Stachys floridana Shuttlw. ex Benth.

FLORIDA BETONY

From fibrous roots, this perennial herb produces a solitary simple or branching, scapelike stem up to 8 dm tall. Arranged in a basal rosette, the petiolate leaves are elliptic, obovate, or lyrate and typically are pinnately lobed. The pale blue bilabiate flowers are arranged in evenly spaced open verticils. Fruits are brown, tuberculate, ellipsoid mericarps. Blooming from winter to spring, lyreleaf sage inhabits open woods, roadsides, gardens, and disturbed sites from eastern TX to eastern KS and east to the Atlantic coastal states as far north as CN. *S. farinacea* Benth., mealycup sage, has purplish flowers densely arranged in spikes and obscurely toothed leaves. This species inhabits prairies and open wet woods, and its range extends from southern NM to central FL.

From a segmented rhizome, this perennial herb produces branching or simple, quadrangular, purplish stems, each up to 5 dm tall. The oppositely arranged leaves are lanceolate, ovate, or oblong with truncate or cordate bases and toothed margins. Arranged in verticils, the bilabiate flowers are pinkish and marked with darker spots. The upper lip is hooded, and the lower one is three-lobed. Fruits are dark brown schizocarps. Blooming from spring to summer, Florida betony inhabits savannas, lawns, gardens, roadsides, and disturbed sites from eastern TX to FL and north to eastern VA. Lacking a rhizome, *S. crenata* Raf., mousesear, is an annual or a biennial. This species inhabits pond margins, stream banks, and disturbed sites; its range extends from eastern TX to northern FL.

Teucrium canadensis L. var. *canadense*

GERMANDER

From a creeping rhizome, this perennial herb produces a branching stem up to 1 m tall. The narrowly elliptic or ovate leaves are oppositely arranged and finely toothed. Bilabiate lavender flowers are densely arranged in a terminal spike. Fruits are nutlets. Blooming from spring to summer, germander inhabits stream banks, marshes, swamps, and lake margins throughout much of the U.S. east of the Rocky Mountains. Although used in traditional folk medicine as a stimulant, antiseptic, and diuretic, recent evidence suggests that this species may be toxic.

Teucrium cubense Jacq. var. *cubense*

COASTAL GERMANDER

From a rhizome, this perennial herb produces several branching stems, each up to 7 dm tall. The oppositely arranged leaves are oblong or obovate with entire or pinnately lobed margins. Bilabiate flowers are borne in the upper leaf axils. The bearded corollas are white and marked with purplish lines in the throat. Fruits are pitted or grooved nutlets. Blooming from spring to fall, coastal germander inhabits coastal prairies and marsh margins along the coast from southeastern TX to southern AL. As a traditional medicinal herb, this species has been used in the treatment of diabetes.

Lemnaceae

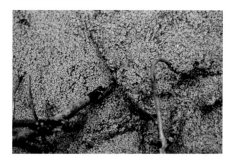

Lemna minor L.

DUCKWEED

Trichostema dichotomum L.

BLUECURLS

From a taproot, this annual herb produces a solitary pubescent stem up to
1 m tall. The oppositely arranged leaves
are ovate or oblong and petiolate with
entire margins. Arranged in axillary
cymes, the bluish flowers are bilabiate
with four prominent, strongly curved
stamens. Fruits are schizocarps that
divide into prominently ridged, reticulate mericarps. Blooming from summer
to fall, bluecurls inhabits open woods,
fields, and stream banks throughout
much of the eastern U.S. *T. setaceum*
Houtt., narrowleaf bluecurls, has linear leaves. This species inhabits open
woods, and its range extends from
eastern TX to FL and north to CT.

This is a freely floating perennial with
a single, unbranched root. The thallus is flattened or slightly convex and
obovate or ovate. Its lower surface is
often mottled with red; its upper surface is dark green or yellowish. Plants
reproduce asexually from reproduc-
tive pouches, and several thalli may be
joined by stipes. An inflorescence consisting of one or two staminate and a
single carpellate flower is borne within
a spathe within one of the pouches.
Fruits are ellipsoid utricles. Blooming
from spring to fall, duckweed inhabits
marshes, lakes, ditches, canals, and sluggish streams throughout much of the
U.S. *L. valdiviana* Phil., valdivia duckweed, has a pale green elliptical thallus.
Its range extends throughout much of
the U.S. excluding the upper Midwest.

Lentibulariaceae

Pinguicula caerulea Walt.

BLUE BUTTERWORT

Pinguicula lutea Walt.

YELLOW BUTTERWORT

This is an insectivorous perennial herb with leaves arranged in a basal rosette. Blades are yellow-green, V-shaped, and copiously clothed with glandular hairs. Flowers are solitary on densely pubescent scapes, each up to 2 dm tall. The tubular, bilabiate corollas are pale or dark violet, prominently veined and spurred. Fruits are globose capsules with pyramid-shaped seeds. Blooming in spring, blue butterwort inhabits wet pinelands and savannas from FL to southeastern NC. *P. ionantha* Godfrey, violet butterwort, has violet flowers, but they are not prominently veined. This species inhabits wet pinelands, savannas, bogs, and canals; its range is restricted to a few counties in northwestern FL.

This is an insectivorous perennial herb with leaves arranged in a basal rosette. The bright yellow-green leaf blades are ovate and involute; the adaxial surfaces are glandular-pubescent. A solitary spurred, sulfur yellow flower terminates each of the one to several glandular-pubescent scapes. Fruits are capsules with oblong brown seeds. Blooming in spring, yellow butterwort inhabits wet pinelands, savannas, and seepage bogs from southeastern LA to FL and north to southeastern NC. *P. primulifolia* Wood & Godfrey, southern butterwort, has violet-colored flowers. This species inhabits shady areas along springs and small creeks, and its range extends from southern MS and AL to northwestern FL and southwestern GA.

Pinguicula pumila Michx.

SMALL BUTTERWORT

From threadlike roots, this annual or perennial herb produces leaves in a basal rosette. Each leaf is involute and densely covered with sticky, glandular hairs. White or purplish flowers terminate each of the one to several scapes. Corollas are bilabiate with a projecting palate on the lower lip that is beset with yellow, knobby hairs. Fruits are capsules containing brown, pitted seeds. Blooming throughout the year, small butterwort inhabits wet savannas, pinelands, and bogs from southeastern TX to FL and north to southeastern NC. With leaves that are greenish red and somewhat translucent, *P. planifolia* Chapm., Chapman's butterwort, produces rosettes that are up to 15 cm wide. This species inhabits wet pinelands, savannas, bogs, and ditches; its range is confined to a few counties in northwestern FL.

Utricularia cornuta Michx.

HORNED BLADDERWORT

This is a rootless, terrestrial, carnivorous annual or perennial herb. The subterranean stems are intricately branched; small emergent stems are filiform and leaflike. Up to 4 dm tall, a wiry green scape bears up to ten fragrant flowers. The corollas are bright yellow and bilabiate with a spur that is about 10 mm long. Fruits are globose capsules with small yellowish seeds. Blooming from winter to summer, horned bladderwort inhabits wet pinelands, savannas, and bogs from eastern TX to FL and north to Canada. With a few-flowered branching scape up to 1 dm tall, *U. juncea* Vahl, southern bladderwort, is a mat-forming aquatic species with purple sepals and spurs that are about 7 mm long. This species inhabits bogs, seeps, and pond margins; its range extends throughout much of the eastern half of the U.S.

Utricularia foliosa L.

LEAFY BLADDERWORT

This is a free-floating, carnivorous perennial herb with straplike, flattened stems, each up to several meters long. The leaves are highly dissected and bear numerous urn-shaped bladders with trigger hairs. Borne from stem nodes, scapes are emergent. A raceme of up to twenty bilabiate, spurred yellow flowers terminates each scape. Fruits are globose capsules with discoid seeds. Blooming throughout the year, leafy bladderwort inhabits ponds, lakes, marshes, ditches, and canals from southeastern TX to FL and north to NC. *U. gibba* L., humped bladderwort, has terete stems and few-flowered racemes. This species inhabits swamps, ponds, and ditches; its range extends throughout much of the eastern U.S.

Utricularia inflata Walt.

FLOATING BLADDERWORT

A free-floating perennial, this herb is carnivorous on small invertebrate animals. On elongated stems, the alternately arranged leaves are several times dichotomously divided into capillarylike segments bearing ovoid bladders. Stimulated by the movement of small invertebrates, trigger hairs around the opening signal the bladder to expand and suck in prey. Up to 3.5 dm wide, a whorl of leaves with inflated petioles supports the emergent scape. A raceme of as many as 18 yellow, bilabiate flowers terminates the scape. The pedicels are recurved in fruit. Blooming from spring to summer, floating bladderwort inhabits swamps, sluggish streams, and lakes from eastern TX to Fl and north to MA.

Utricularia radiata Small

LITTLE FLOATING
BLADDERWORT

This is a free-floating, carnivorous perennial herb. On elongated stems, the alternately arranged leaves are divided into capillary segments bearing ovoid bladders. Up to 1.3 dm wide, a whorl of leaves with inflated petioles supports the emergent scape. A raceme of as many as four yellow, bilabiate flowers terminates the scape. In fruit, the pedicels are erect. Blooming from spring to summer, little floating bladderwort inhabits swamps, sluggish streams, and lakes from eastern TX to FL and north to ME.

Lilium catesbaei Walt.

PINE LILY

From a small, ovoid bulb this perennial herb produces a single stem up to 9 dm tall. The alternately arranged leaves are linear or lanceolate. One to three erect flowers terminate the stem. The clawed tepals are orange-red and marked with yellow and purple spots. Fruits are oblong capsules. Blooming from summer to fall, pine lily inhabits wet pinelands and savannas along the outer coastal plain from southeastern LA to FL and north to southeastern VA. *L. iridollae* M.G. Henry, panhandle lily, is a taller plant with yellow, nodding flowers arranged in umbels. This species inhabits wet savannas, bogs, and stream banks, and its range extends from southern AL to northwestern FL.

Loganiaceae

Lilium michauxii Poiret

CAROLINA LILY

Gelsemium sempervirens (L.) Ait. f.

CAROLINA JESSAMINE

From a scaly bulb, this perennial herb produces a single stem up to 1 m tall. Oblanceolate leaves with undulated margins are arranged in several whorls. Up to four fragrant, nodding flowers are arranged in umbels. Orange tepals splotched with maroon are reflexed. Six prominent stamens are strongly exserted. Blooming in summer, Carolina lily inhabits rich forests from eastern TX to northwestern FL and north to southern VA. *L. superbum* L., turk's-cap lily, has scentless flowers. This species inhabits wet woods, and its range extends from AR and MO east to the Atlantic coastal states as far north as NH.

This evergreen, rhizomatous vine produces red-brown twining stems, each up to 6 m long. Oppositely arranged lanceolate leaves are somewhat leathery. The bright yellow, fragrant, tubular flowers are arranged in axillary clusters. Fruits are elliptic capsules divided into two distinct chambers. Blooming from winter to spring, Carolina jessamine inhabits open woods, swamps, and fencerows throughout much of the Southeast. All parts of the plant are poisonous with active compounds that cause motor nerve depression. *G. rankinii* Small, Rankin's trumpetflower, has scentless flowers. This species inhabits swamps and bogs, and its range extends from LA to FL and north to NC.

Mitreola petiolata (J.F. Gmel.) Torr. & Gray

MITERWORT

From fibrous roots, this annual herb produces a branching stem up to 8 dm tall. The oppositely arranged leaves are narrowly elliptic and petiolate. Small flowers are disposed along one side of a stalked cyme. Fruits are smooth capsules with numerous tiny black seeds. Blooming from summer to fall, miterwort inhabits wet pinelands, savannas, swamps, and ditches from TX and OK to FL and north to southeastern VA. *M. sessilifolia* (J.F. Gmel.) G. Don, swamp hornpod, has papillose capsules and broadly ovate, sessile leaves. This species inhabits wet savannas, prairies, and bogs; its range extends from eastern TX and OK to FL and north to southeastern VA.

Spigelia marilandica (L.) L.

INDIAN PINK

From a rhizome, this perennial herb produces a simple stem up to 6 dm tall. The oppositely arranged leaves are sessile with ovate blades. Tubular, showy flowers are arranged in a secund cyme. Corollas are bright red without and pale yellow within. The five stamens are adnate to the corolla. Blooming from spring to summer, Indian pink inhabits moist woods throughout much of the Southeast. *S. gentianoides* Chapman ex A. DC, purpleflower pinkroot, is a federally endangered species with pale pink flowers. It inhabits rich hardwood forests; only a few populations occur in southern AL and northwestern FL.

Lythraceae

Cuphea glutinosa Cham. & Schlecht.

STICKY WAXWEED

Cuphea carthagenensis (Jacq.) J.F. Macbr.

COLOMBIAN WAXWEED

From fibrous roots, this annual herb produces simple or branching, erect, sticky, pubescent stems, each up to 9 dm long. On short petioles, the oppositely arranged leaves are elliptic, ovate, or obovate. Tubular flowers are solitary in the leaf axils. The greenish purple petals are inserted on the calyx lip. Fruits are capsules with brown, reticulate seeds. Blooming from summer to fall, Colombian waxweed inhabits wet woods, marshes, and ditches from eastern TX to FL and north to eastern NC. *C. aspera* Chapman, tropical waxweed, is a perennial with whorled leaves. This species inhabits wet pinelands and bogs and occurs in a few Florida Panhandle counties.

This introduced perennial herb produces wiry, branching, glandular-pubescent stems. The oppositely arranged leaves are elliptic with entire margins. Purplish bearded flowers are borne in the upper leaf axils. Each tubular calyx is ribbed and bilabiate. Four petals are inserted on one lip and two petals on the other. Fruits are ovoid capsules with several seeds. Blooming in summer, sticky waxweed inhabits fields, roadsides, and disturbed sites in eastern TX and southern LA. *C. viscosissima* Jacq., blue waxweed, is an annual with purplish stems. This species inhabits fields, roadsides, stream banks, and lake margins; its range extends from eastern TX to NE and east to the Atlantic coastal states as far north as NH.

Decodon verticillatus (L.) Ell.

SWAMP LOOSESTRIFE

This is a perennial herb or suffruticose subshrub with arching branches up to 2.5 m long. The lanceolate or elliptic leaves are opposite or whorled with acute tips and entire margins. Tubular magenta flowers are densely arranged in short-stalked axillary cymes. The prominent stamens extend well beyond the corolla. Fruits are globose capsules with glossy, reticulate, pyramid-shaped seeds. Blooming from summer to fall, swamp loosestrife inhabits swamps, marshes, and bogs throughout much of the eastern half of the U.S. With branches that root at their tips, this species produces asexual clones. Its seeds are an important food source for waterfowl.

Lythrum alatum Pursh var. *lanceolatum* (Ell.) Torr. & Gray ex Rothrock

LOOSESTRIFE

From a creeping rhizome, this freely branching perennial herb produces stems up to 1.5 m long. The ovate or lanceolate sessile leaves are opposite below and alternate above. Purple tubular flowers are solitary in the upper leaf axils. Fruits are fusiform, slightly winged capsules with many yellow-brown seeds. Blooming from spring to fall, loosestrife inhabits wet woods, pinelands, savannas, marshes, and ditches from eastern TX and OK to FL and north to southeastern VA. *L. lineare* L., wand lythrum, has linear leaves that are oppositely arranged throughout the length of the stem. This species inhabits saline marshes, and its range extends from TX to FL and north to NY and CT.

Malvaceae

Callirhoe papaver (Cav.) Gray

POPPYMALLOW

From a long woody root, this perennial herb produces ascending or decumbent stems, each up to 6 dm long. The alternately arranged leaves are ovate or deltoid and pedately cleft or entire with cordate or hastate bases. Borne on a long axillary peduncle, each solitary cup-shaped, magenta flower is subtended by three linear bracts. Fruits are elongated capsules with reniform seeds. Blooming from spring to summer, poppymallow inhabits open woods, pinelands, prairies, and roadsides from eastern TX and AR to northern FL and southwestern GA. *C. triangulata* (Leavenworth) Gray, clustered poppymallow, has broadly deltoid leaves that are divided into rounded lobes. This species inhabits open woods and prairies, and its range extends from MS to NC; it also occurs in MO, IL, IN, and MI.

Hibiscus aculeatus Walt.

COMFORT ROOT

From a woody caudex, this perennial herb produces several ascending or erect, stout stems, each up to 1 m long. Harshly pubescent with stellate hairs, the alternately arranged leaves are palmately lobed with irregularly serrated margins. Flowers are cream colored and marked with red from within. Each flower is subtended by an involucre of linear bracts that are apically cleft. Fruits are ovoid, beaked capsules with brown pitted seeds. Blooming from summer to fall, comfort root inhabits wet pinelands, savannas, and ditches from southeastern TX to FL and north to NC. Native Americans used the plant to treat skin irritations and urinary tract infections.

Hibiscus moscheutos L.

ROSE MALLOW

Hibiscus coccineus Walt.

TEXAS STAR

From a robust caudex, this perennial herb produces one to several stout stems, each up to 2 m tall. Alternately arranged leaves are toothed and palmately cleft into as many as seven lobes. Subtended by ten involucral bracts, solitary bright red, funnelform flowers are borne in the upper leaf axils. Fruits are ovoid capsules with brown, pubescent seeds. Blooming from summer to fall, Texas star inhabits swamps, marshes, and ditches from southeastern LA to central FL and southeastern GA. With its large showy flowers that attract hummingbirds and butterflies, this species is planted as a garden ornamental.

This robust perennial herb may exceed 2 m in height. Often palmately lobed, the alternately arranged leaves are broadly ovate and hairy with toothed margins. Large pink or white flowers, often with a red center, are axillary on long peduncles. Sepals are green and leaflike. The involucre is composed of linear, leaflike bracts. Connate stamens form a column through which the style emerges. Fruits are densely hairy capsules with dark brown, water-dispersed seeds. Blooming from summer to fall, rose mallow inhabits fresh and brackish marshes, swamps, pond margins, and ditches throughout much of the eastern U.S. *H. laevis* All., halberdleaf rose mallow, has hastate leaves. This species inhabits swamps, marshes, and riverbanks; its range extends throughout much of the U.S. east of the Rocky Mountains.

Kosteletzkya virginica (L.) K. Presl ex Gray

SEASHORE MALLOW

This is a much-branching shrubby perennial herb with coarsely hairy stems each up to 2 m tall. The leaves are ovate or hastate and densely pubescent. Each showy flower is bright pink with a yellow staminal column. Fruits are pentagonal capsules with smooth seeds. Blooming from summer to fall, seashore mallow inhabits fresh and brackish marshes, swamps, and ditches along the outer coastal plain from TX to FL and north to NY. Native Americans used the plant for the treatment of urinary infections.

Sida rhombifolia L.

CUBAN JUTE

From a taproot, this annual or short-lived perennial produces a single stellate, pubescent stem up to 2 m tall. The oppositely arranged leaves are ovate or rhombic with serrated margins. Solitary pale yellow or orange flowers are axillary on pedicels that are longer than the petioles of the subtending leaf. Fruits are rounded schizocarps with small, dark seeds. Blooming throughout the year, Cuban jute occurs in open woods, fields, and roadsides from TX, OK, and KS to Florida and north to PA and NJ. *S. spinosa* L., prickly fanpetals, has pedicels that are about the same length as the subtending leaf petioles. This species inhabits fields, pastures, and roadsides, and its range extends throughout much of the eastern U.S.

Urena lobata L.

CAESAR WEED

This is a shrubby, stellate-pubescent perennial herb up to 3 m tall. The alternately arranged leaves are broadly ovate with short distal lobes and shallowly toothed margins. The pink or rose-colored flowers are solitary in leaf axils and arranged in short terminal racemes. Each flower is subtended by a cup-shaped, five-lobed involucre. Fruits are bristly schizocarps that separate into one-seeded mericarps at maturity. Blooming from spring to fall, Caesar weed inhabits open woods, swamps, and disturbed sites from southeastern LA to FL. Widely naturalized in tropical and subtropical areas around the world, this species can become an invasive weed.

Thalia dealbata Fraser

POWDERY THALIA

This is an aquatic perennial herb with large rhizomes. The basal leaves have long petioles and ovate or elliptic blades. Leaf sheaths are impregnated with air chambers. Up to 2.5 m tall, the erect, branching inflorescence is held high above the leaves. Arranged in pairs, the self-pollinated flowers are subtended by thick waxy bracts bearing a whitish bloom. Individual flowers are composed of small membranous sepals, dark purple corolla lobes, petal-like staminodes, and a single fertile anther. The complex style is helical-shaped with one appendage. Fruits are capsules, each with a single dark seed. Blooming from spring to fall, powdery thalia inhabits swamps, ditches, and ponds in eastern TX, southeastern OK, southwestern LA, eastern AR, southeastern MO, southeastern GA, and eastern SC. *T. geniculata* L., bent alligator-flag, has floral bracts that are devoid of bloom. This species inhabits swamps and marshes, and it occurs in FL and a few sites in LA.

Melanthiaceae

Lophiola aurea Ker-Gawl.

GOLDENCREST

From a whitish rhizome, this perennial herb produces a solitary simple, erect stem up to 8.5 dm tall. The alternately arranged linear leaves are held erect. The terminal inflorescence is a series of helicoid cymes. The adaxial surfaces of the six perianth segments are bright yellow; the abaxial surfaces are densely beset with white, woolly pubescence. Fruits are ovoid capsules with numerous whitish or yellowish reticulate seeds. Blooming in summer, goldencrest inhabits wet pinelands, savannas, and bogs from southeastern LA to northwestern FL and north to southeastern NC; it also occurs in southern NJ. This species is endangered in NC.

Chamaelirium luteum (L.) Gray

FAIRY WAND

From a stout rhizome, this evergreen, dioecious perennial herb produces a solitary hollow stem up to 3.5 dm tall. Formed in a rosette, the basal leaves are petiolate and may be elliptic or spathulate. Leaves along the stem become reduced distally. The white or yellow flowers are borne in a drooping terminal raceme that gradually becomes erect. Fruits are ovoid capsules with up to four reddish brown seeds. Blooming from spring to summer, fairy wand inhabits mesic woods throughout much of the eastern U.S. from LA and AR to FL and north to CT and MA. This, the only member of the genus, is endangered in CT, IN, and MA and threatened in NY.

Melanthium virginicum L.

VIRGINIA BUNCHFLOWER

From a rhizome, this perennial herb produces a solitary scruffy stem up to 2 m tall. The basally disposed linear leaves are strap-shaped and sheathing. Flowers are arranged in a terminal panicle of ascending racemes. Turning reddish with age, each of the six cream-colored, clawed tepals bears a yellow-green nectar gland. Fruits are ovoid, three-chambered capsules with winged seeds. Blooming from spring to summer, Virginia bunchflower inhabits wet pinelands, savannas, and bogs from eastern TX to IA and east to the Atlantic coastal states as far north as Long Island, NY. *M. woodii* (J.W. Robbins ex Wood) Bodkin, Wood's bunchflower, has purplish or brownish tepals, each with a purple or blackish nectar gland. It occurs in a few counties in northwestern FL.

Stenanthium gramineum (Ker-Gawl.) Morong

FEATHERBELLS

From an ellipsoid bulb, this perennial herb produces a solitary simple stem up to 2 m tall. Basally disposed, the numerous leaves are linear and keeled. Staminate and perfect flowers are arranged in a branching terminal panicle of numerous racemes. Composed of six tepals, each rotate perianth is white or yellowish. Fruits are oblong, ovoid capsules. Blooming in summer, featherbells inhabits open wet woods and roadsides from eastern TX to southern IL and east to the Atlantic coastal states as far north as MD. This uncommon plant is either threatened or endangered in FL, IL, IN, KY, MD, and OH.

Zigadenus densus (Desr.) Fern.

CROW POISON

Zigadenus glaberrimus Michx.

SANDBOG DEATH CAMAS

From a slender, toxic bulb this perennial herb produces a single stem up to 1.5 m tall. Leaves along the lower stem are strap-shaped; those above are reduced and bractlike. Flowers are densely arranged in a simple raceme. Each tepal is white or cream-colored with a single small, obscure gland near the base. Fruits are conical, furrowed capsules with brown seeds. Blooming from spring to summer, crow poison inhabits wet pinelands and savannas from eastern TX to FL and north to southeastern VA. *Z. nuttallii* (Gray) S. Wats., Nuttall's death camas, is a shorter plant with a stem up to 7.5 dm tall; each of its tepals bears a prominent gland. This species inhabits open woods and prairies; its range extends from eastern TX and western LA north to central KS and southern MO.

From a thick, contorted rhizome, this perennial herb produces a solitary stem up to 1.2 m tall. Becoming reduced upward, the alternately arranged leaves are linear and held erect. Showy, creamy white flowers are arranged in loose panicles. The tepals are clawed, and each bears a pair of prominent glands near its base. Fruits are conical-shaped capsules and are partially surrounded by persistent tepals. Blooming in summer, sandbog death camas inhabits wet pinelands, savannas, and bogs from southeastern LA to northern FL and north to southeastern VA. All parts of the plant contain toxic alkaloids.

Melastomataceae

Rhexia alifanus Walt.

SAVANNA MEADOWBEAUTY

From a spongy caudex, this perennial herb produces arching stems, each up to 1 m long. The oppositely arranged lanceolate or narrowly elliptic blue-green leaves are prominently three-veined and glabrous. With prominently curved anthers, the bright pink or lavender flowers are arranged in cymes. Hypanthia are urn-shaped with glandular hairs. Fruits are capsules with lustrous, cuneate seeds. Blooming from spring to fall, savanna meadowbeauty inhabits wet pinelands, savannas, and bogs from southeastern TX to Fl and north to NC. *R. nashii* Small, maid Marian, has hirsute leaves and glabrous hypanthia. This species inhabits wet pinelands, savannas, and bogs, and its range extends from southeastern LA to FL and north to MD.

Rhexia lutea Walt.

YELLOW MEADOWBEAUTY

From a crown, this perennial herb produces quadrangular, hirsute stems, each up to 5 dm long. The oppositely arranged leaves are prominently three-veined and mostly lanceolate-elliptic. Sulfur yellow flowers are arranged in terminal and axillary cymes. Fruits are capsules with numerous strongly curved seeds. Blooming in spring, yellow meadowbeauty inhabits wet pinelands, savannas, and sphagnum bogs from eastern TX to northern FL and north to NC. Members of this genus produce anthers that dehisce through a terminal pore and are adapted for buzz-pollination by bees.

Rhexia mariana L. var. *mariana*
MARYLAND MEADOWBEAUTY

From an elongated rhizome, this colonial perennial herb produces glandular-hairy, quadrangular stems, each up to 1 m long. The short-petiolate, villous leaves are mostly lanceolate. Pale pink flowers with prominent, long-curved anthers are arranged in terminal cymes. The urn-shaped hypanthia are mostly glabrous. Fruits are capsules with many spiral-shaped seeds. Blooming from spring to summer, Maryland meadowbeauty inhabits wet pinelands and savannas throughout much of the eastern half of the U.S. *R. virginica* L., handsome Hairy, has sessile leaves, winged stems, and glandular-hirsute hypanthia. This species inhabits wet pinelands, savannas, bogs, and lake margins; its range extends from eastern TX to northern FL and north to Canada.

Rhexia petiolata Walt.
FRINGED MEADOWBEAUTY

This perennial herb produces square, simple stems up to 6 dm long. The short-petioled, opposite, ovate leaves are strongly three-veined with stiff hairs on the margins and upper surfaces. Rose-colored flowers are arranged in terminal cymes. The hypanthia are glabrous. Fruits are urn-shaped capsules. Blooming in summer, fringed meadowbeauty occurs in wet pinelands, savannas, and sphagnum bogs from southeastern TX to FL and north to southeastern VA. *R. nuttallii* C.W. James, Nuttall's meadowbeauty, has glandular-hairy hypanthia and sessile leaves. This species inhabits wet pinelands, savannas, and ditches, and its range extends from FL to southern GA.

Menispermaceae

Cocculus carolinus (L.) DC.
CAROLINA CORALBEAD

This is a trailing or climbing, dioecious woody vine with stems up to 5 m long. The alternately arranged leaves are ovate or hastate with cordate, truncate, or cuneate bases. Small, creamy white, unisexual flowers are arranged in axillary racemes. Fruits are one-seeded, glossy red drupes. The stony endocarp is flattened with a crescent moon design. Blooming from spring to fall, Carolina coralbead inhabits open woods, stream banks, and roadsides from TX to southeastern KS and east to the Atlantic coastal states as far north as DE. Native Americans used the plant to treat blood disorders.

Menyanthaceae

Nymphoides aquatica (J.F. Gmel.) Kuntze
BIG FLOATING HEART

This is a glabrous, aquatic perennial herb with a thick, stocky rhizome. Floating leaves are broadly ovate with a deep basal cleft; the upper surfaces are yellowish green, and the lower surfaces are purple and pitted. White flowers in umbel-like clusters are borne in the leaf axils. Fruits are ellipsoid capsules with papillose seeds. Blooming from spring to fall, big floating heart inhabits swamps, marshes, and lakes from southeastern TX to FL and north to DE. *N. cordata* (Ell.) Fern., little floatingheart, has smaller cordate leaves and smooth seeds. This species inhabits ponds and sluggish streams, and its range extends from southeastern LA to northwestern FL and north to ME.

Molluginaceae

Mollugo verticillata L.

CARPETWEED

From a slender taproot, this perennial herb produces several prostrate or ascending, dichotomously branching stems. Arranged in whorls, the leaves are linear, elliptic, or spathulate. Borne in the leaf axils, the small flowers are solitary or arranged in umbels. The calyx lobes are white and marked with green lines; the corolla is absent. Fruits are ovoid capsules with many glossy brown seeds. Blooming from summer to fall, carpetweed inhabits fields, gardens, roadsides, and disturbed sites throughout much of the U.S. This edible species has been described as a famine potherb.

Nartheciaceae

Aletris aurea Walter

YELLOW STAR GRASS

This is a rhizomatous perennial herb. The lanceolate or elliptic leathery leaves are densely arranged in a basal rosette. Bright yellow campanulate flowers, each subtended by two unequal bracts, are arranged in an elongated terminal raceme on a scape up to 8 dm long. Perianths are tubular with erect, united tepals. Blooming from spring to summer, yellow star grass inhabits wet pinelands, savannas, and sphagnum bogs from southeastern TX to northern FL and north to VA. *A. lutea* Small, yellow colicroot, has spreading tepals. This species inhabits wet pinelands, savannas, and roadsides, and its range extends from southeastern LA to FL and southern GA.

Aletris farinosa L.

WHITE STAR GRASS

This is a rhizomatous perennial herb. Bright, yellow-green, narrowly lanceolate leaves are arranged in a basal rosette. An elongated raceme of white, granular-textured flowers terminates a scape up to 1 m tall. Perianths are cylindric with spreading lobes. Blooming from spring to summer, white star grass inhabits bogs, prairies, and open woods throughout much of the eastern U.S. *A. obovata* Nash ex Small, southern colicroot, has campanulate flowers with inward-turned lobes. This species inhabits wet pinelands and savannas; its range extends from southeastern LA to central FL and southern GA.

Nelumbo lutea Willd.

LOTUS LILY

This is a rhizomatous, aquatic perennial herb. On stout petioles, orbicular-shaped peltate leaves are floating or held up to 2 m above the water surface. Large, solitary flowers are composed of yellow tepals and numerous free stamens. Separate carpels are embedded in a swollen, conical receptacle. The aggregate fruit consists of a mature receptacle and dark round seeds. Blooming from spring to summer, lotus lily inhabits lakes, marshes, swamps, and floodplains throughout much of the U.S. east of the Rocky Mountains. Native to eastern Asia, *N. nucifera* Gaertn., sacred lotus, has pink or white tepals and is naturalized from eastern TX to MO and east to the Atlantic coastal states as far north as southern NJ.

Nymphaeaceae

Nymphaea elegans Hook.

BLUE WATER LILY

This is a rhizomatous, aquatic perennial herb. The floating ovate or orbicular leaves are green above and purplish below. Pale blue, lavender, or nearly white flowers are held up to 2 dm above the water surface on slender peduncles. Sepals are flecked with black. Fruits are globose berries with many seeds. Blooming from spring to fall, blue water lily inhabits swamps, marshes, lakes, and ditches on the outer coastal plain from eastern TX to southwestern LA; it also occurs in the western part of peninsular FL. *N. mexicana* Zucc., yellow water lily, is an introduction with yellow flowers. This species inhabits marshes, lakes, ditches, and canals; its range extends from eastern TX to FL and north to NC.

Nuphar advena (Ait.) Ait. f.

SPATTERDOCK

From a rhizome, this aquatic perennial herb produces long-petioled leaves that are floating or emergent. Prominently cleft at their bases, the glabrous leaves are broadly ovate or orbiculate. Greenish yellow flowers are held above the water surface on stout peduncles. Fruits are ovoid, ribbed green berries. Blooming from spring to fall, spatterdock inhabits lakes, marshes, canals, and sluggish streams throughout much of the eastern U.S. *N. orbiculata* (Small) Standley, roundleaf spatterdock, has leaves that are densely pubescent on their abaxial surfaces. This species inhabits ponds, swamps, and ditches; its range extends from northern FL to adjacent GA and AL.

Nymphaea odorata Aiton. ssp. *odorata*

WHITE WATER LILY

This aquatic perennial herb produces a large, branching rhizome. Deeply cleft at the base, the ovate or orbicular leaves are green above and purplish below. Fragrant white flowers are floating and open diurnally. Sepals are uniformly green. Fruits are globose capsules with many seeds. Blooming from spring to fall, white water lily inhabits swamps, marshes, and lakes throughout much of the eastern U.S. An introduction from Africa and Asia, *N. lotus* L., white Egyptian lotus, has flowers that open nocturnally. This species inhabits ponds and ditches, and its range extends from southeastern LA to southern MS and in the western part of peninsular FL.

Gaura lindheimeri Engelm. & Gray

BEE BLOSSOM

From a woody caudex, this shrubby perennial herb produces arching or prostrate stems. The alternately arranged, narrowly elliptic leaves are irregularly toothed. Arranged in elongated spikes, the white flowers fade to pink as they age. Fruits are quadrangular, fusiform, sessile capsules. Blooming from spring to fall, bee blossom inhabits prairies, savannas, and pastures from TX and OK to LA. *G. sinuata* Nutt. ex Ser., wavyleaf bee blossom, has fruits that are attached by a slender stipe. This species inhabits fields and pastures, and its range extends from TX and OK to FL and north to SC.

Ludwigia octovalvis (Jacq.) Raven
ssp. *octovalvis*

MEXICAN PRIMROSE

This is a freely branching annual or
perennial herb that produces stems up
to 3 m tall. The alternately arranged
leaves are linear, lanceolate, or narrowly
ovate. Bright yellow flowers are solitary and borne in the leaf axils. Fruits
are linear capsules with glossy brown
seeds. Blooming from summer to fall,
Mexican primrose inhabits swamps,
marshes, and ditches from eastern TX
to FL and north to southeastern NC.
L. decurrens Walt., wingleaf primrose-
willow, has prominently winged stems.
This species inhabits ditches, ponds, and
swamps, and its range extends from
TX, OK, and KS east to the Atlantic
coastal states as far north as MD.

Ludwigia peploides (Kunth) Raven
ssp. *glabrescens* (Kuntze) Raven

WATER PRIMROSE

This aquatic perennial herb produces
trailing or floating stems, up to 6 dm
long. Alternately arranged elliptic or
ovate leaves are simple with entire margins. Borne in the leaf axils, solitary
bright yellow flowers bear four petals
and ten epipetalous stamens. Fruits are
cylindric capsules with many yellowish seeds. Blooming from spring to
fall, water primrose inhabits ditches,
lakes, sluggish streams, and marshes
throughout much of the eastern U.S.
excluding the upper Midwest and
New England. *L. peruviana* (L.) Hara,
Peruvian primrose-willow, is an introduced aquatic shrub with ovoid
capsules that has become naturalized
from TX to FL and north to NC.

Oenothera drummondii Hook.

BEACH EVENING PRIMROSE

This is a mat-forming, suffruticose perennial. The alternately arranged oblanceolate or obovate leaves are silvery green. Solitary in the leaf axils, bright yellow flowers are greater than 5 cm broad. Sepals, petals, and stamens are attached to the rim of a long, slender hypanthium. Fruits are long, slender capsules with many small seeds. Blooming from spring to fall, beach evening primrose inhabits sand dunes and beaches along the coast from TX to FL and north to NC. *O. humifusa* Nutt., seabeach evening primrose, has smaller flowers that are less than 5 cm broad. This species inhabits sand dunes, and its range extends along the outer coastal plain from southern LA to FL and north to southeastern NJ.

Oenothera biennis L.

COMMON EVENING PRIMROSE

From a taproot, this biennial herb produces a stout, erect stem up to 2 m tall. Leaves of the basal rosette are petiolate and pinnately cleft. Leaves along the stem are lanceolate and nearly sessile. Bright yellow four-petaled flowers with well-developed hypanthia are arranged in a spike. Fruits are cylindrical capsules with many reddish seeds. Blooming from summer to fall, common evening primrose inhabits open woods, roadsides, and disturbed sites throughout much of the U.S. excluding the Rocky Mountain States. *O. heterophylla* Spach, variable-leaf evening primrose, is a shorter plant with pinnately lobed leaves. This species inhabits open, sandy woods, and its range extends from eastern TX to western LA and north to MO.

Oenothera speciosa Nutt.

SHOWY EVENING PRIMROSE

This is a sprawling or mounding perennial herb. The alternately arranged leaves are linear, lanceolate, or obovate with margins that are often pinnately cleft into irregularly shaped lobes. Showy white or pink flowers are solitary in the leaf axils. The prominent stamens produce copious amounts of pollen; the stigma is four-lobed. Fruits are obovoid capsules with numerous winged seeds. Blooming from spring to summer, showy evening primrose inhabits open woodlands, prairies, and roadsides throughout much of the southern U.S. Opening at dusk, flowers are adapted for nocturnal pollination, especially by sphinx moths.

Oenothera laciniata Hill

CUTLEAF EVENING PRIMROSE

This is an annual, biennial, or short-lived perennial herb with decumbent stems up to 8 dm long. The alternately arranged leaves are oblanceolate or elliptic with pinnately lobed or entire margins. Solitary bright yellow or reddish flowers are borne in the leaf axils. Fruits are long, cylindrical capsules with brown, angulate seeds. Blooming from spring to fall, cutleaf evening primrose inhabits roadsides, fields, and disturbed sites throughout much of the U.S. east of the Rocky Mountains. *O. linifolia* Nutt., threadleaf evening primrose, is a slender, erect annual herb with filiform leaves. This species inhabits open woods, and its range extends from eastern TX to southern IL and east to the Atlantic coastal states as far north as VA.

Orchidaceae

Calopogon tuberosus (L.) B.S.P. var. *tuberosus*

GRASS PINK

From a globose corm, this perennial herb produces a solitary stem up to 1.1 m tall. Plants typically bear a single linear or lanceolate, prominently veined leaf. One to several magenta, pink, or white flowers open sequentially on the scape. The lip is basally hinged and distally three-lobed; the middle lobe is delta shaped. The lamellae are formed into raised ridges that grade into a brush of white, yellow, or pink hairs distally. Blooming from spring to summer, grass pink inhabits wet savannas, pinelands, and sphagnum bogs throughout much of eastern U.S. *C. oklahomaenis* D.H. Goldman, Oklahoma grass pink, has a forked corm and its flowers open simultaneously. This species inhabits wet pinelands, savannas, and bogs; its range extends from eastern TX and western LA to MN and in southern MS, southern AL, northwestern FL, southwestern GA, and southeastern SC.

Cleistes divaricata (L.) Ames

SPREADING POGONIA

From brittle, tuberous roots, this perennial herb produces a solitary scape up to 7.5 dm tall with a solitary lanceolate or elliptic, sessile leaf positioned near the middle. One to three showy flowers are arranged in a terminal inflorescence. The dark rose or white petals are fused and form a tube; the lip is three-lobed with a fleshy crest. The spreading sepals are greenish brown, bronze, or maroon. Fruits are narrowly cylindrical capsules. Blooming in spring, spreading pogonia inhabits wet pinelands, savannas, and bogs along the outer coastal plain from northern FL to DE. *C. bifaria* (Fern.) Cattling & Gregg, small spreading pogonia, has a slightly shorter lip petal. This species inhabits wet pinelands and savannas, and its range extends from southeastern LA to northern FL and north to eastern NC.

Corallorhiza wisteriana Conrad

WISTER'S CORALROOT

This achlorophyllous perennial herb produces scapes that are purple, yellow, or brown. Flowers are arranged in terminal racemes. The three-veined, brownish sepals and lateral petals collectively form a hood over the column. A white lip petal is often mottled with purple and exhibits two basal lamellae. Fruits are elliptical capsules with many dustlike seeds. Blooming from spring to summer, Wister's coralroot inhabits rich woods from eastern TX to southeastern NE and east to the Atlantic coastal states as far north as NJ.

Cypripedium acaule Ait.

MOCCASIN FLOWER

From a rhizome, this perennial herb produces two basal, prominently plicate, pubescent leaves. Subtended by a green bract, a solitary showy flower terminates the pubescent scape. The spreading, twisted lateral petals and sepals are reddish brown. The inflated labellum is typically pinkish white and marked by darker veins. Fruits are capsules containing numerous dustlike seeds. Blooming from spring to summer, moccasin flower inhabits acidic woods, pine barrens, and bogs from AL to MI and east to the Atlantic coastal states as far north as ME. Native Americans used an infusion of the roots to treat a variety of ailments including venereal disease, urinary infections, stomachache, worms, and colds.

Cypripedium kentuckiense C.F. Reed

KENTUCKY LADY'S SLIPPER

Up to 1 m tall, this is the tallest member of the genus. A single stem produces several ovate leaves that are prominently veined. Flowers are typically solitary and exhibit a pouch-shaped white, cream, or yellow labellum. Sepals and lateral petals are maroon. Fruits are capsules with many seeds. Blooming in spring, Kentucky lady's slipper inhabits deciduous woods, creek banks, and acid-seep forests from northeastern TX and southeastern OK to western AR and northern LA and from eastern MS to western AL with isolated populations in central GA, eastern KY, and northeastern VA.

Encyclia tampensis (Lindl.) Small

BUTTERFLY ORCHID

Attached to trees by its fleshy roots, this epiphytic perennial herb produces ovoid stems called pseudobulbs. One to several coriaceous leaves are linear-lanceolate and sessile. The showy flowers are arranged in a terminal raceme or panicle. Sepals and lateral petals are brownish yellow and suffused with purple. The three-lobed lip is white and marked with a dark purple spot. Fruits are three-ribbed, ellipsoid capsules. Blooming from spring to summer, butterfly orchid inhabits forests and hammocks in peninsular FL. Also native to the West Indies, it has fragrant flowers that attract bee pollinators.

Epidendrum magnoliae Muhl.

GREEN-FLY ORCHID

This is an evergreen perennial with thick, spongy, matted roots. The alternately arranged leaves are oblong, sessile, and coriaceous. Fragrant greenish-translucent flowers are arranged in loose racemes. The lip petal is shallowly three-lobed with two basal calli. Fruits are pendulous, ellipsoid, ribbed capsules. Blooming throughout the year, green-fly orchid is epiphytic or epilithic on trees or rocks situated in mesic to wet sites along the outer coastal plain from southern LA to central FL and north to southeastern NC.

Eulophia alta (L.) Fawcett & Rendle

WILD COCO

This terrestrial perennial herb produces a pseudobulb enclosed in sheaths. Several narrowly elliptic, plaited leaves are clustered atop the short stem. A raceme of showy flowers terminates the scape that arises laterally from near the base of the pseudobulb. Sepals and lateral petals are bronzy green. The three-lobed lip petal is maroon. Fruits are ellipsoid capsules. Blooming from summer to fall, wild coco inhabits wet pinelands, prairies, and ditches in peninsular FL and southeastern GA.

Habenaria repens Nutt.

WATER-SPIDER ORCHID

This is a semiaquatic perennial herb with roots that are scattered along the basal portion of a solitary stem up to 9 dm tall. The lower leaves are sheathing and lanceolate or narrowly elliptic. The upper leaves are reduced and bractlike. Green flowers are densely arranged in a terminal raceme. The lip petal is three-lobed with a spur that is no more than 2 cm long. Fruits are erect, ellipsoid capsules. Blooming from summer to fall, water-spider orchid inhabits bogs, lake margins, and marshes, often in mats of floating vegetation, from eastern TX and southwestern AR to FL and north to eastern NC. *H. quinqueseta* (Michx.) Eat., longhorn bog orchid, has white petals and a spur that is at least 4 cm long. This species inhabits wet pinelands, savannas, and bogs; its range extends from eastern TX to FL and north to southeastern SC.

Hexalectris spicata (Walt.) Barnh. var. *spicata*

CRESTED CORALROOT

Having a stout, branching rhizome, this perennial herb produces no roots or leaves. Up to 8 dm tall, the scapes are brownish purple and sheathing; the bracts are ovate or lanceolate. Arranged in a terminal raceme, the flowers are yellowish and marked with brownish purple parallel lines. The three-lobed lip petal is clawed and exhibits several raised rows of lamellae. Fruits are ellipsoid pendant capsules. Blooming from spring to summer, crested coralroot inhabits mesic woods and stream banks from TX to southern MO and east to the Atlantic coastal states as far north as southern MD. This nongreen species parasitizes fungi to obtain its nutrients.

Isotria verticillata (Muhl. ex Willd.) Raf.

LARGE WHORLED POGONIA

From a rhizome, this colonial perennial herb produces a single purplish green, glaucous stem. Lanceolate, obovate, or elliptic leaves are arranged in a single whorl. The one or two flowers are terminal. Spreading purple-green sepals typically exceed 3 cm long. The white lip is three-lobed; the callus is formed into a green, fleshy crest. Fruits are capsules. Blooming in spring, large whorled pogonia inhabits acid woods, seeps, and sphagnum bogs from eastern TX, AR, and southeastern MO to northwestern FL and north to ME. *I. medeoloides* (Pursh) Raf., small whorled pogonia, has sepals that are less than 3 cm long. This species inhabits deciduous forests, and its range extends from northern GA to southern ME.

Listera australis Lindl.

SOUTHERN TWAYBLADE

From fibrous roots, this perennial herb produces a solitary purplish green, glabrous stem up to 3 dm tall. The two suboppositely arranged leaves are sessile with ovate or elliptic blades. Reddish purple flowers are arranged in a lax raceme. The dorsal sepal is concave, and the two laterals are falcate. Lateral petals are oblong and recurved. The lip is split into two linear lobes with a small tooth in the sinus. Capsules are held horizontally along the rachis. Blooming from winter to summer, southern twayblade inhabits sphagnum bogs and moist woods on the outer coastal plain from eastern TX to FL and north to southern NC.

Malaxis unifolia Michx.

GREEN ADDER'S MOUTH

From a pseudobulb this glossy green, glabrous perennial herb produces a solitary stem up to 5 cm tall. The single leaf is ovate and clasping. Numerous minute, green, resupinate flowers are densely arranged on an elongated raceme. Fruits are persistent ellipsoid capsules. Blooming from spring to fall, green adder's mouth inhabits rich woods, stream banks, and bogs throughout much of the eastern half of the U.S. *M. spicata* Sw., Florida adder's mouth, bears two leaves and its flowers are not resupinate. This species inhabits hammocks, swamps, and rich woods, and its range extends from southern FL to southeastern VA.

Platanthera blephariglottis (Willd.) Lindl. var. *conspicua* (Nash) Luer

WHITE FRINGED ORCHID

From fleshy roots this perennial herb produces a single stout stem up to 1.1 m tall. Spreading or ascending, the lanceolate leaves become reduced upward. Bright white, showy flowers are arranged in a terminal raceme. The lip petal is conspicuously fringed with a slender cylindrical spur that is at least 3 cm long. Fruits are ellipsoid capsules. Blooming from summer to fall, white fringed orchid inhabits wet pinelands, savannas, prairies, and marshes in southeastern TX and also from southern MS to FL and north to eastern NC. *P. blephariglottis* (Wolld.) Lindl. var. *blephariglottis* has a spur that is less than 2.6 cm long. This species inhabits wet pinelands and bogs, and its range extends from southwestern GA to ME.

Platanthera ciliaris (L.) Lindl.

YELLOW FRINGED ORCHID

From tuberous roots, this perennial herb produces a single stem up to 1 m tall. The lanceolate, sessile leaves are sheathing and reduced upward. Bright yellow or orange flowers are arranged in a terminal raceme. The lip petal is three-lobed with a slender linear spur; the central lobe is conspicuously ciliated. The column is short and produces two pollinia. Fruits are cylindric capsules with numerous seeds. Blooming from summer to fall, yellow-fringed orchid inhabits wet pinelands, savannas, bogs, and stream banks from TX to FL and north to NH. *P. integra* (Nutt.) Gray ex Beck, yellow fringeless orchid, is a shorter species with an entire lip petal. This species inhabits wet pinelands and savannas; its range extends from TX to FL and north to NJ.

Platanthera cristata (Michx.) Lindl.

CRESTED FRINGED ORCHID

From fleshy roots, this perennial herb produces a single stem up to 9 dm tall. The alternately arranged linear-lanceolate leaves become reduced and bractlike distally. The bright orange flowers are densely arranged in a terminal spike. The labellum is ciliate-fringed with a slender cylindrical spur. Fruits are capsules with dustlike seeds. Blooming in summer, crested fringed orchid inhabits wet pinelands, savannas, prairies, and bogs from southeastern TX to FL and north to southern MA. This showy species is listed as threatened or endangered in FL, KY, MD, MA, and NY.

Platanthera nivea (Nutt.) Luer

SNOWY ORCHID

From an ellipsoid tuber this species produces a single stem up to 9 dm tall. Linear or lanceolate leaves are ascending to spreading and reduced distally. Showy white flowers are densely arranged in a terminal raceme. Unlike other members of the genus, the flowers of this species are not resupinate. Fruits are capsules with numerous seeds. Blooming from spring to summer, snowy orchid inhabits wet pinelands, savannas, and sphagnum bogs from southeastern TX to FL and north to eastern NC. *P. flava* (L.) Lindl., palegreen orchid, has yellow-green resupinate flowers. This species inhabits cypress swamps and alluvial forests; its range extends from eastern TX to northern FL and north to eastern VA.

Pogonia ophioglossoides (L.) Ker-Gawl.

ROSE POGONIA

From a slender rhizome, this colonial perennial herb produces a stem up to 7 dm tall. Positioned near the middle of the stem is a solitary elliptic or ovate leaf. Subtended by a leaflike bract, one to three rose pink, fragrant flowers terminate the stem. The lip petal is prominently bearded with fleshy yellow bristles. Fruits are ellipsoid capsules. Blooming from spring to summer, rose pogonia inhabits wet pinelands, savannas, seeps, and sphagnum bogs throughout much of the eastern U.S. With its lip petal that falsely appears to bear copious amounts of pollen, this species deceives its pollinators, usually bumblebees, into making unrewarded visits.

Sacoila lanceolata (Aublet) Garay
var. *lanceolata*

SCARLET LADY'S TRESSES

From fleshy, clustered roots, this perennial herb produces a basal rosette of elliptic leaves that is typically absent at
flowering. Up to 6 dm tall, the scape is
terminated by a raceme of densely arranged, coral-red or pale green flowers.
Each lip petal is lanceolate with pubescent calli near the base. Fruits are erect,
ovoid capsules. Blooming from spring
to summer, scarlet lady's tresses inhabits pinelands, fields, and roadsides in
FL. *S. squamulosa* (Kunth) Garay, hoary
beaked orchid, has a white-spotted
scape. This species inhabits open woods
and pinelands and occurs in central FL.

Spiranthes odorata (Nutt.) Lindl.

MARSH LADY'S TRESSES

From slender, spreading roots, this colonial species produces a stem up to 1 m
tall. Elliptic or oblong, the thickened,
sheathing, ascending leaves are abruptly
reduced distally. White flowers are
spirally arranged in a terminal spike.
The labellum is often marked with yellow or green. Fruits are erect, ellipsoid
capsules. Blooming from fall to winter,
marsh lady's tresses inhabits swamps,
marshes, and stream banks from eastern TX and southeastern OK to FL
and north to southeastern MD. *S. cer-
nua* (L.) Rich., nodding lady's tresses, is
a shorter plant with stems up to 5 dm
tall. This species inhabits open woods,
marshes, prairies, and dunes; its range
extends throughout much of the eastern U.S. but is generally absent on the
outer coastal plain from LA to FL.

Spiranthes ovalis Lindl. var *ovalis*

OCTOBER LADY'S TRESSES

From slender roots, this perennial herb produces a solitary stem up to 4 dm tall. The alternately arranged leaves are oblong, elliptic, or oblanceolate; the proximal ones are reduced and strongly recurved. Arranged in spikes, the pure white flowers are tightly spiraled with three flowers per cycle. Each lip petal has a crisped margin. Fruits are erect capsules. Blooming from fall to winter, October lady's tresses inhabits wet woods from eastern TX and southern AR to northern FL. The flowers of *S. ovalis* var. *erostellata* Catling are self-fertile and do not fully open. This species inhabits wet woods and fields; its range extends from eastern TX to southern MI and east to the Atlantic coastal states as far north as MD.

Spiranthes praecox (Walt.) S. Wats.

GREENVEIN LADY'S TRESSES

From a fascicle of thin, fleshy roots, this perennial herb produces a simple stem up to 7.5 dm tall. The alternately arranged leaves are linear or filiform and are gradually reduced upward. A spike of small white flowers terminates a sparsely pubescent rachis. The lip petals are marked with raised green veins. Fruits are erect, ellipsoid capsules. Blooming from winter to spring, greenvein lady's tresses inhabits wet pinelands, savannas, bogs, and marshes from eastern TX and southern AR to FL and north to Long Island, NY. *S. vernalis* Engelm. & Gray, spring lady's tresses, has a densely pubescent rachis with pointed hairs. This species inhabits prairies, savannas, marshes, swamps, and roadsides; its range extends from eastern TX to southern SD and east to the Atlantic coastal states as far north as MA.

Tipularia discolor (Pursh) Nutt.

CRIPPLED CRANEFLY

From a corm, this perennial herb produces a solitary broadly ovate, plicate
leaf. The abaxial surface is dark purple,
whereas the adaxial surface is purplish
green. On a scape up to 6.5 dm tall,
purplish green, resupinate flowers are
arranged in a lax raceme. The three-
lobed lip petal is elongated into a long,
slender spur. Fruits are ovoid, pendant
capsules with numerous seeds. Blooming from summer to fall, crippled cranefly inhabits rich deciduous woods from
eastern TX to southern IL and east to
the Atlantic coastal states as far north
as MA. Emerging in autumn, the leaf
overwinters and withers prior to flowering during the following summer.

Conopholis americana (L.) Wallr.

SQUAW-ROOT

From a coral-shaped root mass, this
achlorophyllous perennial herb produces
stout stems, each up to 2.5 dm tall, that
are covered by imbricate, brownish yellow bracts. Arranged in a spike, the
numerous white, bilabiate flowers terminate the stalk. Fruits are ovoid capsules
with lustrous brown seeds. Blooming in
spring, squaw-root is parasitic on oak
and beech roots in deciduous forests
throughout much of the U.S. east of the
Mississippi River. This species provides
a major food source for black bears.

Epifagus virginiana (L.) W. Bart.

BEECHDROPS

From a spherical mass of coral-like roots, this annual herb produces brownish stems suffused with purple or yellow, each up to 5 dm tall. Leaves are reduced to broadly ovate bracts. The irregularly four-lobed, tubular flowers are brownish and suffused with white and purple. Flowers on the lower part of the stem typically are self-fertile and remain budlike. Fruits are brown capsules with pale yellow, ellipsoid seeds. Blooming from summer to fall, beechdrops is parasitic on the roots of beech trees from southeastern TX to northern FL and north to Canada. The root has been used in traditional herbal medicine to treat sores.

Oxalis rubra St.-Hil.

WINDOWBOX WOODSORREL

This is an introduced, colonial perennial herb with a scaly crown and tuberous roots. The basal leaves are trifoliate and glandular with silky white hairs. Leaflets are broadly ovate with an apical notch; orange glands are situated along the abaxial margins. Arranged in cymes, the white, pink, or lavender flowers are marked with darker veins. Each greenish sepal exhibits an orange gland near its apex. Fruits are ellipsoid capsules with pitted seeds. Blooming from winter to summer, windowbox woodsorrel inhabits lawns and gardens from southeastern TX and OK east to the Atlantic coastal states as far north as eastern VA. Also an escape from cultivation, *O. debilis* Kunth, pink woodsorrel, has a range extending from southeastern TX to FL and north to SC.

Oxalis stricta L.

YELLOW WOODSORREL

From a slender white rhizome, this perennial herb produces glabrous or hairy, erect or decumbent stems, each up to 5 dm long. The alternately arranged leaves are green or purplish and trifoliate. Leaflets are broadly obovate with an apical notch. The bright yellow flowers are arranged in cymes. Fruits are beaked capsules with brownish seeds. Blooming from winter to spring, yellow woodsorrel inhabits open woods, roadsides, gardens, and disturbed sites throughout much of the U.S. excluding the West Coast. *O. corniculata* L., creeping woodsorrel, is a fibrous-rooted perennial herb with trailing stems and yellow flowers. This species inhabits lawns, gardens, and greenhouses, and its range extends throughout much of the U.S.

Oxalis violacea L.

VIOLET WOODSORREL

This is a stoloniferous, colonial perennial herb with a scaly bulb. The trifoliate leaves are petiolate and basal. The green or purplish leaflets are obcordate with entire margins. Up to 1.5 dm tall, the scape is terminated by an umbel of flowers. The pink or violet corolla lobes are greenish-yellow on their bases. Fruits are globose capsules with reticulate seeds. Violet woodsorrel inhabits open woods, roadsides, and prairies throughout much of the U.S. east of the Rocky Mountains. This species has two blooming periods. Leaves are present during the spring period but are absent during the late summer period.

Papaveraceae

Argemone albiflora Hornem. ssp.
texana G.B. Ownbey

WHITE PRICKLY POPPY

From a stout taproot, this annual or biennial herb produces a solitary prickly,
glaucous stem up to 1.5 m tall. The alternately arranged prickly leaves are obovate, sessile, auriculate, and pinnately
lobed. Arranged in cymes, showy white
flowers are subtended by two leaflike
bracts. Fruits are prickly, blue-green, ellipsoid capsules with many reticulate
seeds. Blooming from spring to summer, white prickly poppy inhabits fields,
roadsides, and disturbed sites in eastern
TX, western LA, southern MO, and
northern AR. *A. albiflora* Hornem. ssp.
albiflora has oblong capsules. This species inhabits dunes, fields, roadsides, and
disturbed sites; its range extends from
southeastern LA to to FL and north to
MA. *A. mexicana* L., Mexican prickly
poppy, has yellow petals. It inhabits
fields, roadsides, and disturbed sites, and
its range extends from southern TX to
FL and north to MA and in the Midwest.

Sanguinaria canadensis L.

BLOODROOT

This is a perennial herb with a large,
branching rhizome. Each plant produces
a single prominently veined, reniform
leaf that is palmately lobed. A solitary
white or pinkish flower with numerous
yellow stamens terminates the scape.
Fruits are fusiform capsules with numerous small seeds that are dispersed
by ants. Blooming in spring, bloodroot
inhabits mesic woods and flood plains
throughout much of the eastern U.S.
excluding peninsular FL. Native Americans used the dark orange-red juice
found in all parts of the plant for body
paint and love charms.

Passifloraceae

Passiflora incarnata L.

MAYPOP

This is a trailing or climbing, herbaceous perennial vine with stems up to 2 m long. Palmately three-lobed leaves are alternately arranged on petioles, each bearing a pair of nectar glands. Solitary flowers and tendrils are axillary. Calyx and corolla lobes are whitish green and often tinged with light lavender. A conspicuous corona is composed of lavender or purple filaments banded with white. Three stigmas and five stamens are elevated on a stalk called an androgynophore. Fruits are yellow, inflated, edible berries. Blooming from spring to fall, maypop inhabits fields, roadsides, and fencerows throughout much of the eastern U.S. *P. edulis* Sims, purple granadilla, a native of South America, is grown commercially for its purple passion fruit.

Passiflora lutea L.

YELLOW PASSIONFLOWER

This is a high-climbing, herbaceous perennial vine with slender stems. The three-lobed leaves are broadly ovate. Each cluster of from one to three flowers and a single tendril are borne in leaf axils. Sepals and petals are greenish white. The narrowly linear, coronal lobes are white with pink bases. Fruits are blue-black berries with grooved brown seeds. Blooming from spring to summer, yellow passionflower occurs in wet to mesic woods throughout much of the Southeast and lower Midwest. Mining bees form a spherical mass of yellow passionflower pollen in which the female lays a single egg. Her larva exclusively feeds on the pollen mass prior to pupation.

Phytolaccaceae

Phytolacca americana L. var. *americana*

POKE SALAD

From a stout rhizome, this perennial herb produces stout purple stems up to 3 m long. The alternately arranged leaves are elliptic or lanceolate. Erect or drooping racemes are borne opposite to the leaves. Individual flowers are composed of five white or pink sepals; petals are absent. Fruits are dark purple berries with glossy black seeds. Blooming throughout the year, poke salad inhabits disturbed sites throughout much of the U.S. excluding the Rocky Mountain states. Although most of the plant is poisonous, the young leaves are used as a potherb when properly prepared.

Plantaginaceae

Plantago major L.

COMMON PLANTAIN

This European introduction is a perennial herb with fibrous roots. Arranged in a basal rosette, the broadly ovate or elliptic leaves are strongly ribbed. Up to 3 dm long, densely flowered spikes terminate each of the one to several scapes. The brown corollas are salverform with four reflexed lobes. Broadest near the middle, fruits are ellipsoid, circumscissle capsules with reddish brown, angular seeds. Blooming from spring to summer, common plantain inhabits wet woods, marshes, roadsides, lawns, and fields throughout much of the U.S. *P. rugelii* Dcne., blackseed plantain, has capsules that are broadest below the middle. This species inhabits wet woods, stream banks, lawns, and disturbed sites; its range extends throughout much of the U.S. east of the Rocky Mountain states.

Poaceae

Chasmanthium latifolium (Michx.)
Yates

INDIAN WOODOATS

Plantago virginica L.

VIRGINIA PLANTAIN

This is an annual or biennial herb with a slender taproot. Forming a basal rosette, the oblanceolate or obovate leaves are entire or coarsely toothed. Arranged in spikes up to 3 dm tall, the densely imbricated flowers obscure the upper rachis. The salverform corollas are four-lobed and greenish; the prominent purple anthers are held on elongated filaments. Fruits are ovoid capsules with glossy yellowish brown seeds. Blooming from spring to summer, Virginia plantain inhabits marshes, dunes, roadsides, lawns, and disturbed sites throughout much of the U.S. excluding the upper Rocky Mountain States. *P. sparsiflora* Michx., pineland plantain, has loosely arranged flowers that do not obscure the rachis. This species inhabits savannas, roadsides, and ditches; its range extends from northeastern FL to northeastern VA.

From a mat-forming rhizome, this perennial herb produces arching, sheathed culms each up to 1.3 m long. The alternately arranged leaves are lanceolate with thin, dry margins. Bearing inconspicuous florets and arranged in open panicles, the greenish spikelets are laterally compressed. Fruits are compressed black or reddish caryopses. Blooming in summer, Indian woodoats inhabits wet woods and riverbanks from AZ to MI and east to the Atlantic coastal states as far north as NJ. *C. laxum* (L.) Yates, slender wood oats, has wedge-shaped spikelets that are held erect. This species inhabits wet woods, savannas, and ditches, and its range extends from eastern TX to southern MO and east to the Atlantic coastal states as far north as Long Island, NY.

Polemoniaceae

Uniola paniculata L.

SEA OATS

From straw-colored rhizomes, this colonial perennial herb produces clusters of culms, each up to 2 m tall. The sheathing leaves are linear and attenuated into pointed tips. Small, inconspicuous florets are borne within a golden-brown, flattened spikelet. The numerous spikelets are arranged in a much-branched terminal panicle. The fruit is a linear caryopsis. Blooming in summer, sea oats inhabits coastal sand dunes from TX to FL and north to DE. With its extensive network of rhizomes and roots, this species helps prevent beach erosion.

Ipomopsis rubra (L.) Wherry

STANDING CYPRESS

From a long taproot, this biennial herb produces a solitary simple stem up to 2 m tall. The alternately arranged leaves are pinnately divided into linear and filiform segments. Flowers are arranged in an elongated panicle. The salverform corollas are red or orange and mottled within. Fruits are three-chambered capsules. Blooming in summer, standing cypress inhabits sandhills, riverbanks, and dunes throughout much of the eastern half of the U.S. Copious nectar producers, the flowers are pollinated by ruby-throated hummingbirds.

Phlox drummondii Hook. ssp. *drummondii*

ANNUAL PHLOX

This is a pubescent annual herb with stems up to 5 dm tall. Opposite below, the sessile or clasping leaves become alternate above. Blades are elliptic, oblong, or oblanceolate. The tubular, salverform flowers are arranged in cymes. Corollas may be white, pink, red, or variegated. Fruits are capsules with ellipsoid seeds. Blooming from summer to fall, annual phlox inhabits fields, roadsides, and disturbed sites from eastern TX, OK, and southern MO to FL and north to MD. Seeds are sown along highways for beautification. *P. divaricata* L., wild blue phlox, is a common blue-flowered species that inhabits deciduous woods throughout much of the eastern U.S.

Phlox pilosa L. ssp. *pilosa*

DOWNY PHLOX

This rhizomatous perennial herb produces one to several downy-pubescent stems, each up to 5 dm tall. Oppositely arranged leaves are linear or narrowly lanceolate. Arranged in small cymes, the purple, pink, or white salverform flowers are often marked with a darker center. Fruits are three-chambered capsules. Blooming from spring to summer, downy phlox inhabits open woodlands, savannas, prairies, and roadsides throughout much of the U.S. east of the Rocky Mountains. *P. carolina* L, thickleaf phlox, has thicker and somewhat broader leaves. This species inhabits deciduous woods, savannas, and roadsides; its range extends from eastern TX to FL and north to MD.

Polygalaceae

Polygala cruciata L. var. *cruciata*

DRUMHEAD

This is an annual herb with slender, erect, angular stems up to 4 dm tall. Arranged in whorls, the linear or oblanceolate leaves are sessile and punctate. Racemes of densely arranged pink or purple flowers terminate each stem. Called wings, the petal-like sepals are tipped with a short, rigid point that gives the raceme a brushy appearance. Fruits are orbicular capsules with black, pubescent seeds. Blooming from spring to summer, drumhead inhabits wet pinelands, savannas, and bogs throughout much of the eastern U.S. *P. brevifolia* Nutt., littleleaf milkwort, has a raceme that is not brushy. This species inhabits wet pinelands and savannas, and its range extends from southern MS to northern FL and north to southern NJ.

Polygala incarnata L.

PROCESSION FLOWER

This is a slender, glaucous annual herb with a solitary simple or sparingly branched stem up to 5 dm tall. The alternately arranged leaves are lanceolate and sessile. Rose-colored flowers are arranged in terminal racemes. The tubular corolla is about twice the length of the petaloid wings. Fruits are oblong capsules with black seeds that are clothed in long white hairs. Blooming from spring to summer, procession flower inhabits wet pinelands, savannas, bogs, and prairies from eastern TX to MI and east to the Atlantic coastal states as far north as NY. *P. leptocaulis* Torr. & Gray, swamp milkwort, is a slender, glabrous annual with delicate racemes of rose-colored flowers. This species inhabits wet pinelands, savannas, ditches, and pond margins; its range extends from eastern TX to northern FL.

Polygala mariana P. Mill.

MARYLAND MILKWORT

From a taproot, this annual herb produces a simple or branching stem up to 4 dm tall. Pink or purplish flowers are densely arranged in headlike racemes. Fruits are capsules with pubescent seeds. Blooming from spring to summer, Maryland milkwort inhabits wet pinelands, savannas, bogs, and ditches from southeastern TX and AR to northern FL and north to Long Island, NY. *P. sanguinea* L., purple milkwort, has wings that are about twice as long as the corolla lobes. This species inhabits bogs, prairies, fields, and roadsides; its range extends throughout much of the eastern U.S. excluding FL.

Polygala lutea L.

ORANGE MILKWORT

This glabrous annual or biennial herb produces stems up to 4 dm tall. Arranged in a basal rosette and along the stem, the spathulate or obovate leaves are somewhat succulent. The orange flowers are arranged in a compact terminal raceme. Fruits are capsules with black, pilose seeds. Blooming from spring to summer, orange milkwort inhabits wet pinelands, savannas, and bogs on the outer coastal plain from southeastern LA to FL and north to Long Island, NY. This species is endangered in NY and may be extirpated in PA.

Polygala nana (Michx.) DC.

CANDY ROOT

From a well-developed taproot, this herbaceous annual or biennial produces simple stems, each up to 1.5 dm tall. The succulent basal leaves are mostly obovate and form a rosette. The few leaves along the flowering stem are mostly linear-spathulate. Bright greenish yellow flowers are densely arranged in a cylindrical raceme. Fruits are ovoid capsules with softly pubescent seeds. Blooming from spring to summer, candy root inhabits open sandy woods, savannas, and bogs from TX to FL and north to NC. When pulled from the ground, the roots briefly emit an odor reminiscent of Halloween candy wax.

Polygala polygama Walt.

RACEMED MILKWORT

From a taproot, this biennial herb produces one to several sparsely branched stems, each up to 3 dm tall. The alternately arranged succulent leaves are spathulate, obovate, or linear with mucronate apices. Pinkish or purplish flowers are arranged in a loose terminal raceme. Inconspicuous self-fertile flowers are borne in small racemes near the base of the plant and in the lower leaf axils. Fruits are ovoid capsules with pubescent black seeds. Blooming from spring to summer, racemed milkwort inhabits open woods, bogs, pinelands, and savannas throughout much of the eastern half of the U.S.

Polygala ramosa Ell.

PINE BARREN MILKWORT

From fibrous roots, this annual herb
produces simple or branching stems up
to 4 dm tall. The basal leaves are elliptic
or obovate; those on the stem are linear
or spathulate. Numerous terminal and
axillary racemes of bright yellow flowers form a flat cymose panicle. Fruits are
suborbicular capsules with hairy seeds.
Blooming from spring to summer, pine
barren milkwort inhabits wet pinelands,
savannas, and hillside seeps from southeastern TX to FL and north to NJ. *P.
cymosa* Walt., tall pine barren milkwort,
is a taller species with stems up to 1 m
tall. This species inhabits wet pinelands
and savannas, and its range extends
from LA to FL and north to MD.

Polygala rugelii Shuttlw. ex
Chapman

YELLOW MILKWORT

This annual, biennial, or perennial herb
produces erect stems, each up to 8 dm
tall. Formed in an irregular rosette, the
basal leaves are spathulate with cuneate
bases. Leaves along the stem are mostly
linear-lanceolate. Bright yellow flowers are densely arranged in a terminal
raceme. Fruits are capsules with small
brown seeds. Blooming from spring
to summer, yellow milkwort inhabits
pinelands, savannas, and bogs throughout peninsular and northeastern FL.
This species is listed as threatened by
the Florida Game and Freshwater Fish
Commission.

Polygonaceae

Brunnichia ovata (Walt.) Shinners

EARDROP VINE

This suffrutescent perennial vine climbs by tendrils that terminate lateral branchlets. The bases of the alternately arranged ovate leaves are truncate or subcordate. Greenish flowers are arranged in panicles of spikelike racemes. The fruit is a nutlet contained in an elongated hypanthium and enclosed by the calyx. Blooming in summer, eardrop vine inhabits wet woods, lake margins, and stream banks from eastern TX and OK to northern FL and north to VA. Although this species is grown as an ornamental, it can become invasive.

Coccoloba uvifera (L.) L.

SEAGRAPE

This is a sprawling, dioecious evergreen shrub up to 2 m tall. With orbicular blades and cordate bases, the alternately arranged leaves are coriaceous and prominently veined. Small, white, fragrant flowers are arranged in terminal racemes. Fruits are orbicular achenes that become reddish purple at maturity. Blooming throughout the year, seagrape inhabits sand dunes and hammocks in peninsular FL. In southern FL and the West Indies, this species becomes tree-like and may attain a height of 15 m.

Persicaria glabra (Willd.) M. Gómez

DENSEFLOWER KNOTWEED

The lower stems of this robust perennial herb are decumbent with rooting nodes. The upper stems are held erect. The alternately arranged leaves are mostly lanceolate with entire ocreae. Racemes are arranged in loose, open panicles. Calyx lobes are white or pink and punctate; corollas are absent. Fruits are brown or black, glossy achenes that are oval in cross section. Blooming from summer to fall, denseflower knotweed inhabits swamps, marshes, and ditches from TX to southeastern MO east to the Atlantic coastal states as far north as southern NJ. *P. punctata* (Ell.) Small, dotted knotweed, has ciliated ocreae and achenes that are triangular in cross section. This species inhabits fresh and brackish marshes, and its range extends throughout much of the U.S.

Persicaria hydropiperoides (Michx.) Small

SWAMP SMARTWEED

From a rhizome with fibrous roots, this perennial herb produces decumbent or ascending stems, each up to 7 dm tall. The alternately arranged leaves are lanceolate or linear; the brown, cylindrical ocreae bear appressed bristles. Flowers are arranged in terminal and axillary paniculate fascicles. Perianths are white or pinkish. Fruits are three-sided, brown or black, glossy achenes. Blooming from summer to fall, swamp smartweed inhabits swamps, pond margins, and ditches throughout much of the U.S. *P. setacea* (Bald.) Small, bog smartweed, has ocreae with spreading bristles. This species inhabits wet woods, swamps, and ditches; its range extends from eastern TX to MI and east to the Atlantic coastal states as far north as CN.

Persicaria longiseta (Bruijn) Kitagawa

BRISTLY LADY'S THUMB

From fibrous roots, this introduced annual herb produces decumbent or ascending, branching stems, up to 8 dm tall. The alternately arranged leaves are ovate, lanceolate, or linear and sessile or short-petiolate. In axillary and terminal racemes, the pink or rose-colored flowers are clustered in fascicles. Fruits are ovoid, three-angled, glossy black achenes. Blooming from spring to fall, bristly lady's thumb inhabits wet woods, pond margins, ditches, and disturbed sites throughout much of the eastern half of the U.S. Also an introduction, *P. maculosa* Gray, spotted lady's-thumb, has discoid achenes. It inhabits wet fields and pastures, and its range extends throughout much of the U.S.

Rumex altissimus Wood

PALE DOCK

From a taproot, this perennial herb produces a simple or branching, erect or procumbent stem. The alternately arranged leaves are lanceolate and petiolate with slightly crisped margins. Racemes of greenish flowers are arranged in elongated panicles. Fruits are three-sided, glossy brown achenes. Blooming from spring to summer, pale dock inhabits swamps, marshes, and ditches throughout much of the U.S. east of the Rocky Mountains. *R. crispus* L., curly dock, has leaves that are prominently crisped. This species inhabits fields, roadsides, and disturbed sites, and its range extends throughout much of the U.S.

Rumex hastatulus Baldw.

HEARTWING SORREL

From a taproot, this dioecious annual or short-lived perennial herb produces one to several erect branching stems. The alternately arranged, hastate leaves are pale green with thin ocrea. Fascicles of unisexual flowers are arranged in terminal panicles. The perianth is pink or purple. Each fruit is a glossy brown achene enclosed in the persistent perianth. Blooming from spring to summer, heartwing sorrel inhabits fields, alluvial woods, dunes, and disturbed sites from eastern TX to southern IL and east to the Altantic coastal states as far north as NY. *R. chrysocarpus* Moris, amamastia, has bisexual flowers and thickened dark green leaves. This species inhabits seasonal wet areas, and its range extends along the outer coastal plain from eastern TX to northwestern FL.

Pontederiaceae

Eichhornia crassipes (Mart.) Solms

WATER HYACINTH

Native to tropical America, this free-floating perennial herb is a noxious weed. Arranged in basal rosettes, the ovate to suborbicular leaves have spongy-inflated petioles. Showy flowers are densely arranged in a spike. Corollas are bilabiate; the upper lip exhibits a dark blue splotch with a yellow center. After flowering, the peduncle bends downward so that the capsules can develop under water. Blooming from spring to fall, water hyacinth inhabits lakes, ditches, canals, and marshes from TX to FL and north to VA. This prolific species can quickly clog waterways by producing clones from its stolons. Its root system removes heavy metals and other toxins from the water.

Heteranthera limosa (Sw.) Willd.

BLUE MUDPLANTAIN

This annual aquatic herb produces float-ing or rooting simple stems. Leaves of the basal rosette are sessile and linear or oblanceolate. Leaves on the stem are alternate, petiolate with oblong or ovate blades. Borne in a spathe, each flower is salverform and white or blu-ish. Fruits are elongate capsules with numerous ovoid, winged seeds. Bloom-ing from spring to fall, blue mudplan-tain inhabits pond margins and ditches from TX to SD and east from southern IL to MS; it also occurs in central FL. *H. multiflora* (Griseb.) Horn, bouquet mudplantain, has spikes of white or pur-plish flowers. This species inhabits pond, margins, and ditches; its range extends from northeastern LA to eastern MS and north to southern IL; it also occurs from northeastern NC to southern NJ.

Pontederia cordata L.

PICKERELWEED

This is an aquatic perennial herb with thick, creeping rhizomes. Blades of the long-petiolate basal leaves are narrowly lanceolate or broadly ovate with cune-ate or cordate bases. Terminated by a spike of densely arranged purple-blue flowers, the floral stalk exhibits a single leaflike bract. Each corolla is bilabiate; the upper lip is marked with two yellow spots. Fruits are membranous utricles, each bearing a single seed. Blooming from spring to fall, pickerelweed inhab-its lake margins, swamps, and marshes throughout much of the U.S. east of the Rocky Mountains. Fruits provide an important food source for waterfowl.

Portulacaceae

Claytonia virginica L.

SPRING BEAUTY

From a globose corm, this perennial herb produces one to several succulent stems, each up to 3 dm tall. Each stem bears a pair of oppositely arranged linear leaves. Flowers are arranged in a terminal raceme that is subtended by a single sessile bract. The corolla lobes are white and marked with pinkish veins. Fruits are three-chambered, ovoid capsules with glossy black seeds. Blooming from winter to spring, spring beauty inhabits open woods and prairies throughout much of the eastern half of the U.S. excluding FL. Native Americans cooked and ate the corms.

Portulaca oleracea L.

LITTLE HOGWEED

From a taproot, this introduced glabrous, succulent annual produces freely branching, prostrate stems, each up to 4.5 dm long. The alternately arranged leaves are spathulate or obovate with entire margins. Solitary or arranged in clusters, the small yellow flowers terminate the stems. Fruits are ovoid, membraneous capsules with small black seeds. Blooming from spring to fall, little hogweed inhabits dunes, fields, gardens, and disturbed sites throughout much of the U.S. *P. pilosa* L., kiss me quick, has reddish purple flowers. This species inhabits xeric, often sandy or gravelly sites, and its range extends from AZ and CO east to the Atlantic coastal states as far north as NC.

Potamogetonaceae

Potamogeton diversifolius Raf.

WATERTHREAD PONDWEED

From a freely branching, filiform rhizome, this aquatic perennial herb produces submerged and floating branching stems. Submerged leaves are linear and sessile; the floating leaves are elliptic or ovate and petiolate. Pedunculate spikes of inconspicuous, brownish flowers are borne in the leaf axils. The floating spikes are elongated and bear more flowers than do the subglobose, submerged ones. Fruits are flattened, keeled achenes. Blooming from spring to summer, waterthread pondweed inhabits ponds, lakes, and sluggish streams throughout much of the U.S. *P. nodosus* Poir., longleaf pondweed, has submerged leaves that are lanceolate or elliptic and floating leaves that are lens-shaped or elliptic. This species inhabits lakes, sluggish streams, and canals; its range also extends throughout much of the U.S.

Primulaceae

Anagallis arvensis L. ssp. *arvensis*

SCARLET PIMPERNEL

From a taproot, this introduced annual herb produces one to several prostrate or weakly ascending stems. The oppositely arranged leaves are sessile with ovate or elliptic blades. On long, slender pedicels, the flowers are solitary in the leaf axils. Corollas are typically orange but can be blue or scarlet. Fruits are globose capsules with dark brown seeds. Blooming from spring to fall, scarlet pimpernel inhabits roadsides, pastures, lawns, and disturbed sites throughout much of the U.S. *A. minima* (L.) Karuse, chaffweed, produces minute, inconspicuous, nearly sessile flowers with translucent corollas. This species inhabits open woods, prairies, and disturbed sites; its range extends throughout much of the U.S. excluding the Northeast.

Dodecatheon meadia L. ssp. *meadia*
SHOOTINGSTAR

From thickened, fibrous roots, this perennial herb produces a basal rosette of
oblong or lanceolate leaves. An umbel
of nodding flowers, subtended by small
bracts, terminates the solitary scape up
to 3 dm tall. The reflexed corolla lobes
are white or lavender and marked with
red or yellow near their bases. Fruits
are ellipsoid capsules with many reddish brown, reticulate seeds. Blooming from spring to summer, shootingstar inhabits prairies and open woods
throughout much of the eastern U.S.
Flowers typically are pollinated by bees.

Samolus valerandi L. ssp. *parviflorus*
(Raf.) Hultén
WATER PIMPERNEL

From fibrous roots, this glabrous perennial herb produces a simple or branching stem up to 6 dm tall. The alternately
arranged leaves are obovate, oblanceolate, or spathulate. The lower leaves have
winged petioles, and the upper ones are
sessile. Small, white, campanulate flowers are arranged in simple or paniculate
racemes. Fruits are globose capsules
with tiny reddish brown seeds. Blooming from spring to fall, water pimpernel
inhabits swamps, marshes, stream banks,
and lake margins throughout much of
the U.S. excluding the upper Rocky
Mountain States and the Upper Midwest. The flowers of *S. ebracteatus* Kunth,
limewater brookweed, are pinkish. This
species inhabits dunes and saline prairies,
and its range extends from southeastern
NM to southern KS and east to FL.

Ranunculaceae

Aquilegia canadensis L.

RED COLUMBINE

From a stout caudex, this perennial herb produces several branching stems, each up to 5 dm long. The alternately arranged leaves are palmately divided into lobed leaflets. Nodding flowers are borne on long axillary peduncles. The corolla lobes are yellow and truncate with red spurs. Fruits are aggregates of ellipsoid follicles with persistent styles. Blooming from spring to summer, red columbine inhabits rocky woods, pastures, and disturbed sites throughout much of the eastern half of the U.S. excluding LA. This showy species is planted as a garden ornamental.

Clematis baldwinii Torr. & Gray

PINE HYACINTH

From a slender rhizome, this perennial herb produces one to several erect, pubescent stems, each up to 6 dm tall. The oppositely arranged leaves are elliptic or ovate with entire or lobed margins. Long peduncles, each bearing a solitary nodding flower, emerge from the upper leaf axils. The thickened, lavender or purple calyx lobes are somewhat spongy and reflexed with crisped white margins. Petals are absent. Fruits are ovoid, plumose achenes. Blooming throughout the year, pine hyacinth inhabits wet pinelands and swamp margins in peninsular and northeastern FL. This showy species is planted as a garden ornamental.

Clematis crispa L.

BLUE JASMINE

From a branching rhizome, this herbaceous perennial vine produces stems that climb by tendril-like petioles. The oppositely arranged leaves are pinnately compound. Individual leaflets are elliptic or lanceolate, lobed or entire, and somewhat succulent. Nodding, urn-shaped flowers are solitary and terminate individual stems. The thickened, reflexed calyx lobes are blue or lavender and suffused with white. Fruits are achenes with persistent tail-like styles. Blooming from spring to fall, blue jasmine inhabits wet woods, swamps, and marshes from southeastern TX and OK to FL and north to southeastern VA. *C. galucophylla* Small, whiteleaf leather flower, has red-purple flowers. This species inhabits rich woods, and its range extends from eastern TX and OK to northern FL and north to VA.

Clematis reticulata Walt.

NETLEAF LEATHER FLOWER

This herbaceous perennial vine climbs by tendril-like petioles. The oppositely arranged pinnate leaves are leathery and prominently reticulate. Arranged in axillary inflorescences, each urn-shaped flower exhibits four greenish-pink, recurved sepals. Petals are absent. The numerous stamens are yellow. Fruits are aggregates of spirally arranged achenes. Blooming from spring to summer, netleaf leather flower inhabits dry, sandy woods from eastern TX to central FL and north to SC.

Clematis terniflora DC.

VIRGIN'S BOWER

An introduction from Japan, this climbing or trailing, semi-evergreen woody vine with stems up to 5 m long is a naturalized weed. The oppositely arranged leaves are pinnately compound. Ovate or elliptic leaflets are somewhat leathery with entire margins. White flowers are arranged in paniculate cymes. Sepals are petaloid; corolla lobes are absent. Fruits are achenes with persistent plumose styles. Blooming from summer to fall, virgin's bower inhabits wet woods and disturbed sites throughout much of the eastern U.S. A native species, *C. virginiana* L., devil's darning needles, has leaflets that bear toothed margins. Its range also extends throughout much of the eastern U.S.

Delphinium carolinianum Walt. ssp. *vimineum* (D. Don) Warnock

CAROLINA LARKSPUR

From tuberlike roots, this perennial herb produces a simple stem up to 1 m tall. Palmately divided into numerous linear segments, basal and stem leaves are present at flowering. The blue or bluish white flowers are arranged in a terminal raceme. The upper sepal is elongated into a spur. Fruits are oblong follicles with oblong seeds. Blooming from winter to summer, Carolina larkspur inhabits praires and pinelands in eastern TX, southeastern OK, southwestern AR, and LA. *D. carolinianum* Walt. ssp. *carolinianum* has basal leaves that are usually absent at flowering. This species inhabits open woods and prairies, and its range extends from eastern OK to central IL and east to northwestern FL, GA, and SC.

Ranunculus sardous Crantz

HAIRY BUTTERCUP

From fibrous roots, this naturalized annual herb produces branching, hairy stems, each up to 6 dm tall. The basal and lower stem leaves are ovate or cordate and three-lobed; the individual lobes are deeply divided. Solitary flowers bearing sulfur yellow petals and reflexed sepals are axillary on long pedicels. Fruits are suborbicular, flattened, keeled, smooth achenes, each with a hooked beak. Blooming from winter to spring, hairy buttercup inhabits wet fields, ditches, and disturbed sites from southeastern TX to southeastern KS and east to the Atlantic coastal states as far north as NY. *R. muricatus* L., spiny-fruit buttercup, has spiny fruits. This species inhabits marshes and ditches, and its range extends from eastern TX to northern FL and north to SC.

Ranunculus sceleratus L. var. *sceleratus*

CURSED BUTTERCUP

From fibrous roots, this annual herb produces freely branching hollow stems, each up to 1 m tall. The basal and lower stem leaves are reniform and palmately lobed; each lobe is further divided into rounded segments. On a long pedicel, each solitary shiny yellow flower terminates an upper stem. A cup-shaped nectary is located at the base of each corolla lobe. Fruits are aggregates of ellipsoid, yellowish, tuberculate achenes. Blooming from winter to spring, cursed buttercup inhabits lake margins, stream banks, marshes, and ditches throughout much of the eastern half of the U.S. This species is toxic, and contact with its sap can cause skin irritation.

Rosaceae

Duchesnea indica (Andr.) Focke

INDIAN STRAWBERRY

From a short rhizome, this perennial herb produces prostrate, stoloniferous, hairy stems up to 3 dm long. The alternately arranged leaves are ovate or elliptic and trifoliate. The leaflets are ovate with toothed margins. Subtended by a series of three-lobed bracts, the bright yellow flowers are solitary in the leaf axils. Fruits are bright red aggregates of achenes. Blooming from winter to summer, Indian strawberry inhabits open woods, prairies, fields, gardens, lawns, and disturbed sites throughout much of the eastern U.S. A native of Asia, this species is planted as a groundcover, but it can become invasive.

Rosa bracteata J.C. Wendl.

MACARTNEY ROSE

Introduced from China, this is an evergreen shrub with arching, densely glandular, hairy branches that bear curved prickles. The alternately arranged leaves are pinnately compound with persistent dissected stipules. Leaflets are obovate or oblong and coriaceous with minute teeth. Subtended by pubescent bracts, the white flowers are solitary or borne in few-flowered corymbs. Fruits are aggregates of achenes enclosed in a reddish or blackish hip. Blooming from spring to summer, Macartney rose inhabits roadsides, fields, and disturbed sites from eastern TX and southern AR to the Atlantic coastal states as far north as MD. Also introduced from China, *R. laevigata* Michx., Cherokee rose, has glabrous branches. It inhabits disturbed sites, and its range extends from eastern TX to FL and north to VA.

Rubus trivialis Michx.

SOUTHERN DEWBERRY

A woody vine or subshrub, this perennial produces rooting stems that facilitate asexual reproduction. The alternately arranged leaves are trifoliate and somewhat leathery. Leaflets are coarsely toothed. White or pink flowers are arranged in loose cymes. Fruits are globose or elongate aggregates of black drupes. Blooming from winter to summer, southern dewberry inhabits thickets, roadsides, and fencerows from TX, OK, and KS east to the Atlantic coastal states as far north as MD. *R. persistens* Rydb., persistent blackberry, is an upright, freely branching subshrub with nonrooting stems. This species inhabits open woods, and its range extends from eastern TX to FL and north to SC.

Cephalanthus occidentalis L.

BUTTONBUSH

This is a freely branching shrub up to 3 m tall. The ovate or elliptic leaves are opposite and whorled. Flowers are densely arranged in a spherical head. The white corollas are funnelform with a black gland between each of the four lobes. Styles extend beyond the corolla so that the inflorescence has an overall spiky appearance. Fruits are pyramid-shaped nutlets. Blooming from spring to fall, buttonbush inhabits swamps, marshes, lake margins, and creek banks throughout much of the eastern U.S. A decoction made from its bark was used by Native Americans as a tonic and as a treatment for eye disorders.

Diodia virginiana L. var. *virginiana*
BUTTONWEED

From a woody caudex, this annual or perennial herb produces trailing, pubescent, branching stems. The oppositely arranged elliptic or lanceolate leaves are sessile. Solitary in the leaf axils, the white, four-lobed, salverform flowers are densely pubescent within. The two sepals are narrowly lanceolate. Fruits are leathery, pubescent capsules with prominent ridges. Blooming throughout the year, buttonweed inhabits prairies, savannas, swamps, lawns, and stream banks throughout the Southeast and lower Midwest. *D. teres* Walt., Virginia buttonweed, is an annual with white or pink flowers, each with four sepals. This species inhabits fields, roadsides, and disturbed sites; its range extends throughout much of the U.S. excluding the upper Midwest and Northwest.

Galium aparine L.
GOOSEGRASS

From a slender taproot, this mat-forming annual herb produces trailing or reclining stems that bear hooked prickles. Arranged in whorls, the linear or oblanceolate leaves are sessile with hooked prickles on their margins and midribs. One to several flowers are arranged in axillary cymes. The white corollas are tubular with four lobes. Densely clothed with hooked hairs, the fruits are two-chambered nutlets. Blooming from winter to spring, goosegrass inhabits alluvial woods, roadsides, gardens, and disturbed sites throughout much of the U.S. *G. tinctorium* (L.) Scop., stiff marsh bedstraw, is a perennial herb with corollas that are usually three lobed. This species inhabits wet woods, ditches, and swamps, and its range extends throughout much of the eastern half of the U.S.

Hamelia patens Jacq.

FIRE BUSH

This is an evergreen, suffruticose shrub up to 4 m tall. With reddened veins and petioles, three to several elliptic or ovate leaves are whorled. The bright orange-red flowers are tubular and arranged in terminal cymes. Fruits are red or black berries with many seeds. Blooming throughout the year, fire bush inhabits hammocks and disturbed sites in peninsular FL. With flowers that attract butterflies and hummingbirds, this attractive species is a popular southern ornamental.

Houstonia micrantha (Shinners) Terrell

SOUTHERN BLUET

From a taproot, this clumping annual herb produces erect stems, each up to 3 cm tall. The oppositely arranged leaves are spathulate or ovate with glabrous margins. Solitary white, salverform flowers are terminal. Fruits are two-chambered capsules; each is enclosed partially by a persistent calyx tube. Blooming from winter to spring, southern bluet inhabits pastures, roadsides, lawns, gardens, and disturbed sites from eastern TX and OK to central GA. *H. procumbens* (Walt. ex J.F. Gmel.) Standl., roundleaf bluet, is a creeping perennial with leaves that bear cilia on their margins. This species inhabits pinelands, beaches, and dunes, and its range extends from southeastern LA to FL and north to southeastern SC.

Houstonia pusilla Schoepf

TINY BLUET

Mitchella repens L.

PARTRIDGEBERRY

From a slender taproot, this annual herb produces one to several winged stems, each up to 6 cm tall. The oppositely arranged leaves are ovate, lanceolate, or spathulate with minute translucent teeth on their margins. Flowers are solitary on long axillary peduncles. The salverform corollas are lavender or purple with a reddish center. Fruits are two-chambered capsules with numerous small seeds. Blooming from winter to spring, tiny bluet inhabits pastures, prairies, fields, and lawns from TX to SD and east to the Atlantic coastal states as far north as MD. *H. caerulea* L., azure bluet, has pale blue flowers with yellow centers. This species inhabits alluvial woods, fields, and lawns; its range extends from LA to MI and east to the Atlantic coastal states as far north as ME.

This mat-forming evergreen vine produces several trailing stems that bear adventitious roots. The oppositely arranged ovate or orbicular, coriaceous evergreen leaves have rounded or cordate bases. Two fragrant flowers with united ovaries are borne on a terminal peduncle. The white or pinkish corollas are funnelform and densely bearded within. Each fruit is an aggregate of two bright red drupes with eight seeds. Blooming from spring to summer, partridgeberry inhabits mesic woods, bogs, and stream banks throughout much of the eastern half of the U.S. An extract derived from boiling the leaves was used by Native Americans to facilitate childbirth.

Mitracarpus hirtus (L.) DC.

SMOOTH BUTTONWEED

From fibrous roots, this perennial herb produces simple or branching, erect or decumbent stems, each up to 6 dm long. The oppositely arranged leaves are elliptic or lanceolate and prominently veined. Stipules are sheathing with several filiform bristles. Flowers are densely arranged in sessile, terminal, and axillary headlike clusters. White four-lobed corollas are tubular and bearded within. The fruits are turban-shaped capsules crowned by the persistent calyx lobes. Blooming in summer, smooth buttonweed inhabits wet woods, depressions, and river banks from eastern TX to southeastern KS and east to the Atlantic coastal states as far north as MD. Similar in appearance, *Spermacoce assurgens* Ruiz & Pavón, woodland false buttonweed, has purplish leaves and ellipsoid capsules. This species inhabits gardens, lawns, roadsides, and disturbed sites; its range extends from southern MS to FL.

Oldenlandia corymbosa L.

FLAT-TOP MILLE GRAINES

From a taproot, this annual herb produces erect or decumbent branching stems, each up to 5 dm long. The oppositely arranged leaves are lanceolate or elliptic and sessile. On slender, filiform axillary peduncles, the flowers are solitary or arranged in few-flowered cymes. The corollas are white and rotate. Enclosed by the calyx, each fruit is a capsule with numerous angled seeds. Blooming from summer to fall, flat-top mille graines inhabits lawns and disturbed sites from eastern TX to FL and north to NC. *O. boscii* (DC.) Chapm., Bosc's mille graines, has sessile flowers. This species inhabits lawns and disturbed sites, and its range extends from eastern TX to southern MO and east to the Atlantic coastal states as far north as southern VA.

Richardia scabra L.

MEXICAN CLOVER

This is a branching, pubescent annual with decumbent stems up to 8 dm long. The oppositely arranged hairy leaves are lanceolate or ovate and somewhat coriaceous. White, tubular, funnelform flowers are arranged in terminal heads that are subtended by several leaflike bracts. Fruits are thickened, tuberculate schizocarps. Blooming throughout the year, Mexican clover inhabits roadsides, fields, and disturbed sites from eastern TX to FL and north to NJ. *R. brasiliensis* Gomes, tropical Mexican clover, is a perennial herb with a thickened rhizome and hairy fruit. Its range extends from southern TX to FL and north to NJ.

Sherardia arvensis L.

FIELDMADDER

From slender roots, this annual herb produces several erect or decumbent stems, each up to 4 dm long. Arranged in whorls, the leaves are lanceolate or oblanceolate with hyaline margins. Flowers are borne in axillary and terminal headlike clusters that are subtended by leaflike bracts. Corollas are lavender or pinkish and funnelform. Fruits are pubescent schizocarps with two seeds each. Blooming from winter to spring, fieldmadder inhabits fields, roadsides, and pastures throughout much of the eastern half of the U.S. This weedy introduction is native to Europe, north Africa, and the Middle East.

Stenaria nigricans (Lam.) Terrell var. *nigricans*

DIAMONDFLOWERS

From a stout taproot, this perennial herb produces one to several ascending, branching stems, each up to 5 dm tall. The oppositely arranged leaves are lanceolate, linear, or filiform and sessile. Arranged in terminal cymes, the funnelform flowers are white or pinkish. Fruits are turbinate capsules. Blooming from spring to summer, diamondflowers inhabits open woods and roadsides from AZ to MI and east to the Atlantic coastal states as far north as southwestern VA.

Polygonatum biflorum (Walt.) Ell.

SOLOMON'S SEAL

From an elongated, knotty rhizome, this perennial herb produces a simple arching stem up to 1 m long. The alternately arranged leaves are lanceolate or elliptic, sessile, glabrous, and glaucous. Solitay or in clusters, the pendulous, tubular, greenish white flowers are borne in the leaf axils. Fruits are dark blue berries with yellowish seeds. Blooming in spring and summer, Solomon's seal inhabits rich mesic hardwoods throughout much of the U.S. east of the Rocky Mountains. Native Americans used the plant to treat a wide variety of ailments.

Sapindaceae

Cardiospermum halicacabum L.

LOVE IN A PUFF

This trailing or climbing, herbaceous perennial vine produces stems up to 3 m long. The alternately arranged leaves are twice pinnately compound. Leaflets are ovate, lanceolate, or rhombic and coarsely lobed or toothed. Tendrils are borne in the leaf axils. Arranged in open panicles, the small white flowers have four sepals and four irregularly shaped petals. Fruits are inflated capsules with black seeds. Blooming in summer and fall, love in a puff inhabits disturbed open sites throughout much of the eastern U.S. Although the plants are grown as ornamentals, they can become invasive.

Sarraceniaceae

Sarracenia alata Wood

WINGED PITCHERPLANT

From a rhizome, this insectivorous perennial herb produces erect basal leaves up to 7.5 dm long. The hooded, vaselike leaves are marked with red or purplish veins. A solitary nodding, yellow-green flower terminates the glabrous scape. Each of the five petals hangs across a curved edge of the umbrella-shaped style. Fruits are capsules with numerous small hydroscopic seeds. Blooming in spring, winged pitcherplant inhabits wet pinelands, savannas, bogs, and seeps from central TX to southern AL. Its leaves secrete nectar that attracts insect prey. Once inside the leaf, insects become trapped by retrorse hairs. As enzymes digest the prey, nitrogen-rich compounds are absorbed.

Sarracenia flava L.

YELLOW PITCHERPLANT

This insectivorous perennial herb produces leaves up to 1 m tall. The tubular,
hooded leaves are greenish-yellow with
an irregular-shaped purplish splotch
below the hood. The large yellow, nodding flowers have a musty scent. Blooming in spring, yellow pitcherplant inhabits wet pinelands, savannas, and
sphagnum bogs from southern MS
to northern FL and north to eastern
VA. Native Americans used the leaves
of this and other pitcherplant species
as drinking vessels when traveling.

Sarracenia leucophylla Raf.

WHITE-TOP PITCHERPLANT

From a large rhizome, this insectivorous
perennial herb produces tubular, winged
leaves up to 1 m tall. Green below, leaves
become white with prominent green or
red veins distally. The hoods have ruffled
margins and bear short, stiff white hairs
on their lower surfaces. On a scape up to
8 dm tall, the large, showy flower is maroon or red. Fruits are capsules with numerous reticulate, winged seeds. Blooming in spring, white-top pitcherplant
inhabits wet pinelands, savannas, and
bogs from southeastern MS to northwestern FL and southwestern GA. This
species is endangered in FL and GA.

Sarracenia minor Walt.

HOODED PITCHERPLANT

This is an insectivorous perennial herb with leaves up to 4 dm tall. The winged leaves are green and colored with reddish orange distally. A recurved hood bearing translucent spots arches over the mouth. The bright yellow flower is solitary on a scape up to 5 dm tall. Fruits are capsules with many tuberculate, club-shaped seeds. Blooming in spring, hooded pitcherplant inhabits wet pinelands, savannas, and bogs from southern FL to southern GA and north to southeastern NC. This species is threatened in FL.

Sarracenia psittacina Michx.

PARROT PITCHERPLANT

From a rhizome, this perennial herb produces tubular, winged decumbent leaves in a basal rosette. Inflated, beaked hoods are whitish and prominently veined with red. Their margins are united to form a circular mouth. The maroon or dark red flower is solitary on a scape up to 3.5 dm tall. Fruits are capsules with numerous obovate, reticulate seeds. Blooming in spring, parrot pitcherplant inhabits wet pinelands, savannas, and bogs from southeastern LA to northern FL and southern GA. This species is threatened in FL and GA.

Sarracenia purpurea L. ssp. *purpurea*

PURPLE PITCHERPLANT

From a stout rhizome, this insectivorous perennial herb produces decumbent, urn-shaped leaves. Each leaf is green or purplish with red veins and bears short, stiff hairs from without. A reniform-shaped hood with retrorse hairs partially surrounds the mouth. Up to 7 dm tall, the scape bears a single nodding, reddish or maroon flower. Fruits are five-chambered capsules with numerous seeds. Blooming from spring to summer, purple pitcherplant inhabits wet pinelands, savannas, bogs, and swamps from southeastern LA to northwestern FL and north to NJ. *S. purpurea* L. ssp. *gibbosa* (Raf.) Wherry has leaves that are glabrous from without. This species inhabits pine barrens, savannas, bogs, and swamps; its range extends from VA to MN and north to Canada.

Sarracenia rosea Naczi, F.W. Case & R.B. Case

ROSY PITCHERPLANT

From a stout rhizome, this insectivorous, evergreen perennial herb produces a basal rosette of urn-shaped leaves. Colored green or purplish with red veins, leaves exhibit a bristly, collar-shaped hood around the mouth. A solitary nodding flower terminates the single scape. Sepals are dark red or maroon and the petals are pink. Fruits are capsules with many seeds. Blooming in spring, rosy pitcherplant inhabits wet pinelands, savannas, and bogs from southern MS to northwestern FL.

Sarracenia rubra Walt. ssp. *rubra*

SWEET PITCHERPLANT

Saururus cernuus L.

LIZARD'S TAIL

This insectivorous perennial herb produces basal leaves, each up to 6 dm tall. The hooded green or copper-colored leaves are heavily veined with red. Nectar secreted around the mouth attracts insect prey. A solitary, sweetly fragrant flower is nodding on a glabrous scape that overtops the leaves. Sepals and petals are colored red or maroon on their upper surfaces but are greenish below. Blooming from spring to summer, sweet pitcherplant inhabits wet pinelands, savannas, and sphagnum bogs in scattered populations along the coastal plain from MS to NC. *S. rubra* Walt. ssp. *gulfensis* Schnell has taller leaves, and its range extends from southern AL to northwestern FL. Distinguished by its short and mostly green leaves, *S. rubra* Walt. ssp. *alabamensis* (F.W. & R.B. Case) Schnell from central AL is listed as federally endangered.

Typically occurring in dense colonies, this rhizomatous herb produces stems up to 1.2 m tall. The alternately arranged ovate leaves are basally cordate with acuminate tips. At first nodding, the racemes of densely arranged, fragrant white flowers become erect with maturity. Perianth parts are absent. Fruits are schizocarps that divide into indehiscent mericarps. Blooming from spring to summer, lizard's tail inhabits swamps, wet woods, and fresh to slightly brackish marshes throughout much of the eastern U.S. as far north as Canada. Native Americans made a poultice from its roots for the treatment of wounds and insect bites.

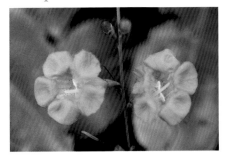

Agalinis fasciculata (Ell.) Raf.
BEACH FALSE FOXGLOVE

This annual herb produces a single branching, scabrous stem up to 1.2 m tall. The oppositely arranged leaves are linear with well-developed fascicles in the axils. Flowers are arranged in elongated racemes. Corollas are bilabiate and pink with darker spots and yellow lines within. Calyxes are campanulate with lobes that are shorter than the tube. Fruits are globose capsules. Blooming from summer to fall, beach false foxglove inhabits wet pinelands, savannas, marshes, and lake margins from eastern TX, OK, and KS to the Atlantic coastal states as far north as Long Island, NY. *A. heterophylla* (Nutt.) Small ex Britt., prairie false foxglove, has calyx lobes that are about as long as the tube and smooth stems. This species inhabits open woods, prairies, and fields; its range extends from eastern TX, OK, KS, and southern MO to GA.

Agalinis oligophylla Pennell
RIDGESTEM FALSE FOXGLOVE

This annual herb produces a solitary wiry, ribbed, branching stem up to 1 m tall. The oppositely arranged minute leaves are linear and ascending. Bilabiate flowers are arranged in numerous axillary racemes. Pink corollas are marked with darker spots and often with yellow lines from within; the lobes are spreading. Fruits are globose capsules with reticulate seeds. Blooming from summer to fall, ridgestem false foxglove inhabits wet pinelands, savannas, prairies, and bogs from southeastern TX to southern AL. *A. aphylla* (Nutt.) Raf., scaleleaf false foxglove, is distinguished by its scalelike leaves that are appressed to the stem. Its range extends from southeastern LA to northern FL and north to southeastern NC.

Agalinis purpurea (L.) Pennell
PURPLE FALSE FOXGLOVE

This branching annual produces glabrous or sparsely pubescent arching stems, each up to 1.2 m long. The oppositely arranged leaves are linear and somewhat revolute. Flowers are borne in elongated racemes. The bilabiate corollas are pink or purple and marked with purple spots and yellow lines from within. Fruits are globose capsules. Blooming from summer to fall, purple false foxglove inhabits wet pinelands, savannas, prairies, and bogs throughout much of the eastern U.S. *A. harperi* Pennell, coastal plain false foxglove, has leaves with involute margins. This species inhabits wet pinelands and savannas, and its range extends from western LA to northern FL and southern GA.

Aureolaria virginica (L.) Pennell
FALSE FOXGLOVE

This perennial herb produces solitary or sparingly branched, pubescent stems, each up to 1 m tall. Opposite below, the coarsely lobed, lanceolate leaves become alternately arranged distally. Terminal and borne in the upper leaf axils, the waxy yellow, campanulate flowers are weakly bilabiate. The four stamens are didynamous. Fruits are ovoid, pubescent capsules with winged seeds. Blooming from summer to fall, false foxglove is partially parasitic on oak trees in deciduous woods from southeastern TX to northern FL and north to NH. *A. pectinata* (Nutt.) Pennell, cornleaf false foxglove, has comb-shaped leaves and glandular-pubescent stems. It inhabits open woods and sandhills, and its range extends from southeastern TX to FL and north to VA.

Bacopa caroliniana (Walt.)
B. L. Robins.

BLUE HYSSOP

This is a mat-forming, aromatic perennial herb with creeping rhizomes. Up
to 3 dm long, the succulent stems are
emergent in shallow water. Oppositely
arranged, the ovate leaves have broad,
clasping bases. Subtended by two linear
bracts, flowers are solitary in the upper
leaf axils. Corollas are blue and bilabiate.
Fruits are capsules with reticulate, irides-
cent seeds. Blooming from spring to
summer, blue hyssop inhabits marshes,
streams, lake margins, and ditches from
eastern TX to FL and north to MD.
B. innominata (G. Maza) Alain, tropical water hyssop, has white flowers and
leaves that are not aromatic. This species inhabits marshes and ditches, and
its range extends from peninsular FL to
southeastern NC.

Bacopa monnieri (L.) Pennell

WATER HYSSOP

This mat-forming perennial herb produces branching, glabrous prostrate
stems. The oppositely arranged succulent
leaves are spathulate or oblanceolate
with entire margins. On slender pedicels, the bilabiate, tubular flowers are
solitary in the leaf axils. Corollas are pale
lavender, pinkish, or white. Enclosed by
the persisting calyx, the fruits are ovoid
capsules with reticulate, olive-colored
seeds. Blooming from spring to fall,
water hyssop inhabits fresh and brackish marshes, ditches, and lake margins
from TX to FL and north to southeastern VA. *B. egensis* (Poepp.) Pennell,
Brazilian water hyssop, is distinguished
by its toothed leaves. A native of tropical America, it has become established
in ponds, marshes, and ditches in LA.

Buchnera americana L.

BLUEHEARTS

This perennial herb has a simple stem up to 8 dm tall. The oppositely arranged leaves are elliptic or lanceolate and sessile with entire or coarsely toothed margins. Arranged in a terminal spike, each salverform flower is subtended by scalelike bracts. Fruits are ovoid capsules with numerous seeds. Blooming from spring to summer, bluehearts inhabits wet pinelands, savannas, and prairies from TX to KS and east to the Atlantic coastal states as far north as NY. Through modified roots called haustoria, this species is hemiparasitic on the roots of neighboring host plants.

Castilleja indivisa Engelm.

TEXAS PAINTBRUSH

From a slender taproot, this annual herb produces a hairy stem up to 4 dm tall. The alternately arranged sessile leaves have lobed or entire margins. Arranged in spikes, the white, pink, red, or green bilabiate flowers are subtended by showy, orange-red entire bracts. Fruits are ovoid capsules with numerous seeds. Blooming in spring, Texas paintbrush inhabits prairies, fields, and roadsides from eastern TX and OK to western LA and western AR. *C. coccinea* (L.) Spreng., scarlet Indian paintbrush, has flowers subtended by three-lobed bracts. This species inhabits wood margins and roadsides, and its range extends throughout much of the eastern half of the U.S. excluding TX. Members of the genus obtain a portion of their nutrients by parasitizing various plants.

Gratiola brevifolia Raf.
STICKY HEDGEHYSSOP

From a slender rhizome, this colonial perennial herb produces a simple or branching, decumbent, glandular-hairy stem up to 6 dm long. The oppositely arranged leaves are lanceolate or linear and clasping with entire or distally toothed margins. On slender axillary pedicels, each solitary bilabiate flower is subtended by a pair of sepal-like bracts. Corollas are white; the tube is greenish yellow and marked with brownish or purplish veins. Fruits are globose capsules with many tiny, reticulate seeds. Blooming from spring to summer, sticky hedgehyssop inhabits wet woods and lake margins from southeastern TX and OK to northern FL and north to southern DE. *G. ramosa* Walt., branched hedgehyssop, has bractless pedicels. This species inhabits wet pinelands, savannas, lake margins, and ditches; its range extends from southwestern LA to FL and north to southeastern NC.

Mazus pumilus (Burm. f.) Steenis
JAPANESE MAZUS

This is an annual herb that produces decumbent basal stems. Leaves on the lower portion of the stem are petiolate and oppositely arranged with irregularly toothed margins. The upper leaves are alternate and bractlike. Flowers are borne in terminal zigzagged racemes. The bilabiate corollas are lavender or purple with yellow markings on the lower lip. Fruits are globose capsules with numerous minute seeds. Blooming throughout the year, this native of southeastern Asia has become naturalized and inhabits lawns, gardens, fields, and roadsides throughout much of the eastern U.S.

Mecardonia acuminata (Walt.)
Small var. *acuminata*

AXILFLOWER

From a woody crown, this perennial
herb produces one to several erect or
ascending, glabrous stems, each up to
7 dm long. The oppositely arranged
leaves are oblanceolate, sessile, and
punctate with toothed margins. Flowers are solitary and borne in the leaf axils. The bilabiate corollas are white and
marked with purple veins; the upper lip
is bearded within. Fruits are capsules
with numerous reticulate seeds. Blooming from summer to fall, axilflower
inhabits wet pinelands, savannas, prairies, swamps, and bogs from eastern
TX, OK, and southeastern KS to the
Atlantic coastal states as far north as
southern DE. *M. procumbens* (P. Mill.)
Small, baby jump-up, has yellow flowers. This species inhabits streams, pond
margins, and ditches, and its range
extends from southern AZ to FL.

Mimulus alatus Ait.

MONKEY FLOWER

This stoloniferous perennial herb produces hollow, square stems that are
winged on the edges. Oppositely arranged petiolate leaves are broadly
lanceolate with toothed margins. Lavender-blue bilabiate flowers are solitary
in the upper leaf axils. The lower lip is
three-lobed with the central lobe ex-
hibiting a yellow beard; the upper lip
is erect. Stamens are didynamous. The
calyx is composed of connate sepals with
mucronate apices. Blooming from summer to fall, monkey flower inhabits wet
woods, swamps, marshes, and ditches
throughout much of the eastern U.S.
M. ringens L., Allegheny monkey flower,
has sessile leaves and wingless stems.
This species inhabits wet woods, and
its range extends throughout much of
the U.S. east of the Rocky Mountains.

Nuttallanthus canadensis (L.)
D.A. Sutton

TOADFLAX

From a small mass of fibrous roots, this
annual or biennial herb produces several
short, sterile basal stems and a solitary
flowering stem up to 7 dm tall. Leaves
are linear. Those along the flowering
stem are alternately arranged, whereas
those on the sterile stems are whorled.
Violet-colored bilabiate flowers are
spurred and arranged in a loose terminal raceme. Each corolla is less than
1 cm long. Fruits are subglobose capsules with sharp-edged seeds. Blooming from spring to summer, toadflax
inhabits open woods, fields, pastures,
roadsides, and disturbed sites throughout much of the eastern half of the U.S.
N. texanus (Scheele) D.A. Sutton, Texas
toadflax, has corollas that exceed 1 cm
long. This species inhabits open woods,
pinelands, and fields; its range extends
throughout much of the U.S. excluding
the Northeast and upper Midwest.

Pedicularis canadensis L. ssp.
canadensis

LOUSEWORT

This hemiparasitic perennial herb produces one to several stems from a short
rhizome. The alternately arranged, narrowly elliptic, pinnately dissected leaves
are fernlike. Yellow, red, or purple flowers are densely arranged in a spike. As
viewed from above, the flowers appear
to be swept in a counterclockwise swirl.
Individual flowers are bilabiate; the upper lip is hood-shaped. Stamens are didynamous. Fruits are capsules, each with
a small beak. Blooming from spring to
summer, lousewort inhabits dry or mesic
woods and prairies throughout much of
the U.S. east of the Rocky Mountains.
Native Americans used an infusion of
the roots to treat stomachaches, coughs,
and dysentery.

Penstemon laxiflorus Pennell

BEARDTONGUE

This is a slender perennial herb with a single stem up to 6 dm tall. The lower leaves are narrowly elliptic or lanceolate and petiolate; the upper leaves are narrowly lanceolate or linear and sessile. Lavender, pink, or nearly white bilabiate flowers are arranged in a terminal panicle. Protruding from the corolla is a single staminode bearing a yellow beard. The four stamens are didynamous. Blooming in spring, beardtongue inhabits woods margins, savannas, and pinelands from eastern TX and southern OK to FL and GA. *P. digitalis* Nutt. ex. Sims, nodding beardtongue, is a taller species with white corollas. This species inhabits open woods, prairies, and fields, and its range extends throughout much of the eastern U.S.

Scutellaria drummondii Benth. var. *drummondii*

DRUMMOND'S SKULLCAP

This annual herb produces an erect stem up to 3 dm tall and several basal, procumbent stems. The leaves are oppositely arranged and ovate. The basal ones are shallowly toothed, whereas the upper ones are entire. Bilabiate flowers are arranged in pairs in the leaf axils. Corollas are violet or purple and bilabiate. The upper lip is hood-shaped; the lower lip is three-lobed and marked with white. Fruits are gray-brown, pubescent schizocarps. Blooming from winter to spring, Drummond's skullcap inhabits open rocky woods, lawns, and disturbed sites from eastern TX to northern FL. *S. cardiophylla* Engelm. & Gray, Gulf skullcap, is a taller plant with deltoid leaves. It inhabits open woods and fields from eastern TX and western LA to southern AR.

Scutellaria integrifolia L.

HYSSOP SKULLCAP

This is a rhizomatous perennial herb
with square-shaped stems, each up to
6 dm tall. The lower leaves are mostly
ovate and often toothed. Becoming
gradually reduced upward, leaves along
the stem are oblong or lanceolate and
entire. Arranged in terminal racemes,
the purple-blue flowers are subtended
by small, leaflike bracts. Flowers are bilabiate; the upper lip is hood-shaped,
and the lower lip is slightly notched
in the middle. The bilabiate sepals become enlarged and spoon-shaped as
the schizocarps mature. Blooming
from spring to summer, hyssop skullcap inhabits wet woods, meadows, and
pinelands from eastern Texas, OK, and
MO east to the Atlantic coastal states as
far north as MA. *S. ovata* Hill, heartleaf
skullcap, is distinguished by its cordate
leaves. It inhabits open, dry woods
throughout much of the eastern U.S.

Verbascum thapsus L.

MULLEIN

This introduced biennial herb is densely
gray-woolly throughout. A basal rosette
of petiolate, oblong or oblanceolate
leaves is produced the first year. A thickened floral stalk up to 2 m tall with
alternately arranged sessile leaves is
produced the second year. Terminating
the stalk is a spike of densely arranged
yellow, fragrant, and slightly irregular
flowers. Fruits are ovoid capsules with
many seeds. Blooming from spring
to fall, mullein inhabits fields, roadsides, open woods, and disturbed sites
throughout much of the U.S. This species is used in traditional herbal medicine to treat a wide variety of ailments.

Veronica persica Poir.

PERSIAN SPEEDWELL

This introduced annual herb has hairy, decumbent stems, each up to 4 dm long. Opposite below and alternate above, the mostly ovate leaves bear rounded teeth on their margins. Borne on long petioles, the flowers are solitary in the upper leaf axils. Corollas are blue with whitish centers and marked with darker lines. Fruits are broadly cleft, flattened capsules. Blooming from winter to spring, Persian speedwell inhabits roadsides, lawns, gardens, and disturbed sites throughout much of the U.S. *V. arvensis* L., corn speedwell, is an introduced annual that bears its flowers in erect terminal racemes. This species inhabits roadsides and disturbed sites, and its range also extends throughout much of the U.S.

Smilacaceae

Smilax laurifolia L.

BAMBOOVINE

From a robust, tuberous rhizome, this high-climbing dioecious vine produces green stems with sharp prickles. The alternately arranged leaves are oblong and coriaceous. Each petiole bears two tendrils. Small, greenish, unisexual flowers are arranged in axillary umbels. Fruits are glossy, glaucous, globose black berries. Blooming from summer to fall, bamboovine inhabits upland swamps, cypress swamps, savannas, bogs, and seeps from eastern TX and OK to FL and north to southern NJ. Also a high-climbing species, *S. walteri* Pursh, coral greenbrier, has nontuberous rhizomes, ovate or lanceolate leaves, and bright red berries. This species inhabits swamps, and its range extends from TX to FL and north to southern NJ.

Smilax smallii Morong

LANCELEAF GREENBRIER

From a large, thick, tuberous rhizome, this evergreen vine produces high-climbing stems with tendrils. The alternately arranged leaves are glossy green with entire margins. Arranged in umbels, inconspicuous greenish, unisexual flowers are axillary in the distal stem nodes. The peduncle is about the same length as the subtending leaf petiole. Fruits are red or black berries, each containing a single seed. Blooming in summer, lanceleaf greenbrier inhabits open woods, thickets, and swamp margins from eastern TX and OK to FL and north to southeastern VA. *S. bona-nox* L., saw greenbrier, has leaf margins that often bear spines and peduncles that are at least 1.5 times as long as the subtending leaf petiole. This species inhabits open woods, thickets, and disturbed sites; its range extends throughout much of the Southeast and lower Midwest.

Smilax pumila Walt.

SARSPARILLA VINE

This trailing or low-climbing evergreen vine produces unarmed stems, each up to 5 dm long. Woolly on their lower surfaces, the basally cordate leaves are ovate, elliptic, or lanceolate. The inconspicuous unisexual flowers are arranged in axillary umbels. Fruits are bright red berries, each containing a single red seed. Blooming in fall, sarsparilla vine inhabits open, sandy woods, pinelands, and stream banks from eastern TX to FL and north to SC. *Smilax herbacea* L., smooth carrionflower, is an herbaceous vine with ovate leaves, ill-scented flowers, and blue-black berries. This species inhabits open woods and roadsides, and its range extends throughout much of the eastern half of the U.S., excluding FL.

Solanaceae

Datura stramonium L.

JIMSONWEED

From a short taproot, this is a branching annual herb up to 1.5 m tall. On long petioles, the leaf blades are ovate or elliptic and irregularly lobed. Both alternately and oppositely arranged leaves may occur on the same plant. Ill-scented flowers are borne singly in the forks of branching stems. The funnelform corollas are white and often suffused with lavender. Fruits are prickly, ovoid capsules with black, pitted, reniform seeds. Blooming from spring to fall, Jimsonweed inhabits disturbed sites throughout much of the U.S. All parts of the plant, especially the seeds, are toxic and hallucinogenic.

Lycium carolinianum Walt. var. *quadrifidum* (Dunal) C.L. Hitchc.

CHRISTMAS BERRY

This is a sparingly branching shrub up to 1 m tall. Young branchlets often bear spines. The alternately arranged leaves are narrowly oblanceolate, sessile, and succulent. Emerging from the leaf axils, short spur shoots bear leafy fascicles. Solitary in the leaf axils, the tubular rotate flowers are blue or lavender. Fruits are bright red berries with numerous seeds. Blooming in fall, Christmas berry inhabits sand dunes and fresh and brackish marshes from southeastern TX to southern MS. Occurring in similar habitats, *L. carolinianum* var. *carolinianum* has a range that extends from southern AL to FL and north to eastern SC.

Physalis angulata L.

CUTLEAF GROUNDCHERRY

This is a freely branching, glabrous annual herb up to 1 m tall. The alternately
arranged leaves are petiolate with lanceolate or ovate blades and irregularly
toothed margins. Solitary flowers are
borne in the leaf axils. The campanulate
corollas are yellow and marked with
brown from within; the anthers are blue.
Fruits are globose, yellow-orange berries with numerous seeds enclosed by
an inflated, ten-ribbed, purple-veined
calyx. Blooming from spring to summer, cutleaf groundcherry inhabits
fields, roadsides, and open woods from
CA to the Atlantic coastal states as
far north as MA. When ripe, fruits of
most groundcherry species are edible;
however, the leaves are poisonous.

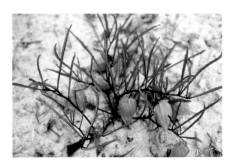

Physalis angustifolia Nutt.

COASTAL GROUNDCHERRY

From a long taproot, this glabrous perennial herb produces freely branching,
ascending, purplish stems. The oppositely arranged leaves are linear or narrowly oblanceolate and folded along
the purplish midrib. The flowers are
solitary on axillary stalks. Corollas are
yellow and marked with purple. Fruits
are globose berries enclosed by an inflated green or yellow calyx. Blooming
from spring to fall, coastal groundcherry
inhabits coastal dunes from southeastern LA to FL. *P. walteri* Nutt., Walter's
groundcherry, is clothed in stellate hairs
throughout and its leaves are ovate or
elliptic. This species inhabits coastal
dunes, roadsides, and wood margins;
its range extends from southern MS
to FL and north to southeastern VA.

Physalis cinerascens (Dunal)
Hitch. var. *spathulifolia* (Torr.)
J. R. Sullivan

SMALLFLOWER GROUNDCHERRY

From a long taproot, this is a freely
branching perennial herb that is densely
beset with stellate hairs throughout.
The alternately arranged leaves are
spathulate, ovate, or lanceolate with
undulate margins and winged petioles.
The nodding flowers are solitary on
axillary stalks. The rotate corollas are
yellow and marked with purple spots
from within. Fruits are globose berries
enclosed by an inflated calyx. Blooming from spring to fall, smallflower
groundcherry inhabits coastal dunes
from eastern TX to southwestern LA.
P. cinerascens (Dunal) Hitch. var. *cinerascens* has ovate or reniform leaves.
This species inhabits xeric, often rocky
sites, and its range extends from TX to
southern MO and east to TN and AL.

Physalis cordata P. Mill.

HEARTLEAF GROUNDCHERRY

Glabrous or with a few short hairs, this
is a branching annual herb up to 1.5 m
tall. The alternately arranged leaves are
ovate and irregularly toothed. Solitary
yellow, campanulate flowers with hairy
throats are borne in the leaf axils. Hairy
filaments support the bluish anthers.
Fruits are spherical berries; each is enclosed by an inflated, five-angled, glabrous calyx. Blooming from spring to
fall, heartleaf groundcherry inhabits
wood margins, roadsides, and disturbed
sites from eastern TX and OK to FL
and north to eastern NC. *P. pubescens* L.,
husk tomato, is a villous species with a
hairy, fruiting calyx. This species inhabits open woods, and its range extends
throughout much of the U.S. excluding
the upper Plains States.

Solanum carolinense L.

SOLANUM CAROLINENSE L.

HORSE NETTLE

From a creeping rhizome, this coarse perennial produces branching erect stems, each up to 1 m tall. Vegetative parts are spiny and pubescent with stellate hairs. Spiny along the main veins, the ovate or lanceolate leaves are often shallowly lobed. Arranged in axillary racemes, the salverform flowers are white or lavender. Fruits are globose yellow berries. Blooming from spring to fall, horse nettle inhabits open woods, fields, roadsides, and disturbed sites throughout much of the U.S. *S. americanum* P. Mill., American black nightshade, has black fruits and smaller flowers. This species inhabits open woods, fields, and disturbed sites; its range extends throughout much of the U.S. excluding the West Coast.

Solanum elaeagnifolium Cav.

SILVERLEAF NIGHTSHADE

Densely covered with stellate hairs, this perennial herb has a silvery appearance. Freely branching stems up to 1 m tall are armed with light brown spines. The alternately arranged leaves are mostly lanceolate. Lavender or purple flowers are arranged in axillary panicles. Large, conspicuous anthers are held erect. Fruits are globose yellow berries. Blooming from spring to fall, silverleaf nightshade occurs in fields, roadsides, and other disturbed sites throughout much of the southern U.S. *S. rostratum* Dunal, buffalobur nightshade, has yellow corollas. This species inhabits fields and disturbed sites, and its range extends throughout much of the U.S.

Sterculiaceae

Melochia corchorifolia L.

CHOCOLATE WEED

From a taproot, this introduced annual herb produces branching stems, each up to 1.5 m long. The alternately arranged leaves are ovate with irregularly toothed margins and linear or lanceolate stipules. Headlike cymes of densely arranged purplish or pinkish flowers are sub-tended by several leaflike bracts. Fruits are globose, hairy capsules. Blooming from spring to fall, chocolate weed in-habits fields, roadsides, and disturbed sites from eastern TX to southern IL and east to the Atlantic coastal states as far north as eastern NC. *M. pyramidata* L., pyramidflower, is a slender native shrub with pink or violet flowers. This species inhabits open woods, ditches, and disturbed sites; its range extends from southern TX to southern LA.

Tofieldiaceae

Triantha racemosa (Walt.) Small

FALSE ASPHODEL

This is a slender perennial herb with a short, creeping rhizome. The basal leaves are linear, erect, and equitant. A raceme of creamy white flowers terminates a solitary glandular scape. A single bract is located near the middle of the scape. Fruits are obovoid capsules with red-dish brown, ellipsoid seeds. Blooming in summer, false asphodel inhabits wet pinelands and savannas from eastern TX to northern FL and north to central NJ. Similar in appearance, *Tofieldia glabra* Nutt., smooth tofieldia, is distinguished by its glabrous scape. This species in-habits savannas and upland sandhill swamps, and its range extends from northeastern SC to southeastern NC.

Trilliaceae

Trillium gracile J.D. Freeman

SABINE RIVER WAKEROBIN

This is a rhizomatous perennial herb that produces a solitary scape. Three ovate or obovate, leaflike bracts are sessile, mottled with various shades of green, and subtended by a solitary terminal, musty-smelling flower. Three lanceolate sepals are dark purple and recurved; the three narrowly elliptic, erect petals are dark purple or maroon. Stamens are about twice the length of the carpel. Mature fruits are green-purple capsules with many seeds. Blooming in spring, Sabine River wakerobin inhabits rich, sandy deciduous woods and stream banks from eastern TX to western LA. *T. foetidissimum* J.D. Freeman, Mississippi River wakerobin, has carrion-scented flowers and its stamens are about as long as the carpel. This species inhabits wet woods, and its range extends from southeastern LA to southwestern MS.

Trillium ludovicianum Harbison

LOUISIANA WAKEROBIN

From a short, thick rhizome, this perennial herb produces a scape up to 2.6 dm tall. Subtending the solitary flower are three mottled, sessile, narrowly ovate, leaflike bracts. Flowers are sessile with the odor of carrion. The erect or spreading petals are greenish maroon and slightly clawed. Fruits are six-angled, ovoid, purplish-green capsules. Blooming in spring, Louisiana wakerobin inhabits wet pinelands, stream banks, and wooded ravines from central Louisiana to southwestern MS. *T. cuneatum* Raf., little sweet Betsy, has erect petals that are not clawed. Its range extends from central MS to central GA and north to western NC and southern KY.

Turneraceae

Piriqueta cistoides (L.) Griseb. ssp. *caroliniana* (Walt.) Arbo

PITTED STRIPESEED

This perennial herb produces colonies from root shoots. Up to 5 dm tall, the stems are densely pubescent with stellate and long, spreading hairs. The alternately arranged leaves are lanceolate or oblong and pubescent on both surfaces. The bright orange-yellow flowers are arranged in a terminal raceme. Fruits are capsules with tan or gray ribbed seeds. Blooming from spring to fall, pitted stripeseed inhabits sandy wood margins, roadsides, and disturbed sites from southern AL to FL and north to southeastern SC. This species is noteworthy for its extensive range that also includes Central America, South America, and the Caribbean.

Typhaceae

Typha latifolia L.

CATTAIL

From a stout rhizome, this perennial herb produces both vegetative and flowering shoots, each up to 3 m tall. The flat, linear leaves are sheathing and are collectively fan shaped. Flowers are unisexual and arranged in a spike. The segment of staminate flowers typically is contiguous with the segment of carpellate flowers. Comose fruits are shed in masses. Blooming from spring to summer, cattail inhabits marshes, ditches, and lake margins throughout much of the U.S. *T. domingensis* Persoon, southern cattail, has noncontiguous staminate and carpellate flower segments and convex leaves. This species inhabits brackish marshes and enriched wetlands along the outer coastal plain, and its range extends from TX to FL and north to MD.

Urticaceae

Boehmeria cylindrica (L.) Sw.

FALSE NETTLE

From a rhizome, this monoecious perennial herb produces a single pubescent stem up to 1.6 m tall. The oppositely arranged leaves are lanceolate, ovate, or elliptic and petiolate with toothed margins. The inconspicuous unisexual flowers are arranged in axillary spikes. Carpellate and staminate flowers are intermixed. Fruits are orbicular achenes enclosed within a persisting perianth. Blooming from summer to fall, false nettle inhabits wet woods, swamps, marshes, and ditches throughout much of the eastern U.S. *B. nivea* Gaud., Chinese grass, has a paniculate inflorescence and its abaxial leaf surfaces are white-tomentose. This species inhabits roadsides and disturbed sites, and its range extends from eastern TX to FL and north to eastern VA.

Valerianaceae

Valerianella radiata (L.) Dufr.

CORNSALAD

Up to 6 dm tall, this annual herb produces dichotomously branched, angled stems. Wings along the angles are pubescent. The leaves are oppositely arranged. The lower leaves are spathulate and somewhat clasping; the upper leaves are ovate or lanceolate and sessile. Small, white, funnelform flowers are arranged in densely bracted cymes. The fruits are three-chambered, pubescent capsules. Blooming from winter to spring, cornsalad inhabits prairies, pastures, roadsides, and disturbed sites from eastern TX to eastern KS and east to the Atlantic coastal states as far north as NJ. Inhabiting oak woods in eastern TX, *V. florifera* Shinners, Texas cornsalad, has entire leaves and glabrous stems.

Verbenaceae

Callicarpa americana L.
FRENCH MULBERRY

This is a freely branching shrub up to
3 m tall. The oppositely arranged leaves
are ovate or elliptic, petiolate, and
coarsely toothed. Flowers are densely
arranged in axillary cymes. Corollas
are white or pink and funnelform.
The showy pink or purple fruits are
four-seeded drupes. Blooming in summer, French mulberry inhabits woods,
swamps, and fencerows from eastern
TX and OK to FL and north to MD.
Berries are eaten by birds but are unpal-
atable to humans. Several cultivars are
commercially available for ornamental
plantings.

Glandularia pulchella (Sweet)
Troncoso
MOSS VERBENA

Introduced from South America, this
spreading perennial herb produces
decumbent stems. The oppositely arranged, triangular-shaped leaves are
finely dissected and featherlike. Showy
pink or purple flowers are densely arranged in terminal spikes. Fruits are
tiny nutlets. Blooming in spring, moss
verbena inhabits fields, roadsides, and
disturbed sites throughout much of the
southern U.S. *G. canadensis* (L.) Nutt.,
rose mock vervain, has less finely dissected leaves. This species inhabits
open woods, fields, and roadsides, and
its range extends across most of the
U.S. east of the Rocky Mountains.

Lantana camara L.

LANTANA

This is a freely branching, aromatic ever-green or deciduous shrub. The oppositely arranged leaves are ovate and pubescent with toothed margins. Flowers are arranged in headlike spikes that are subtended by ovate, pubescent bracts. The salverform corollas are most often pink or yellow but also may be red, orange, or lavender. Fruits are glossy blue-black drupes. Blooming throughout the year, lantana inhabits wood margins, road-sides, fencerows, and disturbed sites from southeastern TX and OK to FL and north to southeastern NC. Numer-ous cultivars of this showy species are commercially available for ornamental plantings. Escape from cultivation is common. All parts of the plant, espe-cially the unripe seeds, are toxic.

Phyla nodiflora (L.) Greene

FROG FRUIT

From freely rooting, four-angled pros-trate stems, this perennial herb produces ascending branches, each up to 1 dm long. Up to 3 cm long, the oppositely ar-ranged leaves are elliptic or spathulate with toothed margins distally. White, pink, or lavender salverform flowers are densely arranged in a globose-shaped spike that becomes elongated with ma-turity. The bracts of the spike are closely imbricate. Fruits are plump schizocarps. Blooming from spring to fall, frog fruit inhabits wet woods, pinelands, savannas, pond margins, and beaches throughout the southern half of the U.S. *P. lanceolata* (Michx.) Greene, lanceleaf frog fruit, has leaves that are typically greater than 3 cm long. This species inhabits coastal marshes, riverbanks, and lake margins; its range extends throughout much of the U.S. excluding the Northwest.

Verbena rigida Spreng.

TUBEROUS VERVAIN

From tuberous roots, this introduction from Brazil produces freely branching erect stems, each up to 6 dm tall. The oppositely arranged lanceolate or narrowly obovate, sessile leaves are sharply toothed with rough, stiff hairs on both surfaces. Spikes of blue-purple salverform flowers are arranged in a terminal panicle. Fruits are small nutlets. Blooming from spring to fall, coarse tuberous vervain inhabits fields, roadsides, and disturbed sites throughout much of the Southeast. Also introduced from Brazil, *V. brasiliensis* Vell., Brazilian vervain, has stems up to 2.5 m tall. This species inhabits fields, pastures, roadsides, and disturbed sites; its range also extends throughout the Southeast.

Verbena halei Small

TEXAS VERVAIN

From a woody root, this perennial herb produces several simple or branching stems, each up to 8 dm tall. The oppositely arranged leaves are pinnately compound and irregularly toothed. Flowers are loosely arranged in terminal spikes. The salverform corollas are pale blue or lavender and about 5 mm across. Fruits are brown schizocarps composed of four oblong mericarps. Blooming from winter to summer, Texas vervain inhabits prairies, fields, pastures, and roadsides from AZ to FL and north to MA. An European introduction, *V. officinalis* L., herb of the cross, has corollas that are about 3 mm across. It inhabits disturbed sites from LA to northwestern FL and north to MA.

Viola lanceolata L. ssp. *vittata* (Greene) Russell

LANCE-LEAF VIOLET

From cordlike rhizomes, this perennial herb produces stolons that form clones. The basal leaves are narrowly lanceolate and shallowly toothed. White flowers are solitary on scapes each up to 1.5 dm tall. The lower three petals are prominently marked with purple lines. Self-fertile flowers that remain closed are produced on the stolons. Fruits are green, elliptical capsules with brown seeds. Blooming from winter to spring, lance-leaf violet inhabits wet sandy woods, sphagnum bogs, and savannas from southeastern TX and OK to FL and north to VA.

Viola pedata L.

BIRDFOOT VIOLET

This is a stemless perennial herb with a short, vertical rhizome. Forming a basal rosette, the leaves are palmately lobed or dissected into linear or spathulate segments. Solitary on peduncles that exceed the length of the leaves, the showy flowers are beardless. In some individuals, all the petals are uniformly lavender; in others, the two upper petals are purple. Fruits are glabrous capsules with many seeds. Blooming from winter to summer, birdfoot violet inhabits open, sandy woods throughout much of the eastern U.S. *V. triloba* Schwein., three-lobe violet, is a stemless species with lobed leaves and large, violet-colored, bearded flowers. This species inhabits rich woods, and its range extends throughout much of the eastern U.S. excluding the upper Midwest.

Viola X *primulifolia* L.

PRIMROSE-LEAVED VIOLET

From a slender rhizome, this perennial herb produces stolons after flowering. The alternately arranged leaves are ovate or lanceolate and closely set near the rhizome. White, beardless flowers are solitary on erect peduncles. The three lower petals are marked with brownish purple veins. Fruits are three-chambered capsules with brown seeds. Blooming from winter to spring, primrose-leaved violet inhabits wet woods, savannas, bogs, and stream banks from southeastern TX to WI and east to the Atlantic coastal states. This plant is thought to be a hybrid between *V. lanceolata* L. and *V. macloskeyi* Lloyd.

Viola septemloba Le Conte

SOUTHERN COASTAL VIOLET

This is a perennial herb with horizontal rhizomes and fleshy roots. Early leaves are mostly deltoid with few or no lobes. Later leaves are sagittate or hastate and pedately lobed. Up to 2 dm tall, the peduncles typically exceed the leaves. Corollas are violet or whitish with darker veins. The spur petal and lateral corolla lobes are densely bearded. Fruits are ellipsoid capsules with yellowish seeds. Blooming in spring, southern coastal violet inhabits wet woods and pinelands on the outer coastal plain from eastern TX to FL and north to NC. *V. sagittata* Ait., arrowleaf violet, has sagittate leaves with basal lobes and peduncles that typically do not exceed the leaves in length. This species inhabits dry, sandy woods, and its range extends throughout much of the eastern half of the U.S. excluding FL.

Viola sororia Willd.

COMMON BLUE VIOLET

This is a stemless perennial herb with a thickened caudex. Leaves are broadly ovate or reniform with rounded apices, cordate bases, and toothed margins. Flowers are solitary on long peduncles. Corollas are pale violet or purple, each with a whitish center that is marked with darker veins. Each of the two lateral petals bear clavate hairs, and the lower petal is short-spurred. Fruits are three-chambered capsules with blackish seeds. Blooming from winter to spring, common blue violet inhabits moist woods, stream banks, and lawns throughout much of the eastern half of the U.S. *V. affinis* Le Conte, sand violet, has leaves that are triangular and often longer than broad. This species inhabits stream banks and wet woods, and its range extends throughout much of the eastern half of the U.S.

Viola walteri House

PROSTRATE BLUE VIOLET

From a slender rhizome, this evergreen, colonial perennial herb produces creeping, matlike stolons. Leaves are orbicular or reniform and slightly toothed. The pubescent upper leaf surface is whitish green with darker veins. The lower leaf surface is purplish and glabrous. Blue or violet flowers are bearded, and each is marked with darker lines on the lower three petals. Fruits are subglobose capsules with brown seeds. Blooming in spring, prostrate blue violet inhabits rich deciduous woods and stream banks from eastern TX to northern FL and north to VA.

Vitaceae

Ampelopsis arborea (L.) Koehne
PEPPERVINE

Cissus trifoliata (L.) L.
SORRELVINE

This is a climbing or sprawling woody vine with stems up to 10 m long. The alternately arranged ovate leaves are pinnately compound; the leaflets are ovate or rhombic with coarse teeth. Tendrils are opposite the leaves. Small greenish yellow flowers are arranged in dichotomously branching cymes. Blooming from spring to summer, peppervine inhabits open woods, fencerows, dunes, and disturbed sites from eastern TX to southern IL and east to the Atlantic coastal states as far north as eastern VA. *A. cordata* Michx., heartleaf peppervine, has simple leaves with cordate or truncate bases. This species inhabits wet woods, and its range extends from TX to NE and east to the Atlantic coastal states as far north as DE.

From tuberous roots, this deciduous woody vine produces sprawling, warty stems, each up to 10 m long. The alternately arranged succulent leaves are simple or trilobed with irregularly toothed margins. On ribbed peduncles, umbellate cymes of small greenish flowers are opposite the leaves and terminal. Some nodes bear tendrils. Fruits are black, obovoid berries with one to several seeds. Blooming from spring to summer, sorrelvine inhabits salt marshes, dunes, stream banks, and roadsides from AZ to southwestern MO and east to FL and southwestern GA. Contact with the stems and leaves of this rank-smelling plant can cause skin irritation.

Parthenocissus quinquefolia (L.)
Planch.

VIRGINIA CREEPER

This is a high-climbing or creeping
woody vine. Up to 30 m long, the stems
produce branching tendrils terminated
by adhesive, disk-shaped holdfasts.
The alternately arranged leaves are palmately compound; the leaflets are elliptic with toothed margins. The small,
greenish white flowers are arranged
in paniculate cymes. Fruits are bluish
berries. Blooming from spring to fall,
Virginia creeper inhabits open woods
and disturbed sites throughout much
of the eastern half of the U.S. Planted
as an ornamental, this species can become invasive. Although toxic to humans, the fruits are eaten by birds.

Xyris ambigua Bey. ex Kunth

COASTAL PLAIN YELLOW-
EYED GRASS

This perennial herb produces linear basal
leaves arranged in fans. Leaf sheath
bases are pale pink or straw colored.
Bright yellow flowers with petal-like,
bearded staminodes are densely arranged in a terminal spike. Up to 1 m
long, scapes are circular in cross section
and bear two prominent ribs. Fruits
are capsules containing translucent
seeds. Blooming from spring to fall,
coastal plain yelloweyed grass inhabits wet pinelands, savannas, and bogs
from eastern TX to FL and north to
VA. There are several yelloweyed grass
species native to the coastal plain,
and they are difficult to distinguish.

Zygophyllaceae

Tribulus cistoides L.

JAMAICAN FEVERPLANT

From a taproot, this introduced perennial herb produces prostrate or ascending, hairy, branching stems each up to 3 m long. The oppositely arranged leaves are pinnately compound. The oblong or elliptical leaflets are densely covered with long, silky hairs. Up to 3.6 cm broad, solitary bright yellow flowers are borne in the leaf axils. A whorl of glands is situated at the base of the ovary. Fruits are spiny schizocarps. Blooming throughout the year, Jamaican feverplant inhabits roadsides, beaches, and disturbed sites on the coast in southeastern LA and also from FL to southeastern GA. *T. terrestris* L., puncture vine, is a prostrate annual with smaller flowers. This species inhabits disturbed sites, and its range extends throughout much of the U.S.

KEYS TO WILDFLOWERS OF
THE COASTAL PLAIN

Dichotomous keys are artificial in that they say nothing about how closely one plant is related to another plant. However, these keys provide a method whereby a particular plant can be identified. Dichotomous keys are designed as a series of paired, mutually exclusive statements that divide a set of plants into progressively smaller subsets until a single plant genus is left. Using these keys takes some practice. But once the technique is mastered, the user can quickly identify many plants encountered on the coastal plain.

To make the process of plant identification easier, the dichotomous keys are divided by flower color. For example, if a plant has flowers that are predominantly red, then the red-flowered key is used.

Individual keys are listed in order as:

A. BROWN OR TAN

B. RED OR MAROON

C. ORANGE

D. GREEN

E. PINK OR ROSE-COLORED

F. BLUE, VIOLET, LAVENDER, OR PURPLE

G. YELLOW

H. WHITE

A. PLANTS WITH BROWN OR TAN FLOWERS

1. Plants without chlorophyll   2
1. Plants with chlorophyll   3
2. Flowers are tubular or remain budlike   *Epifagus*
2. Flowers otherwise   *Corallorhiza*
3. Plants aquatic and not grasslike   4
3. Plants terrestrial or if aquatic then not grasslike   5
4. Inflorescence submergent or floating   *Potamogeton*
4. Inflorescence emergent on a long, sheathing stem   *Typha*
5. Grass or grasslike plants   6
5. Plants not grasslike   *Plantago*
6. Plants inhabiting shallow water or wet soil   *Juncus*
6. Plants inhabiting sand dunes and beaches   *Uniola*

B. PLANTS WITH RED OR MAROON FLOWERS

1. Plant aquatic   *Brasenia*
1. Plant not aquatic   2
2. Plant a shrub   3
2. Plant otherwise   6
3. Plant woody throughout   4
3. Plant woody at the base only   5
4. Plant deciduous   *Aesculus*
4. Plant evergreen   *Illicium*
5. Plant deciduous   *Erythrina*
5. Plant evergreen   *Hamelia*
6. Plant a vine   7
6. Plant otherwise   11
7. Plant evergreen   8
7. Plant deciduous   9
8. Leaves compound   *Bignonia*
8. Leaves simple   *Lonicera*
9. Leaves pinnate   10
9. Leaves trifoliate   *Pueraria*
10. Plant with linear leaflets   *Ipomoea*
10. Plant with ovate leaflets   *Apios*
11. Orchid-type flower with labellum   12
11. Flowers otherwise   13
12. Plants with a pseudobulb   *Eulophia*
12. Plants without a pseudobulb   *Sacoila*
13. Pea-type flowers with standard petal   *Trifolium*
13. Plants otherwise   14
14. Aster-type flowers arranged in heads   15
14. Flowers otherwise   16
15. Ray ligules present   *Gaillardia*
15. Only disk florets present   *Hymenopappus*
16. Flowers arranged in umbels   *Asclepias*
16. Flowers otherwise   17
17. Plants with tubular leaves   *Sarracenia*
17. Leaves otherwise   18
18. Leaves opposite   19
18. Leaves alternate   20
19. Flowers bilabiate   *Salvia*
19. Flowers otherwise   *Spigelia*

20. Flowers subtended by showy bracts   *Castilleja*
20. Flowers otherwise   21
21. Petals spurred   *Aquilegia*
21. Petals not spurred   22
22. Flowers funnelform   *Hibiscus*
22. Flowers otherwise   23
23. Flowers tubular   24
23. Flowers otherwise   *Lilium*
24. Leaves pinnately lobed   *Ipomopsis*
24. Leaves entire   *Lobelia*

C. PLANTS WITH ORANGE FLOWERS

1. Plants aquatic   *Iris*
1. Plants otherwise   2
2. Plant a vine   *Campsis*
2. Plant otherwise   3
3. Plant a shrub   4
3. Plant otherwise   5
4. Plant woody throughout   *Rhododendron*
4. Plant only woody at the base   *Sesbania*
5. Leaves at flowering in a basal rosette   *Polygala*
5. Leaves otherwise   6
6. Leaves whorled   *Lilium*
6. Leaves otherwise   7
7. Leaves opposite   8
7. Leaves alternate   10
8. Aster-type flowers arranged in heads   9
8. Flowers solitary   *Anagallis*
9. Leaves with petioles   *Acmella*
9. Leaves sessile   *Bidens*
10. Plants with milky latex   *Asclepias*
10. Plants otherwise   11
11. Orchid-type flowers with labellum   *Platanthera*
11. Flowers otherwise   12
12. Pea-type flowers with standard petal   *Stylosanthes*
12. Flowers otherwise   13
13. Aster-type flowers in heads   *Krigia*
13. Plants otherwise   14
14. Inflorescence a cyme   *Lithospermum*
14. Inflorescence fan shaped   *Belamcanda*

D. PLANTS WITH GREEN FLOWERS

1. Plant aquatic   2
1. Plant not aquatic   3
2. Plant a tiny thallus with a single root   *Lemna*
2. Plant with a basal rosette and dense roots   *Pistia*
3. Plant a deciduous shrub   4
3. Plant otherwise   5
4. Fruit an inconspicuous aggregate of berries   *Batis*
4. Fruit a conspicuous capsule with scarlet seeds   *Euonymous*
5. Plant a vine   6
5. Plant otherwise   9
6. Plant evergreen   *Smilax*
6. Plant deciduous   7
7. Plant woody   8
7. Plant herbaceous   *Matelea*
8. Flowers arranged in cymes   *Cissus*
8. Flowers arranged in racemes   *Brunnichia*
9. Plant a stoloniferous, mat-forming herb   *Dichondra*
9. Plant otherwise   10
10. Plant epiphytic   11
10. Plant not epiphytic   12
11. Plant with green coriaceous leaves   *Epidendrum*
11. Plant with gray scurfy leaves   *Tillandsia*
12. Orchid-type flowers with a labellum   13
12. Flowers otherwise   17
13. Leaves absent at flowering   *Tipularia*
13. Leaves present at flowering   14
14. More than one leaf present at flowering   15
14. Only a single leaf present at flowering   *Malaxis*
15. Leaves alternate   *Habenaria*
15. Leaves whorled   *Isotria*
16. Plant with pitcher-shaped leaves   *Sarracenia*
16. Plant with normal-shaped leaves   17
17. Leaves palmately lobed   *Arisaema*
17. Leaves otherwise   18
18. Leaves in a basal rosette at flowering   19
18. Leaves otherwise   21
19. Leaves succulent   *Manfreda*
19. Leaves not succulent   20

20. Fruits are siliques   *Coronopus*
20. Fruit a capsule   *Plantago*
21. Leaves alternate   22
21. Leaves opposite   25
22. Flowers perfect   23
22. Flowers unisexual   24
23. Flowers arranged in racemes   *Rumex*
23. Flowers arranged in spikelets   *Chasmanthium*
24. Flowers arranged in panicles   *Amaranthus*
24. Flowers arranged in spikes   *Acalypha*
25. Flowers arranged in umbels   *Asclepias*
25. Flowers otherwise   26
26. Flowers arranged in spikes   27
26. Flowers arranged in cyathia   28
27. Leaves with petioles   *Boehmeria*
27. Leaves sessile   *Salicornia*
28. Leaves subtend the cyathium petal-like   *Euphorbia*
28. Leaves subtending the cyathium not petal-like   *Chamaesyce*

E. PLANTS WITH PINK OR ROSE-COLORED FLOWERS

1. Plant aquatic   *Ottelia*
1. Plant otherwise   2
2. Plant a shrub   3
2. Plant otherwise   9
3. Plant evergreen   4
3. Plant deciduous   6
4. Plant with erect and ascending branches   *Rhododendron*
4. Plant with low creeping or prostrate branches   5
5. Corolla salverform   *Epigaea*
5. Corolla campanulate   *Kalmia*
6. Leaves alternate   *Rhododendron*
6. Leaves opposite or whorled   7
7. Leaves both opposite and whorled   *Decodon*
7. Leaves opposite only   8
8. Salverform flowers arranged in spikes   *Lantana*
8. Funnelform flowers arranged in cymes   *Callicarpa*
9. Plant a vine   10
9. Plant otherwise   13
10. Leaves opposite   *Clematis*
10. Leaves alternate   11
11. Flowers funnelform   *Ipomoea*
11. Pea-type flowers with standard petal   12
12. Leaves trifoliate   *Canavalia*
12. Leaves pinnate   *Vicia*
13. Orchid-type flowers with labellum   14
13. Flowers otherwise   17
14. Labellum inflated   *Cypripedium*
14. Labellum otherwise   15
15. Labellum basally hinged   *Calopogon*
15. Labellum otherwise   16
16. Labellum with a fleshy crest   *Cleistes*
16. Labellum prominently bearded with yellow bristles   *Pogonia*
17. Leaves beset with tentaclelike, glandular hairs   *Drosera*
17. Leaves otherwise   18
18. Leaves pitcher-shaped   *Sarracenia*
18. Leaves otherwise   19
19. Leaves consisting of a petiole but no blade   *Coreopsis*
19. Leaves otherwise   20

20. Leaves whorled   21
20. Leaves otherwise   22
21. Flowers arranged in racemes   *Polygala*
21. Flowers arranged in heads   *Eutrochium*
22. Plant with both alternate and opposite leaves   *Phlox*
22. Plant with opposite or alternate leaves only   23
23. Leaves opposite   24
23. Leaves alternate   31
24. Flowers bilabiate   25
24. Flowers otherwise   28
25. Flowers marked with spots and yellow lines   *Agalinis*
25. Flowers otherwise   26
26. Flowers arranged in a spike   *Teucrium*
26. Flowers otherwise   27
27. Perennial with a segmented rhizome   *Stachys*
27. Annual with a taproot   *Lamium*
28. Anthers prominent and curved   *Rhexia*
28. Anthers otherwise   29
29. Prostrate plant with succulent leaves   *Sesuvium*
29. Plant otherwise   30
30. Flowers bear conspicuous orange, staminodal glands   *Triadenum*
30. Flowers otherwise   31
31. Flowers rotate   *Sabatia*
31. Flowers salverform   *Centaurium*
32. Aster-type flowers in heads   33
32. Flowers otherwise   37
33. Plant with a woody crown   *Pluchea*
33. Plant otherwise   34
34. Plant with a taproot   *Melochia*
34. Plant otherwise   35
35. Plant with a corm   *Liatris*
35. Plant otherwise   35
36. Plant with fibrous roots   *Marshallia*
36. Plant with a rhizome   *Elephantopus*
37. Plant with prickly prostrate stems   *Mimosa*
37. Plant otherwise   38
38. Plant with milky latex   *Asclepias*
38. Plant otherwise   39
39. Ocrea present   40
39. Ocrea not present   41

F. PLANTS WITH BLUE, VIOLET, LAVENDER, OR PURPLE FLOWERS

1. Plant aquatic   2
1. Plant otherwise   7
2. Plant freely floating   *Eichhornia*
2. Plant rooted in substrate   3
3. Leaves floating on water surface   *Nymphaea*
3. Leaves otherwise   4
4. Plant mat-forming   *Bacopa*
4. Plant otherwise   5
5. Inflorescence held well above the leaves   *Thalia*
5. Inflorescence otherwise   6
6. Sharp spines borne in the leaf axils   *Hydrolea*
6. Spines not present in the leaf axils   *Pontederia*
7. Plants without chlorophyll   *Apteria*
7. Plants with chlorophyll   8
8. Plant a vine   9
8. Plant otherwise   15
9. Flowers funnelform   10
9. Flowers otherwise   11
10. Flowers borne in headlike cymes   *Jacquemontia*
10. Flowers otherwise   *Ipomoea*
11. Pea-type flowers with standard petal   12
11. Flowers otherwise   14
12. Leaves with a terminal branching tendril   *Vicia*
12. Leaves otherwise   13
13. Leaves pinnate   *Wisteria*
13. Leaves trifoliate   *Centrosema*
14. Flowers with a conspicuous corona   *Passiflora*
14. Urn-shaped flowers with thickened calyx lobes   *Clematis*
15. Plant a shrub   *Conradina*
15. Plant otherwise   16
16. Plant epiphytic   *Tillandsia*
16. Plant otherwise   17
17. Orchid-type flower with a labellum   *Listera*
17. Flower otherwise   18
18. Solitary flower subtended by three leaflike bracts   *Trillium*
18. Flower otherwise   19
19. Pea-type flowers with standard petal   20

19. Flowers otherwise   21
20. Leaves trifoliate   *Orbexilum*
20. Leaves simple or palmately lobed   *Lupinus*
21. Flowers borne in a spathe   22
21. Flowers otherwise   23
22. All petals the same color   *Tradescantia*
22. Two petals blue and one petal white   *Commelina*
23. Flowers with six petal-like tepals   24
23. Flowers otherwise   27
24. Leaves equitant   25
24. Leaves pleated   26
25. Stem winged   *Sisyrinchium*
25. Stem not winged   *Iris*
26. Flowers secund   *Alophia*
26. Flowers erect   *Herbertia*
27. Flowers spurred   28
27. Flowers otherwise   31
28. Leaves in basal rosettes with sticky glandular hair   *Pinguicula*
28. Leaves otherwise   29
29. Flowers bilabiate   *Nuttallanthus*
29. Flowers otherwise   30
30. Plants without stems   *Viola*
30. Plants with an elongated stem   *Delphinium*
31. Flowers arranged in scorpioid cymes   32
31. Flowers otherwise   34
32. Plants with a basal rosette at flowering   *Cynoglossum*
32. Plants otherwise   33
33. Corollas salverform   *Heliotropium*
33. Flowers campanulate   *Phacelia*
34. Corollas with four lobes   35
34. Corollas otherwise   36
35. Leaves opposite   *Houstonia*
35. Leaves alternate   *Cakile*
36. Aster-type flowers in heads   37
36. Flowers otherwise   48
37. Leaves scalelike   *Lygodesmia*
37. Leaves otherwise   38
38. Phyllaries with conspicuous spines   39
38. Phyllaries otherwise   40
39. Plant biennial with spiny leaves   *Cirsium*

39. Plant perennial with succulent leaves   *Stokesia*
40. Flower heads solitary on peduncles   *Echinacea*
40. Flower heads otherwise   41
41. Flower heads arranged in spikes or racemes   42
41. Flower heads otherwise   43
42. Plants with corms   *Liatris*
42. Plants with a knotty rhizome   *Eurybia*
43. Flower heads arranged in panicles   44
43. Flower heads arranged in corymbs   46
44. Plants freely branching   45
44. Plants with a simple stem   *Carphephorus*
45. Phyllaries with hyaline margins   *Symphyotrichum*
45. Phyllaries without hyaline margins   *Lactuca*
46. Leaves highly fragrant   *Carphephorus*
46. Leaves otherwise   47
47. Leaves opposite   *Conoclinium*
47. Leaves alternate   *Vernonia*
48. Leaves in whorls   *Sherardia*
48. Leaves otherwise   49
49. Plants with both opposite and alternate leaves   50
49. Plants otherwise   53
50. Corolla tubular and attached to the calyx rim   *Lythrum*
50. Corolla bilabiate and not attached to the calyx rim   51
51. Flowers arranged in verticils   *Salvia*
51. Flowers otherwise   52
52. Flowers arranged in racemes   *Mazus*
52. Flowers solitary in leaf axils   *Veronica*
53. Leaves all alternate   54
53. Leaves all opposite   60
54. Flowers arranged in racemes   *Lobelia*
54. Flowers otherwise   55
55. Flowers arranged in umbels   *Oxalis*
55. Flowers otherwise   56
56. Flowers arranged in panicles   *Solanum*
56. Flowers otherwise   57
57. Flowers arranged in cymes   *Amsonia*
57. Flowers otherwise   58
58. Flowers arranged in heads   *Eryngium*
58. Flowers otherwise   59
59. Flowers arranged in axillary fascicles   *Lycium*

59. Flowers solitary in leaf axils   *Triodanus*
60. Flowers bilabiate   61
60. Flowers otherwise   70
61. Flowers arranged in panicles   *Penstemon*
61. Flowers otherwise   62
62. Flowers arranged in cymes   63
62. Flowers otherwise   64
63. Stamens prominent and strongly curved   *Trichostema*
63. Stamens otherwise   *Monarda*
64. Flowers arranged in racemes   65
64. Flowers otherwise   66
65. Fruits are nutlets   *Physostegia*
65. Fruits are schizocarps   *Scutellaria*
66. Flowers arranged in spikes   67
66. Flowers otherwise   69
67. Stems circular in cross section   *Justicia*
67. Stems square in cross section   68
68. Plants blooming in spring   *Prunella*
68. Plants blooming in summer and fall   *Salvia*
69. Solitary flowers in leaf axils   *Mimulus*
69. Paired flowers in leaf axils   *Scutellaria*
70. Corolla lobes forming a closed tube   *Gentiana*
70. Corolla otherwise   71
71. Petals inserted on the calyx lip   *Cuphea*
71. Petals otherwise   72
72. Flowers campanulate   73
72. Flowers otherwise   74
73. Flowers erect   *Eustoma*
73. Flowers nodding   *Clematis*
74. Corollas funnelform   *Ruellia*
74. Corollas salverform   75
75. Flowers arranged in cymes   *Phlox*
75. Flowers arranged in spikes   76
76. Stems decumbent   *Glandularia*
76. Stems erect or ascending   77
77. Stems simple   *Buchnera*
77. Stems branching   78
78. Leaves simple   *Phyla*
78. Leaves pinnate   *Verbena*

G. PLANTS WITH YELLOW FLOWERS

1. Plant aquatic   2
1. Plant otherwise   7
2. Carnivorous plant with bladder-shaped traps   *Utricularia*
2. Plants otherwise   3
3. At least some leaves floating on the water surface   4
3. Leaves otherwise   5
4. Leaves cleft at base   *Nuphar*
4. Leaves not cleft at base   *Nelumbo*
5. Flowers embedded in a spadix   *Orontium*
5. Flowers otherwise   6
6. Flowers composed of four petals and no staminodes   *Ludwigia*
6. Flowers composed of three petals and staminodes   *Canna*
7. Suffruticose shrub   8
7. Plants otherwise   9
8. Flowers pea-type with standard petal   *Sesbania*
8. Flowers not pea-type   *Hypericum*
9. Plant a vine   10
9. Plant otherwise   20
10. Plant woody   11
10. Plant herbaceous   12
11. Leaves opposite   *Gelsemium*
11. Leaves alternate   *Ampelopsis*
12. Leaves opposite   *Tribulus*
12. Leaves otherwise   13
13. Aster-type flowers in heads   *Calyptocarpus*
13. Flowers otherwise   14
14. Flower with conspicuous corona   *Passiflora*
14. Flower otherwise   15
15. Fruit a legume   16
15. Fruit otherwise   18
16. Leaves pinnate   *Neptunia*
16. Leaves trifoliate   17
17. Flowers often tinged with purplish brown   *Rhynchosia*
17. Flowers not tinged with purplish brown   *Vigna*
18. Fruit a pepo   *Cucumis*
18. Fruit otherwise   19
19. Fruit a berry   *Melothria*
19. Fruit an aggregate of achenes   *Duchesnea*

40. Legumes thin, curved, and elongated   *Senna*
40. Legumes erect and not elongated   *Chamaecrista*
41. Legumes beaked   *Baptisia*
41. Legumes otherwise   42
42. Legumes coiled   *Medicago*
42. Legumes flattened   *Melilotus*
43. Aster-type flowers in heads   44
43. Flowers otherwise   82
44. Basal leaves present at flowering   45
44. Basal leaves absent or withered at flowering   53
45. Flower heads arranged in panicles   46
45. Flowers otherwise   47
46. Flower heads campanulate   *Silphium*
46. Flower heads cylindrical   *Youngia*
47. Flower heads arranged in corymbs   48
47. Flower heads solitary   49
48. Flower heads campanulate   *Pityopsis*
48. Flower heads cylindrical   *Bigelowia*
49. Flower heads conical   *Rudbeckia*
49. Flower heads otherwise   50
50. Flower heads subglobose   *Coreopsis*
50. Flower heads otherwise   51
51. Flower heads cylindrical   *Taraxicum*
51. Flower heads hemispheric   52
52. Leaves alternate   *Helenium*
52. Leaves opposite   *Borrichia*
53. Plant with both alternate and opposite leaves   *Helianthus*
53. Plant with alternate or opposite leaves only   54
54. Plants with opposite leaves   55
54. Plants with alternate leaves   64
55. Heads arranged in glomerules   *Flaveria*
55. Heads otherwise   56
56. Heads arranged in spikes   *Iva*
56. Heads otherwise   57
57. Heads arranged in corymbs   58
57. Heads solitary   60
58. Flower heads campanulate   *Bidens*
58. Flower head otherwise   59
59. Flower heads subglobose   *Coreopsis*
59. Flower head cylindrical   *Flaveria*

60. Flower heads campanulate   *Coreopsis*
60. Flower heads hemispheric   61
61. Leaves palmately lobed   *Smallanthus*
61. Leaves otherwise   62
62. Involucral bracts leaflike   *Tetragonotheca*
62. Involucral bracts otherwise   63
63. Achenes winged   *Coreopsis*
63. Achenes not winged   *Helianthus*
64. Heads arranged in cymes   *Packera*
64. Heads otherwise   65
65. Heads arranged in racemes   *Solidago*
65. Heads otherwise   66
66. Heads arranged in corymbs   67
66. Heads otherwise   71
67. Heads campanulate   *Heterotheca*
67. Heads otherwise   68
68. Heads turban shaped   *Euthamia*
68. Heads otherwise   69
69. Heads obconic   *Sonchus*
69. Heads cylindrical   70
70. Annual with taproot   *Pyrrhopappus*
70. Perennial with rhizome   *Solidago*
71. Heads arranged in panicles   72
71. Heads solitary   76
72. Heads campanulate   *Solidago*
72. Heads otherwise   73
73. Heads globose   *Helenium*
73. Heads hemispheric   74
74. Leaves succulent   *Rayjacksonia*
74. Leaves not succulent   75
75. Plant a perennial with a fleshy crown   *Berlandiera*
75. Plant an annual with a taproot   *Helenium*
76. Heads obconic   *Thymophylla*
76. Heads otherwise   77
77. Heads conic   *Rudbeckia*
77. Heads hemispheric   78
78. Plant with fibrous roots   79
78. Plant with taproot   80
79. Perennial with linear leaves   *Balduina*
79. Annual with ovate, elliptic, or lanceolate leaves   *Rudbeckia*

80. Perennial with a simple stem   *Helenium*
80. Annual with branching stems   81
81. Stem leaves sessile and lanceolate   *Gaillardia*
81. Stem leaves petiolate and ovate   *Helianthus*
82. Plant with pitcher-shaped leaves   *Sarracenia*
82. Plant otherwise   83
83. Plant with pad-shaped stems bearing spines   *Opuntia*
83. Plant otherwise   84
84. Plant with basal leaves   85
84. Plant otherwise   92
85. Leaves equitant   **Iris**
85. Leaves otherwise   86
86. Flowers solitary   *Ranunculus*
86. Flowers otherwise   87
87. Flowers arranged in racemes   88
87. Flowers arranged in spikes   90
88. Flowers composed of six tepals   89
88. Flowers composed of five petals   *Polygala*
89. Tepals united   *Aletris*
89. Tepals free   *Schoenolirion*
90. Flowers composed of three petals   *Xyris*
90. Flowers otherwise   91
91. Flowers with four regular petals   *Oenothera*
91. Flowers with five slightly irregular petals   *Verbascum*
92. Leaves opposite   93
92. Leaves alternate   95
93. Flowers solitary   *Sida*
93. Flowers arranged in cymes   94
94. Fruits are capsules   *Rhexia*
94. Fruits are schizocarps   *Monarda*
95. Flowers arranged in racemes   *Piriqueta*
95. Flowers otherwise   96
96. Flowers arranged in spikes   *Stillingia*
96. Flowers otherwise   97
97. Flowers arranged in cymes   98
97. Flowers solitary   99
98. Leaves trifoliate   *Oxalis*
98. Leaves simple   *Helianthemum*
99. Plant succulent   *Portulaca*
99. Plant otherwise   100

100. Flowers with six tepals   *Uvularia*

100. Flowers otherwise   101

101. At least some leaves pinnately lobed   *Oenothera*

101. All leaves entire   *Ludwigia*

H. PLANTS WITH WHITE FLOWERS

1. Plants strictly aquatic   2
1. Plants otherwise   12
2. Plant with primary leaves submerged below water surface   3
2. Plant otherwise   4
3. Leaves fan-shaped   *Cabomba*
3. Leaves linear   *Egeria*
4. Plant with leaves emergent and submergent   *Myriophyllum*
4. Plant otherwise   5
5. Plant with floating leaves   6
5. Plant emergent   8
6. Some leaves also emergent   *Limnobium*
6. All leaves floating   7
7. Lower leaf surface pitted   *Nymphoides*
7. Lower leaf surface smooth   *Nymphaea*
8. Plant mat-forming   *Bacopa*
8. Plant otherwise   9
9. Leaves forming a basal rosette   *Heteranthera*
9. Leaves otherwise   10
10. Flowers arranged in fascicles   *Persicaria*
10. Flowers arranged in whorls   11
11. Scape arching or decumbent   *Echinodorus*
11. Scape erect   *Sagittaria*
12. Plant a vine   13
12. Plant otherwise   25
13. Plant woody   14
13. Plant herbaceous   20
14. Plant evergreen   15
14. Plant otherwise   16
15. Corollas funnelform   *Mitchella*
15. Corollas bilabiate   *Lonicera*
16. Plant semi-evergreen   17
16. Plant deciduous   18
17. Leaves pinnate   *Clematis*
17. Leaves simple with coarse teeth   *Pachysandra*
18. Leaves simple   *Cocculus*
18. Leaves compound   19
19. Leaves palmately divided   *Parthenocissus*
19. Leaves trifoliate   *Rubus*

40. Flowers borne in a cyathium   *Euphorbia*
40. Flowers otherwise   41
41. Flowers with spathe and spadix   *Peltandra*
41. Flowers otherwise   42
42. Flowers arranged in scorpioid cymes   *Heliotropium*
42. Flowers otherwise   43
43. Orchid-type flowers with labellum   44
43. Flowers otherwise   45
44. Flowers arranged in spikes   *Spiranthes*
44. Flowers arranged in racemes   *Platanthera*
45. Pea-type flowers with standard petal   46
45. Flowers otherwise   49
46. Leaves trifoliate   47
46. Leaves pinnate   *Tephrosia*
47. Plant mat-forming   *Trifolium*
47. Plant otherwise   48
48. Legume inflated   *Baptisia*
48. Legume not inflated   *Lespedeza*
49. Flowers bilabiate   50
49. Flowers otherwise   56
50. Leaves pinnate   *Teucrium*
50. Leaves simple   51
51. Flowers arranged in axillary glomerules   *Lycopus*
51. Flowers otherwise   52
52. Flowers arranged in heads subtended by bracts   53
52. Flowers otherwise   54
53. Floral bracts whitened   *Pycnanthemum*
53. Floral bracts not whitened   *Hyptis*
54. Flowers arranged in spikes   *Froelichia*
54. Flowers solitary   55
55. Leaves clasping   *Gratiola*
55. Leaves not clasping   *Mecardonia*
56. Flowers with four petals   57
56. Flowers otherwise   67
57. At least some leaves in whorls   58
57. Leaves otherwise   59
58. Flowers arranged in spherical heads   *Cephalanthus*
58. Flowers arranged in cymes   *Galium*
59. Stem leaves alternate   60
59. Stem leaves opposite   62

60. Fruit a silicle   *Lepidium*
60. Fruit a silique   61
61. Siliques jointed   *Cakile*
61. Siliques not jointed   *Cardamine*
62. At least some flowers arranged in cymes   63
62. Flowers otherwise   65
63. Flowers funnelform   *Stenaria*
63. Flowers rotate   64
64. Capsules rounded   *Oldenlandia*
64. Capsules flattened   *Polypremum*
65. Flowers arranged in headlike clusters   *Mitracarpus*
65. Flowers solitary   66
66. Stems erect   *Houstonia*
66. Stems trailing   *Diodia*
67. Aster-type flowers in heads   68
67. Flowers otherwise   81
68. Basal leaves present at flowering   69
68. Leaves otherwise   71
69. Flower heads arranged in cymes   *Erigeron*
69. Flowers heads solitary   70
70. Flower heads hemispheric   *Marshallia*
70. Flower heads campanulate   *Chaptalia*
71. Stem leaves opposite   72
71. Stem leaves alternate   76
72. Flower heads arranged in panicles   *Eupatorium*
72. Flower heads arranged in corymbs   73
73. Flower heads obconic   *Eupatorium*
73. Flower heads otherwise   74
74. Flower heads campanulate   75
74. Flower heads ellipsoid   *Eupatorium*
75. Stems decumbent   *Eclipta*
75. Stems erect   *Bidens*
76. Flower heads solitary   *Aphanostephus*
76. Flower heads otherwise   77
77. Flower heads arranged in spikes   *Gamochaeta*
77. Flower heads otherwise   78
78. Flower heads arranged in corymbs   79
78. Flower heads arranged panicles   80
79. Flower heads cylindrical   *Arnoglossum*
79. Flower heads turban shaped   *Verbesina*

80. Leaves pinnately lobed   *Parthenium*
80. Leaves entire   *Symphyotrichum*
81. Flowers arranged in umbels   82
81. Flowers otherwise   97
82. Plants with milky latex   *Asclepias*
82. Plants otherwise   83
83. Leaves whorled   *Mollugo*
83. Leaves otherwise   84
84. Basal leaves present at flowering   85
84. Leaves otherwise   90
85. Leaves pinnate   *Limnosciadium*
85. Leaves entire   86
86. Flowers with five reflexed petals   *Dodecatheon*
86. Flowers with six tepals   87
87. Flowers with a conspicuous corona   *Hymenocallis*
87. Flowers otherwise   88
88. Leaves thick and strap-shaped   *Crinum*
88. Leaves thin and terete or linear   89
89. Three or four spathes subtend each umbel   *Allium*
89. Two spathes subtend each umbel   *Nothoscordum*
90. Leaves peltate   *Hydrocotyl*
90. Leaves otherwise   91
91. Leaves palmately lobed   *Sanicula*
91. Leaves otherwise   92
92. Leaves with petiole but blade absent   *Oxypolis*
92. Leaves pinnate   93
93. Bracts subtending umbels all pinnate   *Daucus*
93. Bracts otherwise   94
94. Bracts subtending umbels pinnate and simple   *Ptilimnium*
94. Bracts otherwise   95
95. Bracts subtending umbels ovate   *Chaerophyllum*
95. Umbels not subtended by bracts   96
96. Robust perennial   *Cicuta*
96. Slender annual   *Cyclospermum*
97. Both alternate and opposite leaves present   *Datura*
97. Leaves otherwise   98
98. Basal leaves present at flowering   99
98. Leaves otherwise   114
99. Hinged leaves modified for trapping insects   *Dionaea*
99. Leaves otherwise   100

100. Leaves palmately lobed   *Sanguinaria*
100. Leaves otherwise   101
101. Flowers arranged in spikelets   *Rhynchospora*
101. Flowers otherwise   102
102. Flowers arranged in cymes   *Sisyrinchium*
102. Flowers otherwise   103
103. Flowers arranged in panicles   *Zigadenus*
103. Flowers otherwise   104
104. Flowers solitary   105
104. Flowers otherwise   106
105. Salverform flower composed of six tepals   *Zephyranthes*
105. Irregular shaped flower composed of five petals   *Viola*
106. Flowers in heads subtended by bracts   107
106. Flowers in racemes   109
107. Leaves thickened with marginal bristles   *Eryngium*
107. Leaves not thickened and without bristles   108
108. Male flowers with four stamens   *Eriocaulon*
108. Male flowers with three stamens   *Lachnocaulon*
109. Plant evergreen   *Chamaelirium*
109. Plant deciduous   110
110. Tepals free   111
110. Tepals fused   112
111. Tepals clawed   *Melanthium*
111. Tepals not clawed   *Triantha*
112. Perianth rotate   *Stenanthium*
112. Perianth cylindrical   113
113. Plants with a bulb   *Zigadenus*
113. Plants with a rhizome   *Aletris*
114. Leaves opposite   115
114. Leaves alternate   125
115. Flowers arranged in racemes   *Claytonia*
115. Flowers otherwise   116
116. Flowers solitary   *Podophyllum*
116. Flowers otherwise   117
117. Flowers arranged in spikes   *Alternanthera*
117. Flowers otherwise   118
118. Flowers arranged in heads subtended by bracts   *Richardia*
118. At least some flowers arranged in cymes   119
119. Ellipsoid flowers with petals absent   *Paronychia*

119. Flowers otherwise   120
120. Petals notched or divided   121
120. Petals otherwise   122
121. Capsule slender   *Cerastium*
121. Capsules ovoid   *Stellaria*
122. Flowers rotate   *Sabatia*
122. Flowers otherwise   123
123. Flowers funnelform   *Valerianella*
123. Flowers campanulate   124
124. Roots fibrous   *Mitreola*
124. Roots fleshy and brittle   *Obolaria*
125. Flowers arranged in pendulous axillary clusters   *Polygonatum*
126. Flowers otherwise   127
127. Flowers in headlike clusters   *Desmanthus*
127. Flowers otherwise   128
128. Flowers solitary   129
128. Flowers otherwise   130
129. Leaves pinnate   *Proserpinaca*
129. Leaves palmately lobed   *Hibiscus*
130. Flowers arranged in cymes   131
130. Flowers otherwise   133
131. Flowers salverform   *Cnidoscolus*
131. Flowers otherwise   132
132. Leaves small and bractlike   *Burmannia*
132. Leaves prickly and not bractlike   *Argemone*
133. Flowers arranged in spikes   134
133. Flowers arranged in racemes   136
134. Plant a perennial with a woody caudex   *Gaura*
134. Plant an annual   135
135. Plant with fibrous roots   *Sphenoclea*
135. Plant with a taproot   *Caperonia*
136. Flowers unisexual   *Croton*
136. Flowers perfect   137
137. Perianth absent   *Saururus*
137. Perianth present   138
138. Petals absent   *Phytolacca*
138. Both sepals and petals present   139
139. Flowers salverform   *Solanum*
139. Flowers campanulate   *Samolus*

APPENDIX

Illustrations of Plant Structures

FLORAL STRUCTURES

Inflorescence Types

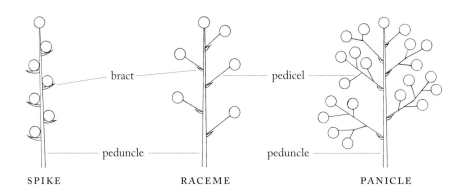

SPIKE — RACEME — PANICLE

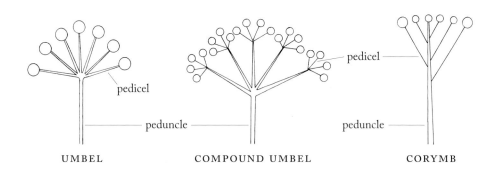

UMBEL — COMPOUND UMBEL — CORYMB

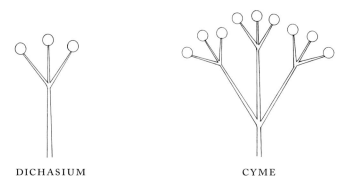

DICHASIUM — CYME

FLORAL STRUCTURES

Basic Flower Structure

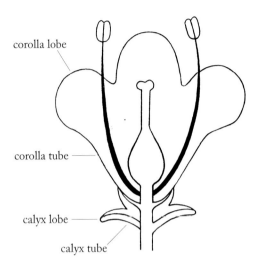

corolla lobe

corolla tube

calyx lobe

calyx tube

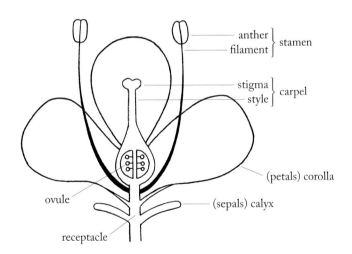

anther
filament } stamen

stigma
style } carpel

(petals) corolla

(sepals) calyx

ovule

receptacle

FLORAL STRUCTURES
Specialized Structures

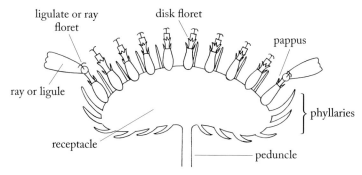

ligulate or ray floret

disk floret

pappus

ray or ligule

phyllaries

receptacle

peduncle

ASTER-TYPE FLOWERS IN A HEAD
(ASTERACEAE)

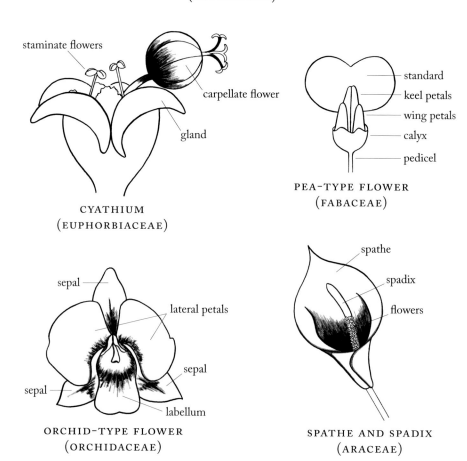

staminate flowers

carpellate flower

gland

CYATHIUM
(EUPHORBIACEAE)

standard

keel petals

wing petals

calyx

pedicel

PEA-TYPE FLOWER
(FABACEAE)

sepal

lateral petals

sepal

sepal

labellum

ORCHID-TYPE FLOWER
(ORCHIDACEAE)

spathe

spadix

flowers

SPATHE AND SPADIX
(ARACEAE)

FRUITING STRUCTURES

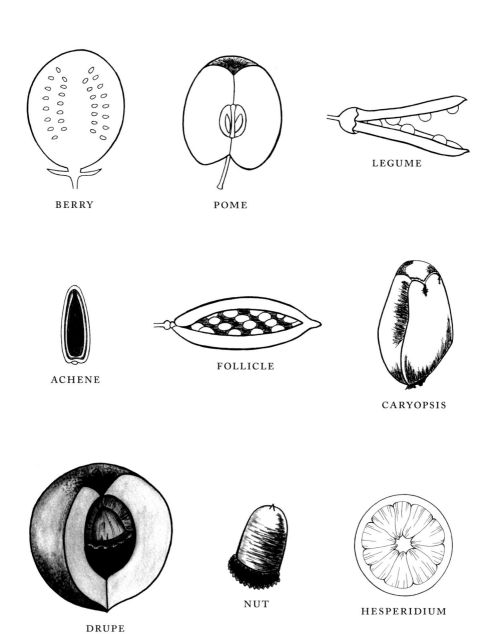

BERRY

POME

LEGUME

ACHENE

FOLLICLE

CARYOPSIS

DRUPE

NUT

HESPERIDIUM

continued on next page

FRUITING STRUCTURES

(continued)

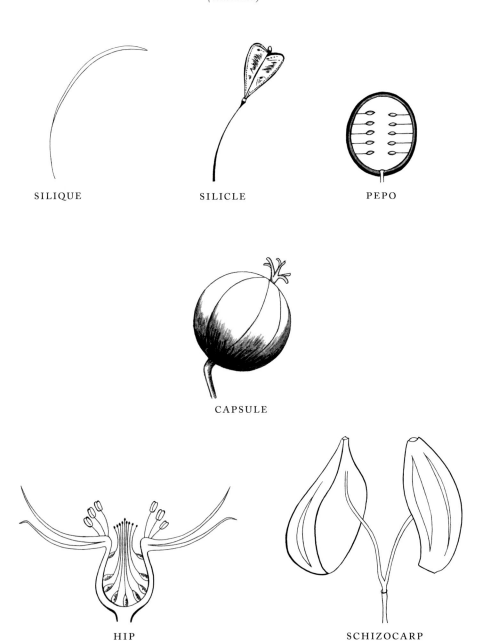

SILIQUE

SILICLE

PEPO

CAPSULE

HIP

SCHIZOCARP

VEGETATIVE STRUCTURES
Leaf Shapes

blade shapes

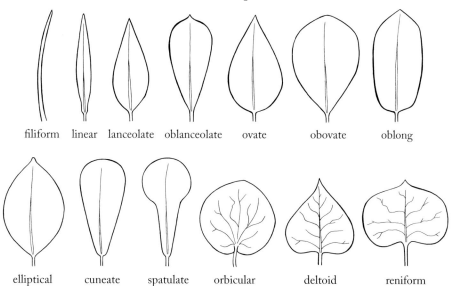

filiform   linear   lanceolate   oblanceolate   ovate   obovate   oblong

elliptical   cuneate   spatulate   orbicular   deltoid   reniform

tip shapes

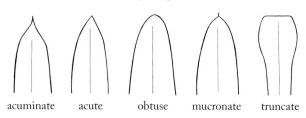

acuminate   acute   obtuse   mucronate   truncate

base shapes

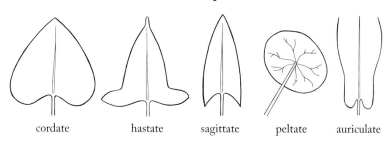

cordate   hastate   sagittate   peltate   auriculate

VEGETATIVE STRUCTURES
Leaf Arrangements

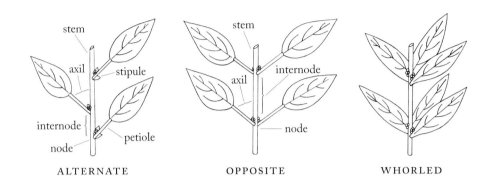

ALTERNATE   OPPOSITE   WHORLED

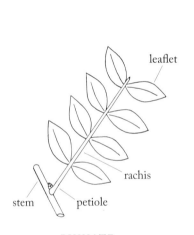

PINNATE

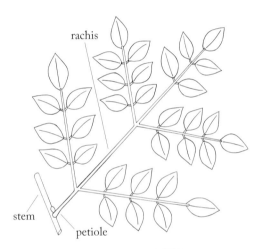

BIPINNATE

TRIFOLIATE

PALMATE

VEGETATIVE STRUCTURES
Specialized Leaf Attachments and Shapes

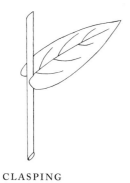

CLASPING

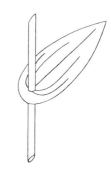

PERFOLIATE

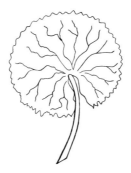

ORBICULAR

PALMATELY LOBED

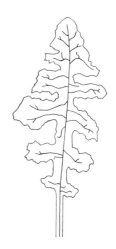

PINNATELY LOBED

GLOSSARY

The terms marked with an asterisk (*) are illustrated in the appendix.

Abaxial. Located on the underside of a structure such as a leaf.

***Achene.** A dry, one-seeded fruit that does not split open; the seed is attached to the fruit wall by the ovule stalk.

***Acuminate.** Gradually tapering to an attenuate point.

***Acute.** Sharply pointed with an angle of less than 90°.

Adaxial. Located on the upper side of a structure such as a leaf.

Adnate. Fusion of dissimilar parts such as petals attached to sepals.

Adventitious. Occurring in other than the usual location, such as roots appearing from a node of a stem.

***Alternate leaves.** Only one leaf is attached to a single node.

Androgynophore. A support structure on which stamens are borne.

Annual. A plant that completes its life cycle in one growing season.

Anther. A pollen sac.

Antrorse. Directed upward or forward, such as hairs.

Apically. Situated at an apex.

Appressed. Lying flat against a surface.

***Auricle.** Having an ear shape.

Awn. A slender bristle.

***Axil.** The point where stem and leaf meet.

Axillary bud. A lateral bud borne in a leaf axil.

***Berry.** A fleshy fruit that does not split open.

Biennial. A plant that completes its life cycle in two growing seasons.

Bipinnately compound leaf. A compound leaf that is twice divided.

Bract. A modified leaf often associated with an inflorescence.

Bracteate. Having bracts.

Bulb. A short, vertical stem with large storage leaves attached.

Callus. A thickened area on a plant surface.

*Calyx. The flower part consisting of the sepals.

Campanulate. Bell-shaped.

*Capsule. A dry fruit that splits open and is derived from two or more fused carpels.

Carpel. The female part of a flower, consisting of the ovary, style, and stigma.

*Carpellate. Having only female functional flowers.

*Caryopsis. A dry, one-seeded fruit that does not break open; the seed is completely attached to the fruit wall.

Caudex. The thickened base of an herbaceous perennial.

Cauline. Growing on a stem.

Cilia. Minute, short, marginal hairs.

Circumscissile. Splitting open around the hemisphere of a fruit or anther.

*Clasping. Refers to a sessile leaf with lobes of blade tissue projecting backward from the stem.

Clavate. Club shaped.

Comose. Having a tuft of hairs.

Compound leaf. A leaf with more than one leaflet per petiole.

Connate. Having similar parts fused, such as anthers or petals.

*Cordate. Having the shape of a heart.

Coriaceous. Leathery.

Corm. A solid, erect, enlarged underground stem used for starch storage.

*Corolla. The flower whorl, consisting of the petals.

Corona. A crown-shaped outgrowth or appendage of a flower part.

*Corymb. Flat-topped inflorescence in which the upper pedicels are shorter than the lower ones.

Crisped. Irregularly curled, as a margin.

Culm. A hollow or pithy stem of the families Poaceae and Cyperaceae.

*Cuneate. Wedge-shaped.

*Cyathium. A specialized inflorescence in the family Euphorbiaceae, consisting of a cup-shaped structure bearing a nectary gland, several male flowers, and a single female flower.

*Cyme. A usually flat-topped inflorescence in which each floral axis is terminated by a single flower.

Decumbent. Prostrate with ascending tips, such as a stem.

Decurrent. Refers to a wing or ridge that extends down below the point of attachment of a leaf or ligule.

Dehiscent. Refers to a fruit or anther that splits open to release seeds or pollen, respectively.

*Deltoid. Shaped like a triangle.

*Dichasium. A cyme that is divided into two axes.

Didynamous. Having four stamens in two unequal-length pairs.

Dioecious. Having unisexual flowers on separate plants.

Discoid. A flower head of family Asteraceae bearing only disk flowers.

Disjunct. Geographically separated plant populations.

*Disk floret. A tubular flower without a ligule of the family Asteraceae.

Distinct. Refers to parts that are not fused.

*Drupe. A fleshy fruit with a stony pit that does not split open along a seam.

Echinate. Prickly.

*Elliptic, elliptical. Shaped like an oval or ellipse.

Entire. Having an undivided margin, such as a leaf.

Epilithic. A plant that grows directly on stone.

Epipetalous. Stamens attached to the petals.

Epiphyte. A nonparasitic plant that grows upon another plant.

Equitant. Folded lengthwise, as a leaf.

Exserted. Projecting beyond the surrounding parts, as a stamen.

Falcate. Shaped like a sickle.

Fascicle. A tight cluster of flowers, leaves, roots, or stems.

Fibrous root. A thin root arising from another root or from stem tissue.

Filament. The thread-shaped structure bearing an anther.

*Filiform. Shaped like a thread.

Fimbriate. Having a fringe.

Floret. A small flower in a larger cluster of flowers as in families Poaceae and Asteraceae.

Foliaceous. Having leaves.

*Follicle. Dry fruit splitting open along one seam.

Fruit. Mature ovary containing seeds and any floral or vegetative structures attached to it.

Funnelform. Shaped like a funnel.

Fusiform. Shaped like a spindle.

Glabrous. Without hairs.

Gland. Any structure that secretes a fluid.

Glaucous. Appearing whitish due to wax deposition.

Globose. Spherical.

Glomerule. A compact cyme of almost sessile flowers.

Gynostegium. A structure consisting of the joining of anthers and stigmas in family Asclepiadaceae.

*Hastate. Shaped like an arrowhead with the bases turned outward.

Helicoid. Arranged in or having the shape of a flattened coil or spiral.

Hemiparasite. A partially parasitic green plant that procures water and minerals from a host plant.

*****Hesperidium.** A fruit with a leathery rind embedded with oil glands.

*****Hip.** An aggregate fruit of some members of family Rosaceae in which the hypanthium becomes enlarged but does not become attached to the individual fruits.

Hirsute. Bearing rough, coarse hairs.

Hood. The petal-like corona lobes in some members of family Asclepiadaceae.

Horn. A slender, pointed appendage emerging from the corona in some members of family Asclepiadaceae.

Hyaline. Translucent tissue.

Hypanthium. A structure, often urn-shaped, formed by the fusion among sepals, petals, and stamens.

Imbricate. Overlapping, as in tiles on a roof or scales on a fish.

Inflorescence. The arrangement of flowers that are borne in groups.

Infrutescence. The inflorescence in fruit.

*****Internode.** The part of a stem axis between nodes.

Involucre. A whorl of bracts underneath a flower cluster.

Involute. Having the margins rolled upward, as in a leaf.

*****Keel.** The two lower, united petals in some members of family Fabaceae; any linear, ridge-shaped structure.

*****Labellum.** A modified lip petal in the family Orchidaceae.

Lamella. A thin layer of tissue.

*****Lanceolate.** Shaped like a lance.

*****Leaflet.** Segment of a compound leaf.

*****Legume.** Dry fruit splitting along two seams in family Fabaceae.

*****Ligule.** A strap-shaped structure.

*****Linear.** A narrow, elongated shape with parallel sides.

Loment. A flat legume that is constricted between the seeds.

Lyrate. Shaped like a lyre.

Mericarp. One segment of a multi-segmented fruit.

Mesic. A moderately moist habitat.

Monoecious. Having both kinds of unisexual flowers on the same plant.

*****Mucronate.** A short, abrupt tip, as in a leaf.

*****Node.** The position on a stem where one or more leaves are attached.

*****Nut.** Dry fruit with a hard fruit wall that does not split open.

Nutlet. Dry fruit that splits into one-seeded segments.

Ob. Prefix indicating *the reverse of,* as in a leaf or bract (e.g., lanceolate, oblanceolate).

*****Oblong.** An elongated shape with parallel sides.

*****Obtuse.** Blunt or rounded with an angle greater than 90 degrees.

Ocrea. A sheath-like stipule that surrounds the stem in some members of family Polygonaceae.

*Opposite leaves. Two leaves attached at the same node.

*Orbicular. Circular in outline.

Ovary. The part of the carpel that contains the ovules.

*Ovate. Shaped like an egg.

Ovule. Unfertilized seeds contained within the ovary.

*Palmate leaf. Compound leaf with leaflets radiating from a common point of attachment.

Pandurate. Shaped like a fiddle.

*Panicle. A loose compound inflorescence of flowers.

Papilla. A minute conical or nipple-shaped projection.

*Pappus. The modified calyx of bristles or scales of the family Asteraceae.

Pedate. Having palmately divided lobes with the lobes cleft.

*Pedicel. An individual flower stalk.

*Peduncle. An inflorescence stalk.

*Peltate. Having the stem or petiole attached to the lower surface rather than at the base or margin, as in a leaf.

*Pepo. A fruit derived from an inferior ovary with a leathery rind in family Cucurbitaceae.

Perennial. A plant that lives for more than two growing seasons.

Perfect. Refers to a flower that contains both male and female parts.

*Perfoliate. A sessile leaf with the stem passing through the blade.

Perianth. The set of sepals and petals surrounding the stamens and carpels.

*Petal. One of the segments of the set of parts positioned second from the outside of a flower.

*Petiole. The stalk of a leaf.

*Phyllary. An individual involucral bract of family Asteraceae.

Phyllode. A leaf that consists of a petiole but no blade.

Pilose. With soft, spreading hairs.

*Pinnate leaf. A compound leaf with leaflets attached like the vanes of a feather.

Plait. A folded structure like that in a fan.

Plicate. Folded like a fan; pleated.

Pollinium. A pollen mass.

*Pome. A fruit derived from an inferior ovary and a fleshy hypanthium.

Prickle. Nonwoody, sharp outgrowth from the epidermal (outer) cell layer, as in a leaf or stem.

Procumbent. Trailing or lying on the ground, as some stems.

Pseudobulb. A thickened, bulblike stem found in family Orchidaceae.

Puberulent. With soft, downy hairs.

Pubescent. Having hairs.

Punctate. Dotted with glands or colored spots.

*Raceme. Elongate inflorescence in which the flower pedicels are approximately equal in length.

*Rachis. The axis of a compound leaf or inflorescence.

*Ray floret. Ligulate flowers in heads of some members of family Asteraceae.

*Receptacle. That part of the stem to which floral parts are attached.

*Reniform. Shaped like a kidney.

Resupinate. Twisted 180 degrees on its axis.

Reticulate. Netlike.

Retrorse. Bent backward or downward, as in hairs.

Revolute. Having margins rolling downward, as in a leaf.

Rhizome. A horizontal underground stem.

Rhombic. Diamond-shaped.

Rotate. Radially spreading in a single plane, such as flower petals.

*Sagittate. Shaped like an arrowhead.

Salverform. Refers to a tubular corolla that expands at the open end.

Scabrous. Pubescent with short, stout hairs.

Scape. A leafless peduncle arising from the ground.

*Schizocarp. Fruit that breaks into one-seeded segments called mericarps.

Scorpioid. An inflorescence coiled in bud that unfurls as it matures.

Scurfy. Having a rough surface.

Secund. Arranged on one side only.

*Sepal. One of the segments of the outermost set of floral parts.

Sessile. Directly attached, such as a leaf attached to a stem without a petiole.

Sheathing. A leaf blade or petiole that is prolonged into a tube that partially or completely surrounds the stem.

*Silicle. A short silique having a length less than three times its width.

*Silique. A long, narrow, dry, dehiscent fruit whose outer walls break away from a central papery partition.

*Spadix. A fleshy spike of numerous small flowers (typical of Araceae).

*Spathe. Green, colored, or dry sheath enclosing the inflorescence (typical of Araceae).

*Spathulate. Shaped like a spatula.

*Spike. Elongate inflorescence in which the flowers have no pedicels.

Spikelet. The ultimate flower cluster in families Poaceae and Cyperaceae.

Spine. Woody, sharp leaf homologue.

Spur. A tubular or sac-shaped extension of the corolla or calyx.

Staminal column. A column formed by the fusion of filaments in family Malvaceae.

*Staminate. A flower in which only the stamens are functional.

Staminode. Sterile stamen.

*****Standard.** The upper petal of the flowers of some members of family Fabaceae.

Stellate. Pubescent with hairs that branch at or near the base, resulting in a starlike appearance.

Stigma. The upper, receptive part of the carpel onto which the pollen grains are received.

Stipe. The stalk beneath an ovary.

Stipitate. Having a stipe as an elevated gland.

*****Stipule.** One of a pair of appendages situated at the base of the petiole or leaf blade.

Stolon. A horizontal stem near ground level that gives rise to a new plant.

Strigose. Pubescent, with short hairs that lie flat against the surface.

Style. The contracted portion of a carpel between the ovary and stigma.

Suffruticose. Having stems with only the lower parts woody.

Taproot. A root system consisting of a single main root.

Tepal. A name given to a perianth segment when the distinction between sepals and petals is not apparent (e.g., when they are all the same color and shape).

Terete. Circular in cross section.

Terminal bud. A bud borne at the end of a stem.

Ternate. Arranged in threes.

Thallus. A plant body not differentiated into root, stem, and leaf.

Thorn. A sharp, woody process emanating from a stem.

Tomentose. Pubescent, with curly, matted, soft, white, woolly hairs.

Trifoliate leaf. Compound leaf divided into three leaflets.

*****Truncate.** Having the end square or even.

Tuber. A solid, horizontal underground stem used for starch storage.

Turbinate. Inverted cone-shaped.

*****Umbel.** An inflorescence in which the pedicels all attach at a central point.

Undulate. Wavy margined.

Urceolate. Urn-shaped.

Utricle. A type of achene that is bladder-shaped.

Verticil. A whorl of organs such as leaves or flowers on a central axis.

Villous. Covered with long, soft hairs.

*****Whorled.** Refers to three or more leaves symmetrically attached at the same node.

*****Wing.** The lateral petals in some members of family Fabaceae; a thin extension.

Xeric. Dry, as in a habitat.

SELECTED REFERENCES

Angiosperm Phylogeny Group. 2003. An update of the Angiosperm Phylogeny Group classification for the orders and families of flowering plants: APG II. Botanical Journal of the Linnean Society 141: 399–436.

Austin, D. F. 2004. Florida Ethnobotany. CRC Press, Boca Raton, FL.

Brummitt, R. K., and C. E. Powell. 2004. Authors of plant names. Royal Botanic Gardens, Kew, UK.

Correll, D. S., and M. C. Johnston. 1979. Manual of the vascular plants of Texas. The University of Texas at Dallas, Richardson, TX.

Flora of North America Editorial Committee, eds. 1997–. Flora of North America North of Mexico. 10+ vols. New York and Oxford. Vol. 3, 1997; vol. 4, 2003; vol. 5, 2005; vol. 19, 2006; vol. 20, 2006; vol. 21, 2006; vol. 22, 2000; vol. 23, 2002; vol. 25, 2003; vol. 26, 2002.

Godfrey, R. K., and J. W. Wooten. 1979. Aquatic and wetland plants of the southeastern United States. Monocotyledons. The University of Georgia Press, Athens, GA.

———. 1981. Aquatic and wetland plants of the southeastern United States. Dicotyledons. The University of Georgia Press, Athens, GA.

Guccione, M. J., and D. L. Zachary. 2006. Geologic history of the southeastern United States and its effects on soils of the region. Southern Cooperative Bulletin #395. http://soilphysics.okstate.edu.

Long, R. W., and O. Lakela. 1971. A flora of tropical Florida. University of Miami Press, Coral Gables, FL.

Radford, A. E., H. E. Ahles, and C. R. Bell. 1964. Manual of the vascular flora of the Carolinas. University of North Carolina Press, Chapel Hill, NC.

Takhtajan, Armen. 1986. Floristic regions of the world. University of California Press, Berkeley, Los Angeles, London.

USDA, NRCS. 2006. The PLANTS Database (http://plants.usda.gov). National Plant Data Center, Baton Rouge, LA.

INDEX TO FLOWERS

Wood's bunchflower, 187
wooly chaff head, 41
wooly sunbonnets, 42
woolywhite, 58
wreath goldenrod, 72
Wright's morning glory, 106
wrinkleleaf goldenrod, 73

X

Xyridaceae, 274
Xyris ambigua, 274

Y

yankeeweed, 49
yellow anisetree, 159

yellow butterwort, 174
yellow colicroot, 192
yellow flag, 162
yellow fringed orchid, 206
yellow fringeless orchid, 206
yellow meadowbeauty, 189
yellow milkwort, 222
yellow passionflower, 214
yellow pitcherplant, 244
yellow puff, 137
yellow star grass, 192
yellow star-grass, 158
yellow sweetclover, 137
yellow water lily, 194
yellow wild indigo, 127
yellow woodsorrel, 212

Youngia japonica, 79
Yucca aloifolia, 10
Yucca filamentosa, 10

Z

Zephyranthes atamasca, 17
Zephyranthes chlorosolen, 18
Zephyranthes citrina, 16
Zephyranthes drummondii, 18
Zephyranthes treatiae, 17
Zigadenus densus, 188
Zigadenus glaberrimus, 188
Zigadenus nuttallii, 188
zigzag iris, 162
Zizia aurea, 25
Zygophyllaceae, 275